W9-AHP-906

THE PERSONAL INTERNET SECURITY GUIDEBOOK

A Volume in The Korper and Ellis E-Commerce Books Series

GRACE LIBRARY CARLOW COLLEGE
PITTSBURGH PA 15213

THE PERSONAL INTERNET SECURITY GUIDEBOOK

KEEPING HACKERS AND CRACKERS OUT OF YOUR HOME

Timothy Speed
Juanita Ellis
Steffano Korper

TK
5105.875
I57
S675
2002

ACADEMIC PRESS
A Division of Harcourt, Inc.
San Diego San Francisco New York Boston
London Sydney Tokyo

CATALOGUED

This book is printed on acid-free paper. ♾

Copyright © 2002 by Academic Press

All rights reserved.
No part of this publication may be reproduced or transmitted in any form or by any means, electronic or mechanical, including photocopy, recording, or any information storage and retrieval system, without permission in writing from the publisher.
Requests for permission to make copies of any part of the work should be mailed to the following address:
Permissions Department, Harcourt, Inc., 6277 Sea Harbor Drive, Orlando, Florida 32887-6777.

Academic Press
A division of Harcourt, Inc.
525 B Street, Suite 1900, San Diego, CA 92101-4495, USA
http://www.academicpress.com

Academic Press
Harcourt Place, 32 Jamestown Road, London, NW1 7BY, UK
http://www.academicpress.com

Library of Congress Catalog Card Number: 2001091437

International Standard Book Number: 0-12-656561-9

Printed in the United States of America
01 02 03 04 05 06 IP 9 8 7 6 5 4 3 2 1

To Linda Speed—still my favorite wife

Contents

Foreword

Thanks to high-speed DSL and cable technology and PCs everywhere, the road to the Internet is fast becoming the highly trafficked resource it was meant to be. However, with everyone scrambling to get online with high-speed Internet access; it's not surprising to see an equally explosive need for Internet security. It is a simple fact: Any computer that is connected to the Internet is at risk of security threats, including targeted hacker attacks, crackers, spyware, Internet-borne Trojan horses, viruses, and other malicious code. But there *are* ways to protect your computers from unwanted intrusions, and the path to security begins with knowledge.

Since Ethernet was developed in the 1970s, it has quickly become the basis for the Internet, Local Area Networks (LANs), and enterprisewide networks that span an entire geographic area, called WideArea Networks, or WANS. These networks have in turn led to the growth of the Internet as a global exchange capable of handling communication and commerce 24 hours a day, seven days a week. But in the beginning LANs were not built and designed to handle digital communication over long distances or with the use of the Internet. IBM had designed the networking technology into Windows called NetBIOS and NetBEUI. These two application interfaces were designed for an internal LAN to communicate between IBM PCs and compatible hardware within one central location—thus, the operative term *local.* LANs were constructed so that computers could communicate with each other to share files, printers, and other hardware. Today, sharing broadband Internet access has become the leading reason for building networks in the home or office. There are over 10 million broadband account subscribers, with millions more that are sharing the ISP accounts and another 30 million that will have cable or DSL access by 2004. So while Internet connectivity is on the rise, the amount of network intrusions continues to soar.

The recent Anna Kournikova and LoveBug viruses, the Code Red worm, and the DDOS attacks on sites sponsored by Yahoo and Microsoft have all been in the headlines. With these highly publicized attacks and scare tactics, Internet security is rapidly becoming an important consideration when building a network. Mainstream America is beginning to appreciate the control a single individual can gain by quietly sneaking into a network and downloading personal files, data, and information. Identities are stolen, businesses are shut down for hours or days, and billions of dollars are lost. Also alarming is the number of people who freely give out their credit card information to scammers through promotions in e-mails and on Web sites. The Federal Trade Commission reported that nearly 70,000 American Internet users have reported some kind of identity theft between November 1999 and June 2001, mostly from some kind of credit card fraud. To many Internet intruders, it's not only a challenge, it's a business.

Computers aren't the only devices that can be tampered with by intruders. Any device that uses the Internet to communicate is at risk. Handheld devices such as PDAs are open to attacks. The first viruses were launched in 2000, and mobile phones became victims in 2001. Open source codes in servers, handhelds and set-top boxes give Trojan Horse gateways to offices, pockets, and TVs. As our reliance on the World Wide Web to communicate and access information grows, the Internet will become more tightly interwoven with our daily lives. Security will be an essential tool in keeping information safe and allowing us to conduct business privately.

The latest trend in networking is networking without wires. Wireless LANs allow users to perform all the same networking tasks as a wired network but without the restrictions of cables. With new technology comes issues, just as when cell phones, satellite TVs, and networked computers were new. Problems were resolved as the technology became advanced and went mainstream. Today, security issues relevant to wireless LANs are a hot topic. But wireless LANs are secure if users follow the appropriate precautions in vendor manuals and enhance their security with additional hardware and software available on the market, such as routers and gateways, firewall software, and antivirus software. Enhancing security will also become important as more wireless LAN environments are offered to the public in schools, airports, strip malls, and coffeehouses. Wireless access to the Internet through public sources will become as common as the cell phone, but connecting to open access networks can be even more risky if users don't protect their systems.

The value placed on security is up to the user or the company. Research groups report that the average cost of network penetration by an outsider and the resulting damage is over $400,000. But it can be more than that if the information lost or stolen is an entire customer database, personal bank account information, or proprietary information that is crucial to company business. So the $20 antivirus software license, the $100 broadband router for the home or business, or the $100,000 security system with an experienced IT person pays for itself many times over if it stops an intruder just once.

The more you know about network protection, the less chance you will someday be a victim of malicious attacks. This book educates and informs users about the risks and solutions to protecting a network of any size. The authors have researched all types of security issues related to home, businesses, and workgroup environments and provide clear explanations on how information is taken, deleted, or embedded with viruses or worms that can cause computer problems. The book discusses different software, hardware, and service options available. This book along with vendor manuals, experienced IT personnel for business networks, and updated patches will provide readers with all the precautions they need to enhance the security of their networks. If you are connected, get protected.

Victor Tsao
President/CEO/Co-Founder
Linksys

Victor Tsao is president and chief executive officer of The Linksys Group, Inc., in Irvine, California. Linksys is a leader in the development of broadband, wireless, and networking hardware solutions for the small office/ home office (SOHO), small/medium business (SMB), and enterprise environments. Linksys has been the leading manufacturer of networking hardware in the retail channel for over four years and currently owns 30 percent of the market. Through this position, Linksys has become the fastest-growing networking hardware manufacturer in the distribution channel as well as the leading seller of networking hardware online through E-tailers.

Prior to joining Linksys, Tsao served as the director of MIS Strategic Systems Development for Taco Bell Corp. from 1984 to 1991. Tsao played a key role in the implementation of networking the restaurants to the headquarters for daily run reports. When Pepsi Corporation acquired Taco Bell, Tsao implemented the marketing strategies of the cola giant. He also served as supervisor of technical services for Santa Fe International Inc., as a systems programmer for TRW, as a software engineer for Kraft, Inc., and as a database administrator for Montgomery Ward & Co.

Victor has an MBA, an MS, and a BA in computer science from Pepperdine University, Illinois Institute of Technology, and Tamkang University, Taiwan, respectively. He was also named Orange County Enterpreneur of the Year by Deloitte and Touche in 1999 and one of the most successful Orange County businessmen by the American Electronics Association in 2001. Linksys has been named as an Inc. 500 fastest-growing company in America for four consecutive years and has won many awards in the marketing and innovation of new technologies for the consumer.

Acknowledgments

Knowledge is based on many different facets—what you know, knowing where information can be found, and who you know. The information in this book is a combination of all these facets. Data sources have been referenced in this book, including references to people, URLs, and other books. But much of the knowledge that is in this book comes from very smart people. Not all the people listed in this "acknowledgment" section actually participated in the writing of this book, but they have influenced and guided me and this has resulted in this work. First and foremost I need to thank my wife for helping me with this book and providing some of the editing in the various chapters. Next, I want to thank Johnny Speed, a great son for providing not only his support but also some editing of various chapters in this book. I thank my daughter, Katherine, for tolerating me during the months I worked on this book. Next, I want to thank my mother, Lillian Speed, for teaching me to "think big." It is great to have a mother's support. My brothers and my sister have all been an inspiration to me and helped me to strive for a better life. I am very grateful to Juanita Ellis for asking me to participate in writing this book. Special thanks to Julio G. Esperas, Production Editor of my last book. Also thanks to Chris Cotton, who has supported me (at least mentally) during some crazy times. Thanks to Joel Claypool for publishing this book. Special thanks to Lotus Development, Steve Mohr, and Jamie Chisholm for allowing me to coauthor this book.

Now to talk about the really smart people—due to legal issues, the people listed here could not directly contribute to this book, but I have learned a lot from them both through work and in their friendships:

Andy Howe; Andy Nietupski; Azim Tirmizi; Barry Heinz; Bill Kulduff; Bond Carter; Boris Vishnevsky; Brad Schauf; Candace Brenner; Carl Radino; Carlos Gonzalez (Sam I am); Carmen Pascual; Chris Cotton; Carol Crosby; Charles Carrington; Cliff Sokol; Craig Levine; Daniel Suster; Dave Erickson; Dave Martin; David Bell; Danny Suster; David Leaser; David Noble; David Winters; Dawn Rose; Debra Filla; Denise La Grouw; Dennis Archibald; Donald Bridges; Doug Johnson; Dwight A. Wilbanks; Glen Steffens; Gregory

Green; Jack Kelly; Jana Reynolds; Jennifer Strait; Jim Jameson; John Kistler; John Norton (left John out of the last book, sorry John); Jon P. Dodge; Jonathan Poulter; Juanita Ellis; Karen Rigione; Kent McKitrick; Kevin Smith; Kiki Forsythe; Kim Schettig; Larry A. Anglin; Leon Hutcheson; Leslie K. Versey; Lori Williams; Louis DePadova; Luc Groleau; Luis Nieves; Maria Albright (another wonderful person left out of the last book); Mario Figueroa; Mark Leaser; Mary A. Bostic; The other John Norton; Mary Joesph (this was a big oversight on my part from the last book—Mary is the best); Michael Cowan; Michael Dennehy; Michael Flores; Michael Lamparty (Dr. Lamparty); Michael Vollmer; Mike Stover; Pat Fleming; Pattie Abbott; Randy Parrett; Rob McAuley; Robert Thietje; Roy Hudson; Shahir Daya; Shannon Siebert; Shelley K. Rychlik; Steffano Korper; Stephen Cooke; Steve Houchin; Steve Shelton; Susie Darbonne; Takeshi Suzuki; Ted Lewis; Tom Agoston; Tom Haynie; Tony Chong; Tracy Dent; Vahik Gharibian; Valarie Gray; Wanda Brewster; Wanda Rodgers (the better half of the Rodgers gang); William Crowell; Dr. Jose Burbano; and Pastor Greg Gerendas.

Acknowledgment to Johnny Speed (developmental editor of this book); Nuchjaree Khunchana.

Special thanks to Randy Parrett.

Finally, sorry if I missed you on this book, I will get you in the next. Sorry, Titus, you don't get an acknowledgment in this book.

Company Copyright Notices and Statements

Although the authors and editors have attempted to provide accurate information in this book, we assume no responsibility for the accuracy of the information. The following listing is not exhaustive. The names of actual companies and products mentioned herein may be the trademarks of their respective owners.

For the purposes of this book, the companies used as examples (e.g., The Company), as well as all organizations, products, people, and events depicted herein are fictitious. No association with any real company, organization, product, person, or event is intended or should be inferred.

Microsoft

Copyright © 2000 Microsoft Corporation, One Microsoft Way, Redmond, Washington 98052–6399 USA. All rights reserved. See www.microsoft.com for more information.

Trademarks: Microsoft, Windows, Windows NT, MSN, Outlook,The Microsoft Network, Windows98, Windows95, and/or other Microsoft products referenced herein are either trademarks or registered trademarks of Microsoft. See www.microsoft.com for more information.

Verisign

Copyright © 2000 VeriSign, Inc. All rights reserved. VeriSign, the VeriSign logo, Digital ID, OnSite, and Go Secure! are trademarks and service marks or registered trademarks and service marks of VeriSign, Inc. All other trademarks and service marks are property of their respective owners. See www.verisign.com for more information.

Armadillo Multimedia Enterprise LTD

http://www.armadillo.com.hk/legal.html

INTEL

http://www.intel.com/sites/corporate/tradmarx.htm?iid=intelhome+legal&

XEROX

http://www.xerox.com/go/xrx/template/004.jsp?view=Legal&Xcntry=USA &Xlang=en_US&Xseg=corp

DEC/Compaq

http://www.compaq.com/copyright.html

3COM

http://www.3com.com/legal/index.html

Spam (this is trademarked)

http://www.spam.com/ci/ci_in.htm

spam (this is not trademarked)

http://www.spam.com/ci/ci_in.htm

GE

http://www.ge.com/

Zone Labs

http://www.zonealarm.com/aboutus/legal.html

LinkSys

http://www.linksys.com/contact/coinfo.asp

Network ICE

Network ICE, the Network ICE logo, the Defender logo, BlackICE, BlackICE Sentry, BlackICE Defender, BlackICE Auditor, ICEpac, Enterprise ICEpac, ICEcap, ICEcap Auditor, advICE, "Collective Awareness," "The Future of Network Security . . . Today," "We Stop Hackers Cold," Intrusion Countermeasure Enhancements (ICE), Intrusion Defense System, and "Intrusion Detection at the Speed of Light" are trademarks or registered trademarks of Network ICE or its licensees in the USA and other countries.

APPLE

http://www.apple.com/legal/default.html

MICROWAREHOUSE

http://www2.warehouse.com/

IBM

The list for IBM is too extensive to present here. See this URL: http://www.ibm.com/legal/copytrade.phtml

RSA

For the purpose of promoting interoperability among products implementing S/MIME, the 'S/MIME-Enabled' logo is trademarked, http://www.rsasecurity.com/ and vendors must demonstrate S/MIME compliance before using the logo on product packaging, promotional materials, advertising, signage, and/or Web sites. See www.rsa.com for more information. The S/MIME logo can be found at http://www.rsasecurity.com/standards/smime/logos.html

Baltimore Technologies

Baltimore Technologies, Global E|Security, Global E-Security, E-Security, E|Security, TrustedWorld, PKI World, Zergo, ZSA, and Baltimore product names including UniCERT, MailSecure, PKI-Plus, W/Secure, X/Secure, and J/CRYPTO are all trademarks of Baltimore Technologies plc and its subsidiaries. http://www.baltimore.ie/legalnotices.html

Netscape

Netscape, Netscape Certificater Server, Netscape FastTrack Server, Netscape Navigator, Netscape ONE, SuiteSpot, and the Netscape N and Ship's Wheel logos are registered trademarks of Netscape Communications Corporation in the United States and other countries.

Netscape Trademarks

An ® following a name indicates that the trademark has been registered in the USA. This list is not exhaustive. Netscape may own other trademarks that are not included here.

AutoConfig, AutoUpdate, BeanConnect, Client Registry, Client Version Registry, Collabra®, Collabra Share®, Contact, CoolTalk, Expert Alliance, ExpertDesk, Expert-to-Expert, In-Box Direct, ISP Select®, Live 3D, LiveCall, LiveConnect, Live Objects, LiveType, LiveWire, LiveWire Pro, MailCaster, Mozilla, Netcaster, Netcenter, NetHelp, Netscape®, Netscape® Administration Kit, Netscape AffiliatePlus, Netscape® AgentXpert, Netscape Alliance, Netscape® AppFoundry, Netscape® Application Builder, Netscape® Application Server, Netscape® AutoAdmin, Netscape Business Community, Netscape Business Journal, Netscape® BuyerXpert, Netscape® Calendar, Netscape® Calendar Express, Netscape® Calendar Link, Netscape® Calendar Server, Netscape CaseTracker, Netscape® Cash Register, Netscape Catalog Server®, Netscape Certificate Server®, Netscape® Channel Finder, Netscape Charters Program, Netscape® Chat, Netscape® Client Customization Kit, Netscape® Collabra®, Netscape® Collabra® Server, Netscape® Commerce Server, Netscape® CommerceXpert, Netscape® Commercial Applications, Netscape® Communications Server, Netscape® Communicator, Netscape® Communicator Deluxe Edition, Netscape® Communicator Internet Access Edition, Netscape® Communicator News, Netscape Community, Netscape® Community System, Netscape® Compass Server, Netscape® Component Builder, Netscape® Composer, Netscape® Conference, Netscape® Console, Netscape® Content Management Server, Netscape DevEdge®, Netscape DevEdge® Application Builder, Netscape DevEdge® Online, Netscape DevEdge® Open Studio, Netscape® DeveloperXpert, Netscape Direct, Netscape® Directory Server, Netscape® ECXpert, Netscape® Enterprise News, Netscape® Enterprise Server, Netscape® Enterprise Server with FORTEZZA, Netscape® Extension Builder, Netscape FastTrack Server®, Netscape Guide, Netscape Industry Watch, Netscape Insight, Netscape® Install Builder, Netscape® Internet Applications, Netscape® Internet Foundation Classes, Netscape Internet Learning Academy, Netscape® Internet Service Broker, Netscape® Istore, Netscape® JAR Installation Manager, Netscape® JAR Packager, Netscape® LiveMedia, Netscape® LivePayment, Netscape® Mail, Netscape® Mail Server, Netscape® Mailing List Manager, Netscape® Media Converter, Netscape® Media Player, Netscape® Media Server, Netscape® Merchant System, Netscape® MerchantXpert, Netscape® Messaging Server, Netscape® Messenger, Netscape® Messenger Express, Netscape® Migration Toolkit, Netscape® Mission Control, Netscape® Mission Control Desktop, Netscape Navigator®, Netscape Navigator® with FORTEZZA, Netscape Navigator® Gold, Netscape Navigator® News, Netscape Navigator® Personal Edition, Netscape Netcenter, Netscape Netcenter Small Business Source, Netscape® News Server, Netscape ONE®, Netscape® Payment Kit, Netscape® Power Pack, Netscape® Process Manager, Netscape Professional Community, Netscape® Proxy Server, Netscape® Proxy Server with FORTEZZA, Netscape® Publishing Suite, Netscape® Publishing System, Netscape® PublishingXpert, Netscape® SellerXpert, Netscape Services Network, Netscape® Site Manager, Netscape Site Sampler, Netscape® SmartUpdate, Netscape Software Depot, Netscape Solution Expert, Netscape Subscribers Advantage, Netscape® SuiteTools, Netscape SupportEdge, Netscape® Update, Netscape Virtual Office, Netscape® WebTop, Netshare, ONE Stop Software, PowerStart®, ResponseDesk, ResponseLine, Secure Courier, ShopTalk Direct, SmartMarks, Suite Solutions, SuiteSpot®, SuiteSpot® Hosting Edition, and TechVision.

Netscape Trade Names

Following are Netscape trade names: Netscape; Netscape Communications; and Netscape Communications Corporation.

Cisco

See http://www.cisco.com/public/copyright/trademark.html for a list.

Sun

JavaScript is a trademark of Sun Microsystems, Inc., used under license for technology invented and implemented by Netscape.

CERT

CERT® is a registered trademark and service mark of Carnegie Mellon University.

Computer Security Institute

Copyright © 2000, Computer Security Institute, 600 Harrison Street, San Francisco, CA 94107. See http://www.gocsi.com/

Excerpted from RFC2026:

ftp://ftp.isi.edu/in-notes/rfc2026.txt

(C) The following copyright notice and disclaimer shall be included in all ISOC standards-related documentation:

"Copyright (C) The Internet Society (date). All Rights Reserved.

This document and translations of it may be copied and furnished to others, and derivative works that comment on or otherwise explain it or assist in its implmentation may be prepared, copied, published and distributed, in whole or in part, without restriction of any kind, provided that the above copyright notice and this paragraph are included on all such copies and derivative works. However, this document itself may not be modified in any way, such as by removing the copyright notice or references to the Internet Society or other Internet organizations, except as needed for the purpose of developing Internet standards in which case the procedures for copyrights defined in the Internet Standards process must be followed, or as required to translate it into languages other than English.

The limited permissions granted above are perpetual and will not be revoked by the Internet Society or its successors or assigns.

Excerpted from RFC2223:

ftp://ftp.isi.edu/in-notes/rfc2223.txt

11. Copyright Section

Per BCP 9, RFC 2026 [2], "The following copyright notice and disclaimer shall be included in all ISOC standards-related documentation." The following statement should be placed on the last page of the RFC, as the "Full Copyright Statement."

"Copyright (C) The Internet Society (date). All Rights Reserved.

This document and translations of it may be copied and furnished to others, and derivative works that comment on or otherwise explain it or assist in its implementation may be prepared, copied, published and distributed, in whole or in part, without restriction of any kind, provided that the above copyright notice and this paragraph are included on all such copies and derivative works. However, this document itself may not be modified in any way, such as by removing the copyright notice or references to the Internet Society or other Internet organizations, except as needed for the purpose of developing Internet standards in which case the procedures for copyrights defined in the Internet Standards process must be followed, or as required to translate it into languages other than English.

The limited permissions granted above are perpetual and will not be revoked by the Internet Society or its successors or assigns.

This document and the information contained herein is provided on an "AS IS" basis and THE INTERNET SOCIETY AND THE INTERNET ENGINEERING TASK FORCE DISCLAIMS ALL WARRANTIES, EXPRESS OR IMPLIED, INCLUDING BUT NOT LIMITED TO ANY WARRANTY THAT THE USE OF THE INFORMATION HEREIN WILL NOT INFRINGE ANY RIGHTS OR ANY IMPLIED WARRANTIES OF MERCHANTABILITY OR FITNESS FOR A PARTICULAR PURPOSE."

Warning and Disclaimer

Every effort has been made to make this book as complete and accurate as possible, but no warranty or fitness is implied. The security of any site is the responsibility of the owners. The authors and publishers are not liable for the security of any person, company or site. The authors and the publisher shall have neither liability nor responsibility to any person or entity with respect to loss or damages arising from the information contained in this book. Purchase and read this book at your own risk. Every effort has been attempted to obtain permissions for extracts and quotes whenever possible. See listed URLs for quote sources. The products referenced or mentioned in this book are listed for informational purposes only. The publisher and authors may have received demonstration copies to review. The publishers and authors have not received any compensation from the software or hardware vendors mentioned in the book. Many different vendors are mentioned in this book and many vendor products are used for reference. The publisher and authors do not recommend any product, software, or hardware. You, the owner of your hardware, software, and data are responsible for determining what is best for you. The authors DO advise that you take careful consideration in determining your security needs and review more than just one vendor. Remember, you own your security, we do not!

INTRODUCTION

The government has for years been sending out radio signals to our brains with secret messages. The messages tell us to "pay our taxes," "drive slowly," and "eat fatty foods." I have found a method to block these signals; I have created a hat made out of aluminum foil. I wear this hat whenever I go out of the house.

We need to protect our computers from "the evil bad dude hackers" much as I protect my mind from the government. While the aluminum hat seems to work for me, it does not work for my computer. Unfortunately, most any connection to the Internet exposes our computer to the bad dude hackers. Cable modem and DSL provides an always-on and high-speed link to the Internet. And these "always-on" connections from our homes can be easy prey for the bad dudes. Corporate DMZs, firewalls, and armed guard dogs do not sufficiently protect the home computer. In fact, if the hacker is really successful in his or her attempts to take over your machine, then your computer can be used to attack other systems back on your corporate network. To see how these numbers are increasing each year in some major areas, take a look at the figure provided here on Internet fraud.[1]

1. Chart source is http://www.fraud.org/internet/1t00totstats.htm

FIGURE 1.1 *Internet Fraud*

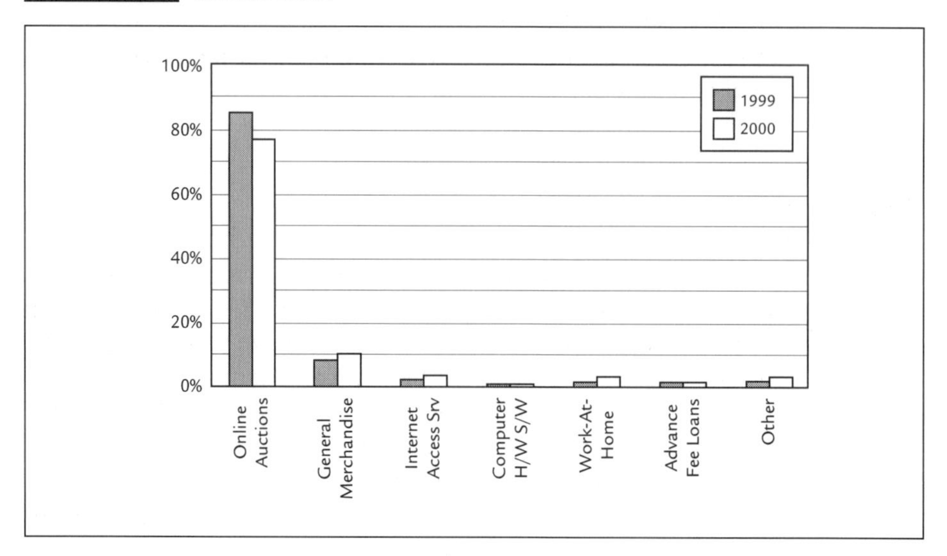

Hackers use various methods to attack systems connected to networks and especially to the Internet. Here are some of the attacks that as a home PC user you could experience:

1. Virus
2. Worms
3. Trojan Horse
4. Port Scanning
5. File Share Attacks
6. DOS
7. O/S Attacks
8. SCAMs
9. And There Is More

Virus

A computer virus is a program that spreads itself by replicating itself and sending the copies from computer to computer, creating havoc on each computer it visits. The term "virus" is used loosely to cover any sort of program that tries to hide its possibly malicious function as it tries to spread to as many computers as possible. A virus can spread itself via a number of mechanisms: a floppy, a CD, an e-mail message, even an application. Viruses can even use your computer's internal clock to trigger the actual program on a certain date.

Worms

A worm gestates in a networked environment and then spreads by spawning copies of itself on other computers on the network. Worms eat up computer resources like memory and even network bandwidth. Worms can also sometimes delete data and then spread themselves via e-mail. Here again, the transport of choice is e-mail. One of the earliest worms that caused great disruption on the Internet was the Morris worm in 1988. This worm was a harbinger of things to come. The Morris Internet worm burrowed through the Internet world of 1988; it had an impact on only 6,000 of the 60,000 computers in use at the time. Stop and think for a second—only 60,000 computers were on the Internet at that time, not that many by today's numbers, but that worm hit 10% of the existing community. The Love Bug hit 100 times that. As the technology has been growing so have the worms; bummer, dude.

Trojan Horse

A Trojan horse is a program that appears legitimate but contains secondary hidden functions that can (and many times will) cause damage. E-mail with the aim of stealing passwords from a victim's computer and then e-mailing the stolen data to a targeted recipient often illustrates one of the most common of the Trojan horses. Back Orifice is one of these types of tools (or virus—you make the call).

There are many vendors working to provide information and tools to combat viruses. Here are a few:

- http://www.symantec.com/
- http://www.mcafee.com/
- http://www.drsolomon.com/

For more information about viruses check out. http://www.bocklabs.wisc.edu/~janda/virl_faq.html#B01.

Port Scanning

There are hundreds if not thousands of tools that can be used to "scan" a system or Web page. These tools can be downloaded by almost anyone and used with little or no modification. These tools will search a network or operating systems looking for vulnerabilities and reporting them back to the hacker. The hacker can then take advantage of these "open doors." With the results of the port scanning tools the hackers can then use that information to attack specific ports, for example, 137 or 139, the ports used for file sharing.

File Share Attacks

Windows provides the ability to share files over a network. In order to use file sharing, two different protocols are used:

1. Netbeui is a proprietary protocol created by Microsoft and
2. TCP/IP is the protocol that allows us to communicate on the Internet.

A computer with file sharing enabled by TCP/IP can easily become a target for the bad dudes. You can have a directory that can be written to and have all of the data on your hard drive removed, or some bad dude can print all types of junk on your "shared" printer.

DOS

This stands for Denial of Service Attacks. This is an indirect attack to the site. The hackers are not trying to get into the site itself. They are keeping everyone else from getting into the site. One of the most famous of these attacks, the "IP Ping of Death," was documented as early as January 1998 (CERT® Advisory CA-98.01 "smurf" IP Denial-of-Service Attacks [http://www.cert.org/advisories/CA-98.01.smurf.html]). A DOS attack can keep you from using your home computer on the Internet.

Operating Systems (OS) Attacks

This is where a set of tools can be used to attack the OS, try to damage the OS and/or extract passwords from the OS. A combination of approaches is used for these attacks, including port scanning to find an open port, Virus, and Trojan horses.

Scams

Scams are nothing new, I was about 10 years old and had five dollars scammed from me at a carnival in George West, Texas. At 50 cents a throw the attendant had me convinced that I would double my money on the next ball. That was the best $5.00 lesson of my life. The Internet is a spawning ground for scams. Here is an example: You may receive an e-mail that looks like your service provider sent it. This request may look very "official." The request has your name and your e-mail address. The request may read something like this:

```
From: Your Service Provider
To: Joe Smith
Subject: Please update your account information

Dear Joe Smith:

It is time for you to update your account information.
Please go to this URL and enter your credit card
information and your expiration date. Also please enter
your password when you enter the site.

http://192.9.201.200/ISP.html

Thanks for your cooperation
```

Now is this a fake message or a real message? Here is what you do: Contact your service provider and ask them if they actually sent this message. Also notice the URL in the message in our example. It has an IP address. The ISP should never use an IP address for account information updates. Why? Something called SSL. (More on SSL later in this chapter). A secure server should always have the name of the service in the URL. For example, when I connect to purchase a book from *Amazon.com* they take me to a secure area and the name remains *Amazon.com*.

Therefore, if you receive any message via e-mail that requests personal information, social security numbers, credit card numbers, and a password, contact the source directly (and not via e-mail). Please take the time to protect yourself. Check out the stats below for Internet fraud before you peruse the next chapter.

And, There Is More

Check out these sites for more information about the various attacks to which your computer can be exposed:

1. http://www.icsa.net/html/library/whitepapers/crime.pdf
2. http://advice.networkice.com/Advice/default.htm
3. http://www.cablemodeminfo.com/index.html-ssi
4. http://www.speedguide.net/index.shtml
5. http://www.cablemodemhelp.com
6. http://www.cablelabs.com
7. http://www.cablemodem.com
8. http://www.firewallguide.com/hardware.htm
9. http://www.practicallynetworked.com/sharing/sharing.htm
10. http://www.dslreports.com/
11. http://www.firewallguide.com/faq.htm
12. http://www.dslreports.com/r3/dsl/secureme
13. http://www.fraud.org/internet/lt00totstats.htm
14. http://www.fraud.org/internet/intset.htm
15. http://www.consumer.gov/idtheft/

Okay, we have made our point. There are lots of threats, exposures and, in general, bad dudes. How can we protect ourselves from all this stuff? This book will cover the major issues and security threats you need to know in order to protect your computing asset. In addition, we will include both the software and hardware needed to do the job, as well as a process to review the different products on the market.

CHAPTER 1

The Internet

1.1 Introduction

Before we get started let's take a step back and look at what this thing known as the Internet actually is. At first glance you might think it is a single big computer network out in the ether: Some large wonderful safe place to send and receive data and everyone is happy on the planet. Not quite right—other than the fact that the Internet is big, there is no one network and it isn't necessarily safe. In fact the Internet is changing every minute of every day. The Internet has revolutionized the computer and communications world like nothing before it. However, the telegraph, telephone, radio, and computer set the stage for the Internet to even exist. What many people don't know is that the Internet is actually more than 27 years old but that this whole WWW thing is fewer than 10 years old. Even older than the WWW world we know is the WORM—the first worm to burrow throughout the Internet occurred in 1988. As you can see, the Internet itself has been around for many years, thanks to the technology from the Telco world, but the http://www.Iwanttolookatawebpage.com is really new. As we have said, the Internet is not a single agency, network, or company but rather a collection. So, what is the glue that makes the Internet work? At first it was the "protocol" known as transmission control protocol/internet protocol (TCP/IP). (We have a chapter on this later.) The other parts of the puzzle include some magic known as DNS, and dedicated software—also known as browsers. Put all of these ingredients together and you get the Internet.

The first recorded description of these technical discussions about networked computers came from memos written by J.C.R. Licklider of MIT in August, 1962. Licklider discussed his "Galactic Network" concept and envisioned a globally interconnected set of computers through which everyone could access data and programs from any site. Now back in those days there were no video games. At that time I was in the second grade and worried that the bomb had targeted my school, so I hid under the desk to protect myself from the radiation. Back to our friend Licklider. Old bubba Licklider was the first head of the computer research program at the Defense Advanced Research Projects Agency.

Meanwhile at MIT, Leonard Kleinrock published the first paper on packet switching theory in July 1961 and a book on the subject in 1964. In 1964 the bomb was not so much a threat, but I had a new fear — Mary Martin Smith—she threw rocks at my head (this now accounts for many of my personality quirks). Mr. Kleinrock had convinced his peers of the theoretical feasibility of communications using packets rather than circuits. A series of experiments were created to test these concepts. Only circuit-type connections were tested, but the results of these experiments showed the need for packet switching.

In the mid-1960s people were writing all types of papers on this subject of networks. One of the first papers on the ARPANET[1] was published by Lawrence G. Roberts[2]. Also at this time were papers on packet switching networks. One of these papers came from a gentleman known as Donald Davies, the British inventor of packet switching, who was theorizing at the British National Physical Laboratory (NPL) about building a network of computers to test his packet switching concepts. About the same time Paul Baran and others at the RAND group had written a paper on packet switching networks for secure voice in the military in 1964. With all of these papers being floated, it happened that the work at MIT[3] (1961–1967), the RAND corporation (1962–1965), and NPL (1964–1967) had occurred simultaneously without the researchers knowing about each other's work. The

1. ARPANet was the network that became the basis for the Internet. It was funded by the US military and consisted of many different individual computers connected by leased lines or a network.
2. http://www.landfield.com/rfcs/rfc2235.html
3. Massachusetts Institute of Technology: "a coeducational, privately endowed research university — is dedicated to advancing knowledge and educating students in science, technology, and other areas of scholarship that will best serve the nation and the world in the 21st century." http://web.mit.edu/about-mit.html.

word "packet," adopted from the work at NPL, means a unit of data that is routed between a network source and a network destination on any network. Then in August of 1968, a Request For Quote (commonly called an RFQ) was released by DARPA[4] for the development of the key components for the ARPANET. Part of the RFQ was the definition and creation of a device known as the IMP.[5] The IMP's job was to manage the packets and provide an interface to the computer at each site. The RFQ was won in December 1968 by a group headed by Frank Heart at Bolt Beranek and Newman (BBN). The team at BBN worked on the IMPs with Bob Kahn playing a major role in the overall ARPANET architectural design.

The Network Measurement Center at UCLA was selected to be the first device (or node) on the ARPANET. In 1969 this was brought to fruition when BBN installed the first IMP[6] at UCLA and the first computer was connected. Another computer at Stanford Research Institute (SRI) provided a second node. One month later the first host-to-host message was sent across the network. Two more nodes were added at University of California, Santa Barbara, and the University of Utah. Finally, by the end of 1969, four host computers were connected together into the initial ARPANET, and the future Internet was underway.

In 1969 a film was released known as *Colossus: The Forbin Project*. An American super computer Colossus and its Russian counterpart, Guardian, got together to rule the world. This film was shot at The Lawrence Hall of Science, Berkeley, California, USA. A great film that was years ahead of its time, *The Forbin Project* showed two computers that became "aware" or "alive" and then decided to connect themselves together—in other words, they formed a network. Here are some of the concepts you can find in the film:

1. Computer virus
2. Network
3. Artificial intelligence
4. Voice activation response

Many of the technologies we have today were alluded to in that science fiction film. If you discover any others send a message to tim-speed@home.

4. The defense Advanced Research Projects Agency is an independent research branch of the US Department of Defense. Originally called ARPA (the "D" was added to its name later), DARPA came into being in 1958 as a reaction to the launching of Sputnik, Russia's first manned satellite.
5. Interface message processor.
6. http://info.internet.isi.edu:80/in-notes/rfc/files/rfc18.txt

com. And FYI—you can purchase *Colossus: The Forbin Project* at www.amazon.com—just search for *The Forbin Project.*

Back to the history. At this point, we now have four computers on the ARPANET. A team of dudes got together to work on the software that would enable the computers to communicate. At UCLA, the first site on the network, Vint Cerf, Steve Crocker, and Jon Postel worked with Leonard Kleinrock[7] to create the software. On April 7, Crocker sent around a memo entitled "Request for Comments." This was the first of many future RFCs that would document the design of the ARPANET and the Internet. This team called itself the "Network Working Group" (aka, RFC 10). The team took it upon itself to develop something called a "protocol." This first network protocol was a collection of programs that came to be known as NCP (Network Control Protocol). From 1970 to 1973 several events occurred:

1. Bob Metcalfe[8] built a network interface between the MIT IMP and a PDP-6 to the ARPANET. Metcalfe builds another network interface for Xerox PARC's PDP-10.[9]
2. The Network Working Group[10] completes the Telnet protocol and makes progress on the file transfer protocol (FTP) standard.
3. Kahn and Cerf design a net-to-net connection protocol. Cerf now leads the International Network Working Group. In September 1973, the two give their first paper on the new Transmission Control Protocol (TCP) at a meeting at the University of Sussex in England.
4. Ray Tomlinson,[11] a programmer at Bolt Beranek and Newman invented e-mail in late 1971. He created e-mail to send messages over a network to fellow programmers.
5. About this time I graduated from high school with several dents in my head, but now I was free of Mary Martin Smith.

At this point in 1973 we are at a critical juncture. Although NCP was the dominant protocol, it did not have the ability to address networks (or computers) farther down the network than a destination IMP on the ARPANET. Therefore, NCP needed either to be updated or replaced. Here

7. Leonard Kleinrock created a doctoral dissertation at MIT on queuing theory in communication networks.
8. Bob Metcalfe later created Ethernet.
9. PDP 10 — From Digital Equipment — now Compaq.
10. http://info.internet.isi.edu:80/in-notes/rfc/files/rfc85.txt
11. http://info.internet.isi.edu:80/in-notes/rfc/files/rfc561.txt

was the problem: If a packet was lost then the application using the network could crash.

For the most part NCP had no end-end host error control and because the ARPANET was to be the only network around, it would need to be so unfailingly reliable that no error control would be required. So Cerf (yes, dudes, not SERF!) and Kahn developed a new protocol, which would eventually be called the transmission control protocol/internet protocol (TCP/IP).

1.2 The Beginning of TCP/IP

The TCP/IP was the glue that the future Internet needed. This single protocol was able to solve many different issues and problems:

1. The TCP/IP was able to stand on its own within each distinct network. As a result no internal changes were required to "connect" the network together.
2. Communications within the network would be on a best effort basis. If a packet didn't make it to the final destination, it would shortly be retransmitted from the source.
3. Special boxes would be used to connect these disparate networks; these would later be called gateways and routers.
4. There would be no global control at the operations level.
5. Defined gateway functions would forward packets as needed to the correct network.
6. Check Sums were used and packets could be "fragmented"[12] or sent out of order and at the destination be put back into the correct order.

It is amazing to look at how scalable the original TCP/IP protocol was. Today we call the protocol IP(v4), or version 4 of the IP protocol. You see, the original model that Cert and Kahn put together was designed to accommodate only the requirements of the ARPANET and the idea of 1000s of networks was not really on their minds. Because the IP protocol uses a 32-bit base, if you factor out the numbers available you have approximately 4 billion possible addresses (2^{32}). The original idea was to use a 32-bit IP address and cut it into chunks. The first 8-bits were used by the network and the remainder (24) were to be used by the hosts (or computers). With 2^8, you have 256 possible combinations that you could use for networks. In the

12. http://info.internet.isi.edu:80/in-notes/rfc/files/rfc815.txt

1970s that was plenty, but today we are out of network numbers. (We will be discussing TCP/IP addressing in Appendix 2, TCP/IP Reference, and a bit on IP(v6).) (We will not be discussing User Datagram Protocol (UDP)—ever—well OK maybe a bit later on.) In the 1970s the addressing scheme was genius work—I don't know whether Cert and Kahn were lucky or brilliant, but in any case we benefited from their design. Thanks Mr. Cert and Mr. Kahn!

The early implementations of TCP were done for large timesharing[13] systems such as Tenex and TOPS 20. Good old TOPS 20, this software ran on a system known as the KL-10 from digital equipment. The KL-10 was a 36-bit "mainframe" from DEC. I worked on the machines types many years ago (yes, just aged myself). When desktop computers first appeared, it was thought by some that TCP was too big to run on a personal computer. This dude named David Clark (as far as I know he was not part of the Dave Clark 5) and a research group from MIT set out to show that a compact and simple implementation of TCP was possible. The first implementation was for the Xerox Alto and the IBM PC.

From 1974 to 1980 several events occurred in the history of the Internet:

- By 1974 daily traffic on the ARPANET exceeds 3 million packets and the Ethernet was demonstrated at Xerox PARC.
- In 1975 the ARPANET geographical map shows 61 nodes.
- In 1976 the packet satellite project went into use. SATNET, Atlantic packet Satellite network, was born. This network linked the United States to Europe.
- In 1977 Steve Wozniak and Steve Jobs announce the Apple II computer. Also introduced is the Tandy TRS-80. These off-the-shelf machines create the consumer and small business markets for computers.
- Continuing their work at DARPA on TCP/IP, in 1978 Vint Cerf expands the vision of the Internet, forming an International Cooperation Board chaired by Peter Kirstein of University College, London.
- In 1979, Newsgroups are created, also known as USENET.

1.3 TCP/IP and the Internet

In 1980 TCP/IP was adopted as a defense standard. This enabled the military-industrial complex of the USA to begin sharing in the DARPA Internet technology base. By 1983, ARPANET was being used by a significant number of defense research and development (R&D) and operational organizations. As of

13. http://www.landfield.com/rfcs/rfc2235.html

January 1, 1983 the ARPANET moved over to a single protocol, TCP/IP. All hosts converted simultaneously. The transition was carefully planned[14] within the community over several years before it actually took place. Another critical event for the Internet occurred in 1983: the domain name system (DNS) was invented. Here is the issue—every computer has an address, for example, 192.9.200.123—OK, we could keep track of these numbers if we had about 30–40 computers, but if we have 1000s of computers, how do we (humans) keep track of all those numbers? Numbering the Internet hosts and keeping tabs on the host names simply failed to scale with the growth of the Internet. In November of 1983, Jon Postel and Paul Mockapetris of USC/ISI and Craig Partridge of BBN develop the DNS. The DNS system provided an on-line mechanism to track the names of computers in relation to their IP address. Previously each computer needed to maintain its own list and if you then added a computer to the network you needed to edit each list on each computer. In the case of DNS all you needed to do was to edit the list in one place.

By 1984, the DNS system was introduced across the Internet, with domain suffixes (you have seen these before) .gov, .mil, .edu, .org, .net, and .com. The Internet was starting to mature by 1985 and was already well established as a technology supporting a broad community of researchers and developers; it was also beginning to be used by other communities for daily computer communications. Electronic mail (via SMTP[15]) was being used broadly across several communities, often with different systems, but interconnection between different mail systems was demonstrating the utility of broad-based electronic communications between people.

By the end of 1985, the number of hosts on the Internet (TCP/IP interconnected networks) reached approximately 2000. Also at this time there were several RFCs created that described a concept known as subnetting. This process involved a mask number being placed along with an IP address, which in effect would divide an IP network into several networks.[16] Between the beginning of 1986 and the end of 1987 the number of networks grew from 2000 to nearly 30,000. TCP/IP[17] was available on workstations and PCs such as the Compaq portable computer. Ethernet[18] was starting to grow and

14. http://info.internet.isi.edu:80/in-notes/rfc/files/rfc801.txt
15. http://info.internet.isi.edu:80/in-notes/rfc/files/rfc821.txt
16. http://info.internet.isi.edu:80/in-notes/rfc/files/rfc932.txt and http://info.internet.isi.edu:80/in-notes/rfc/files/rfc936.txt and http://info.internet.isi.edu:80/in-notes/rfc/files/rfc940.txt
17. http://info.internet.isi.edu:80/in-notes/rfc/files/rfc983.txt
18. http://info.internet.isi.edu:80/in-notes/rfc/files/rfc826.txt and http://info.internet.isi.edu:80/in-notes/rfc/files/rfc894.txt

become available across college campuses. In 1986, the US National Science Foundation (NSF) initiated the development of the NSFNET, which provided a major backbone communication service for the Internet.

When we look at the 1980s the question comes up about Al Gore and the Internet. There is no explanation better than the one from Cert and Kahn. Here is an extract:

> As a Senator in the 1980s Gore urged government agencies to consolidate what at the time were several dozen different and unconnected networks into an "Interagency Network." Working in a bipartisan manner with officials in Ronald Reagan and George Bush's administrations, Gore secured the passage of the High Performance Computing and Communications Act in 1991. This "Gore Act" supported the National Research and Education Network (NREN) initiative that became one of the major vehicles for the spread of the Internet beyond the field of computer science. (http://www.isoc.org/internet-history/gore.shtml)

The question for us to ponder then is, "Who really invented the Internet?" The answer is "I did, yes, I invented the Internet, I also invented popcorn, gravy, and pizza." So now you know and can quote me. :-)

1.4 Okay, Back to Reality

A great deal of support for the Internet community has come from the US federal government, since the Internet was originally part of a federally funded research program and, subsequently, has become a major part of the US research infrastructure. Over the history of the Internet it has provided a platform for collaboration and communication. The Internet Activities Board (IAB) was created in 1983 to guide the evolution of the TCP/IP Protocol Suite and to provide research advice to the Internet community. During its short existence, the IAB has reorganized many times and now has two primary components: the Internet Engineering Task Force (IETF) and the Internet Research Task Force. The IETF[19] has responsibility for further evolution of the TCP/IP protocol suite and its standardization.

As we continue with the history, we find The Morris WORM. In 1988, this worm burrowed into the Internet and into 6000 of the 60,000 hosts now on the network at this time. This is the first worm experience and

19. http://info.internet.isi.edu:80/in-notes/rfc/files/rfc1539.txt

DARPA forms the computer emergency response team (CERT[20]) to deal with future such incidents.[21]

By the end of 1989 the number of hosts has increased to 160,000 and we also see the advent of commercial e-mail relays. Network speeds are up to 45 Mbps and 100 Mbps is on the horizon based on FDDI. Now we hear the first rumblings of the "WEB." In Switzerland at CERN,[22] Tim Berners-Lee addresses the issue of the constant change in the currency of information and the turnover of people on projects. Berners-Lee[23] proposed something called "Hypertext," which is a system that will run across distributed systems on different operating systems.

From 1990 to 1992 we see a number of changes and enhancements to the Internet:

1. The number of networks exceeds 7500 and the number of computers connected grows beyond 1,000,000.
2. The Internet now connects more than 100 countries.
3. The Web is born. The Stanford Linear Accelerator Center (SLAC) in California becomes the first Web server in the USA. It serves the contents of an existing, large database of abstracts of physics papers.

In 1993 we saw some of these events:

1. The US White House comes on-line http://www.whitehouse.gov/
2. RFC 1437: The Extension of MIME content-types to a new medium
3. RFC 1438: IETF statements of boredom (SOBs) (this is really good)
4. Marc Andreessen and NCSA and the University of Illinois develop a graphical user interface to the WWW, called "Mosaic for X."

No major changes were made to the physical network in 1994, but the most significant event was its growth. Other events from this year include:

1. Pizza Hut offers pizza ordering on its Web page.
2. Shopping malls arrive on the Internet.
3. Internet traffic passes 10 trillion bytes/month.

20. http://www.cert.org/
21. http://www.apcatalog.com/cgi-bin/AP?ISBN=0122374711&LOCATION=US&FORM=FORM2
22. http://cern.web.cern.ch/CERN/
23. http://www.w3.org/People/Berners-Lee/ShortHistory.html

4. RFC 1607: A VIEW FROM THE 21ST CENTURY; this is another great RFC—check it out—http://info.internet.isi.edu:80/in-notes/rfc/files/rfc1607.txt
5. First Virtual, the first cyberbank, opens.
6. The URI is defined—http://info.internet.isi.edu:80/in-notes/rfc/files/rfc1630.txt
7. The URL is defined—http://info.internet.isi.edu:80/in-notes/rfc/files/rfc1738.txt

On October 24, 1995, the FNC unanimously passed a resolution defining the term "Internet." A resolution was drafted that stated the following (from the the Federal Networking Council (FNC)):

the term "Internet" refers to the global information system that

(i) is logically linked together by a globally unique address space based on the Internet Protocol (IP) or its subsequent extensions/follow-ons;

(ii) is able to support communications using the transmission control protocol/Internet protocol (TCP/IP) suite or its subsequent extensions/follow-ons, and/or other IP-compatible protocols; and

(iii) provides, uses or makes accessible, either publicly or privately, high-level services layered on the communications and related infrastructure described herein.

And 1995 also saw these events:

1. The National Science Foundation (NSF) announced that as of April 30, 1995 it would no longer allow direct access to the NSF backbone and contracted with four companies that would be providers of access to it (Merit). These companies would then sell connections to groups, organizations, and companies.
2. A $50 annual fee is imposed on any domains, excluding .edu and .gov domains, that are still funded by the National Science Foundation.
3. The world wide web surpasses ftp-data in March as the service with highest amount traffic.
4. RFC 1825—Security Architecture for the Internet Protocol—http://info.internet.isi.edu:80/in-notes/rfc/files/rfc1825.txt
5. RFC 1882—you need to see this one. –> http://info.internet.isi.edu:80/in-notes/rfc/files/rfc1882.txt

The Internet has changed significantly since it came into existence. This ubiquitous network was designed before LANs were even thought up and yet today it can accommodate a massive amount of traffic. From 1996 to 2001 the Internet continued to grow. New applications and features were developed and implemented. And security became the "hot topic." In fact, from 1996 to today we have seen:

1. The US Communications Decency Act (CDA) become law in the US in order to prohibit distribution of indecent materials;
2. various ISPs suffer extended service outages, bringing into question whether they will be able to handle the growing number of users;
3. a malicious program is released on USENET that wipes out more than 25,000 messages;
4. human error at Network Solutions causes the DNS table for .com and .net domains to become corrupted;
5. viruses
    a. Melissa
    b. ExploreZip
    c. Love Letter;
6. more stolen Identities, denial of service attacks, child pornography, and the famous dot-com crashes of 2001; and the very sad death of the sock puppet—why—because pets can't buy things (or use a credit card for that matter). The fact that pets can't drive is a moot point.

At first glance you may say, the Internet started off great, but now it is just dead business and trash; but take a look at the billions of dollars that are spent yearly on e-commerce, and at the track record from GE, where Jack Welch has shown all of us how to do the Internet.

1.5 Why Ethernet?

Why give the Ethernet its own section and provide a separate history for it? Because many of the examples that we will be discussing will pertain to "The Ethernet," it is necessary. The Ethernet is a system for connecting computers within a building (or your house) using dedicated hardware and software running from machine to machine. Robert Metcalfe, a member of the research staff for Xerox at their Palo Alto Research Center (PARC), where some of the first personal computers were created, was asked to build a networking system for PARC's computers. Xerox's motivation for the computer network was that they were also building the world's first laser printer and wanted all of the PARC's computers to be able to print with this printer. Mr. Metcalfe had two challenges:

1. The network had to be fast enough to drive the new laser printer; and
2. the network needed to connect hundreds of computers within the same building.

There are several contradictory stories about when the Ethernet was really invented. For us it really does not matter, so if you want a date use the one given by Metcalfe, who said, "gradually over a period of several years." In about 1979, Metcalfe left Xerox to evangelize the use of personal computers and local area networks (LANs). Metcalfe was able to sell Digital Equipment, Intel, and Xerox Corporations on the concept and get them to work together to promote Ethernet as a standard. In fact, one of the orginal connectors that was used was called a DIX connector—get it? **D**igital, **I**ntel, **X**erox.

CHAPTER 2

Got DSL, Got Cable, May Have Trouble (Connecting to the Internet Today): The Internet and the Home User

We have a need for speed, more and more speed. We just can't download those pictures from the Internet fast enough. Faster and faster we go. Our search for the Holy Grail of speed drives us toward newer and faster technologies. Remember 300-baud[1] modems?[2] This was the "fast" speed just a few years ago. I remember getting excited about purchasing a modem that transmitted at 1200 baud—wow, was that fast. Today we have analog[3] modems that can reach speeds of 56k (bits per second). In comparison to 300 baud this is lighting fast. As the access to the Internet gets faster, we do more. Think about this, could you play that interactive Internet network game if your access speed to the Internet was just 300 bps? No, because you are accustomed to using 56,000 bps and even more with cable and DSL. There is a direct correlation between the value of the Internet and the speed of the Internet.

1. Baud was the term used to reflect a measurement of transfer speed for data transmission. Today's term is *bits per second*. The term baud was named after the French engineer, Jean-Maurice-Emile Baudot. It was first used to measure the speed of telegraph transmissions.
2. A modem is a modulator / demodulator — the modem converts outgoing digital signals from a computer and places these signals onto an analog signal. At the receiving end of the transmission the digital signal is removed or demodulated.
3. Analog transmission, in the case of modems, refers to electronic transmission signals that vary the frequency or amplitude to carrier waves of a given frequency.

FIGURE 2.1

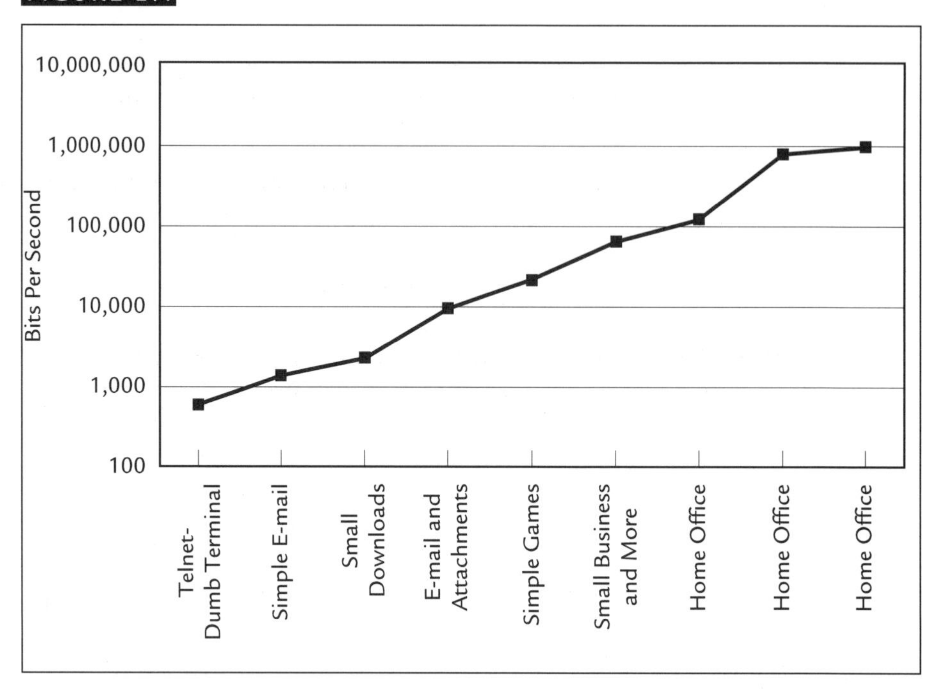

As you can see from the chart in Figure 2.1, the faster the speed the more you can do with the Internet. Once we get into the realm of "Home Office," then the whole world opens up. We cannot run a business from our home, host a Web server, or connect to a corporate network at 300 bps. With each of these advances in speed come more products, tools, and applications. Associated with each advance in value is more risk.

Thus, as more and more professionals are working at home, more computer security is needed for their home-based computers. We have categorized the level of security according to two scenarios:

- Personal computer (PC) at home, and
- Business Computer at home.

At this point you may be asking, what is the difference between a personal computer and a business computer? The answer is risk and loss. At the end of the day you may lose all of the data on your computer. Okay, in any case this is no fun and can really make you mad; you also need to look at your losses and determine the financial impact, if any. If you open an e-mail message with a virus and all of your data are destroyed, then what is the impact to you?

- If it takes maybe four hours to reinstall all of your programs, then the impact is minimal,
- But if it takes four hours to reinstall all of your programs, **AND** your small business payroll data is lost, including your data for the IRS, then you have a big problem.

In the end the difference between a business computer and a home PC is the value that the computer has to you, and what you can lose if the data were to be lost. Before we get into the various scenarios let's look at one more question—"Can I get 100% security for my personal PC or my business PC?"—The answer is NO. Much like life itself, there are no absolutes. If you are looking for 100% security then don't purchase the PC in the first place.

Before we address different security options available to the home PC, let's take a look at some of the configuration options that you may be currently using at your home. These scenarios include:

- The personal computer at home as a single PC or in a network; and
- The business computer at home as a single PC or in a network. (See the drawing in Figure 2.2.)

FIGURE 2.2

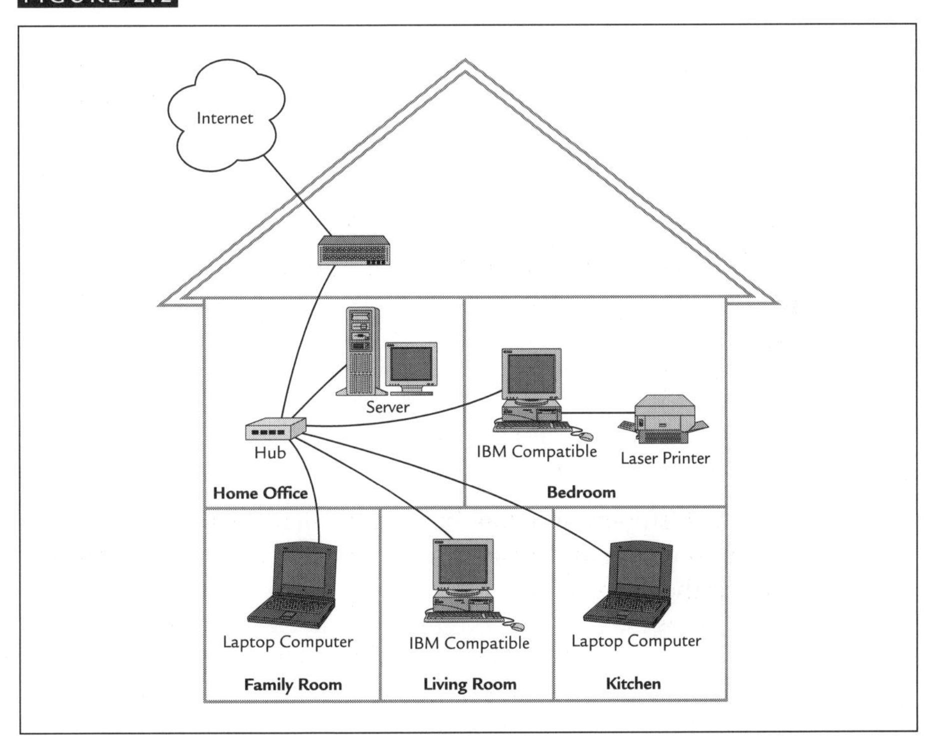

2.1 The Personal Computer at Home

There are two basic configurations that we will discuss as part of the single PC at home:

1. Low-speed connections; and
2. high-speed connections.

Low-speed connections to the Internet is established via a dial-up mechanism. This is accomplished by using a modem and a service provider. The provider, also known as an ISP (Internet service provider), establishes access to the larger Internet. The modem dials the provider and the provider returns information to the computer that grants access, addressing, and in some cases applications services. Figure 2.3 shows a user accessing a service provider to access the Internet and receive e-mail.

In this example a user at a computer (1) will access the ISP, via a modem (2). This modem will dial another modem via a phone line. A bank of modems at the service provider will be listening for calls from end-users. One of the modems (3) will answer the call and establish a connection to the Internet (6). If the user is authorized then he or she will be able to browse Web sites, send e-mail, and do other interesting things (like play games). The ISP also may house the user's e-mail(5). That way the user can send and receive e-mail via the service provider. Connection speeds typically max out at about 56k. Later we will be discussing a protocol known at TCP/IP. For now we will discuss how a computer is known on the Internet by starting with a simple analogy. Most of us live at some type of address,

FIGURE 2.3

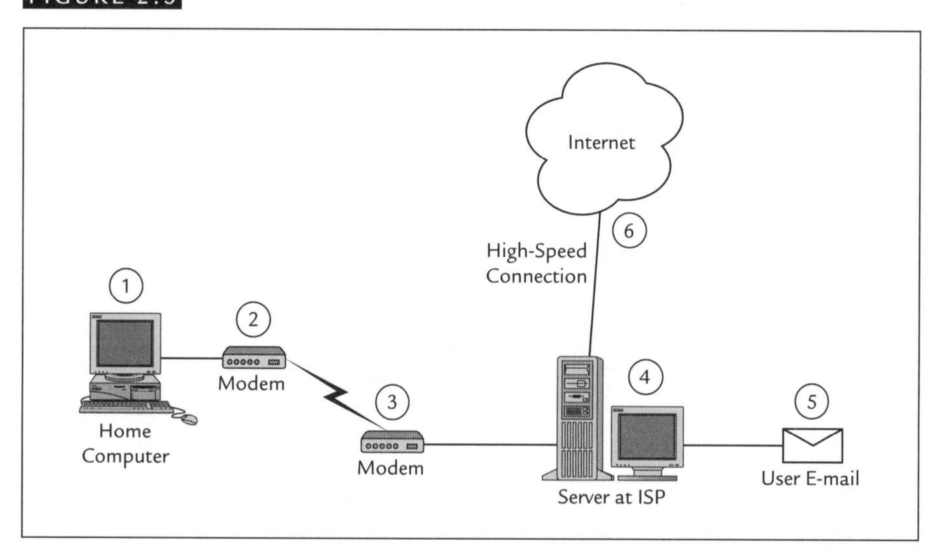

house, apartment, tent, you get the idea. Most of these locations have some type of address, your street, and your house on the street. Thanks to the US post office, those of us in the United States have a thing known as a zip code. You combine these factors and you have a method to locate someone and even send a package or a piece of mail (a.k.a. snail mail). Guess what, the Internet uses a similar method to locate your machine. The TCP/IP is the address scheme used to assign addresses. Every computer will have one of these IP addresses. The service may assign you a temporary address, via Dynamic Host Configuration Protocol (DHCP), or may assign a static address. In any case you will have one of these addresses.

A dial-up connection typically has a limited connection time. You dial-up, do your business and then you finish the connection by logging off or shutting down your computer. In most cases the home computer initiates the connection and, therefore, if the computer is off then your connection to the Internet is also off.

Figure 2.4 shows you the connection process. You sit down at your computer; you need to purchase that new security book on Amazon.com. You open your Internet dial-up software, and dial the service provider. (These are steps 1–3.) The server at the ISP (4) assigns an IP address to your computer (5). This address stays in place until you break the connection or shut down your computer. Many ISPs will have a series of tools and processes that will automatically disconnect you if you don't use the system; for example, if you don't have any activity for an hour then the service provider will hang up the modem on their side and your computer will be off of the Internet.

FIGURE 2.4

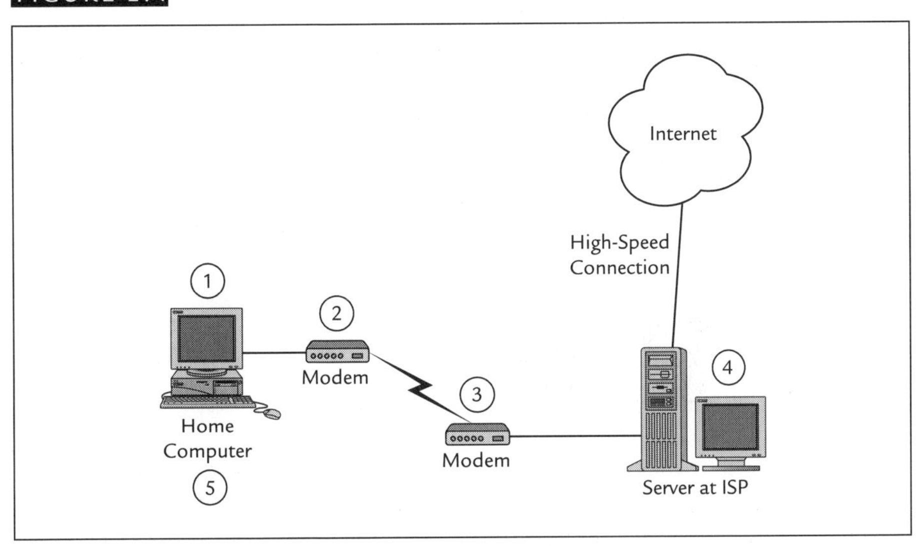

Okay, you are saying, I know all of this stuff, so tell me something new. Hold on there, bubba. We need to discuss these basics so that you understand the difference between a dial-up connection and a constant connection. Both ISDN and cable can provide constant connections—more to follow on this!

2.2 The Business Computer at Home

One example of a business computer at home is the laptop you have at work. Laptops are easy to unplug from the office and take back to the house. Now you can use your computer from home, in fact you may even have your office at home. Before we get too far let's look at some of the issues computing at home involves. If you have a computer at work you may have several security features that protects this computer, for example, virus software on the servers, a DMZ,[4] on-line IntrAnet with instant information about issues, and problems relating to security. In other words you have the company's security protections available to you. When you bring that computer home you may not have all of these features available to you. We hope that you have some virus software that lives on your PC, but you may not. In fact, you could possibly bring your computer home, infect it with a virus, and then bring that virus back to work. Okay, we know you would not do this on purpose, but this could (and does) happen. And if your computer at home is also used for business purposes, you need to protect that system from various security exposures and issues.

Figure 2.5 provides an example of a home network. In this example you have several computers on a private network. Each of these computers communicates with each other via a network protocol. There are various protocols, TCP/IP, Netbios, IPS/SPX, and others. For our discussions we will focus on TCP/IP. Thanks to this 30-year-old technology we can set up computers quickly on a network. You may have noticed that the physical network type used in our figure is the Ethernet. Ethernet will be our network of choice for the examples in this book. (We will discuss some MAC issues—later.) In this simple network you will notice there are no connections to the Internet. In order to connect to the Internet you need some type of access point.

In the diagram in Figure 2.6 you see one of many different methods for connecting to the Internet. In this case one computer connects to the Internet and routes messages (actually packets) from the private network to the

4. In computer networks, a DMZ (demilitarized zone) is a computer host or small network inserted as a "neutral zone" between a company's private network and the outside public network. It prevents outside users from direct accessing a server that contains company data.

FIGURE 2.5

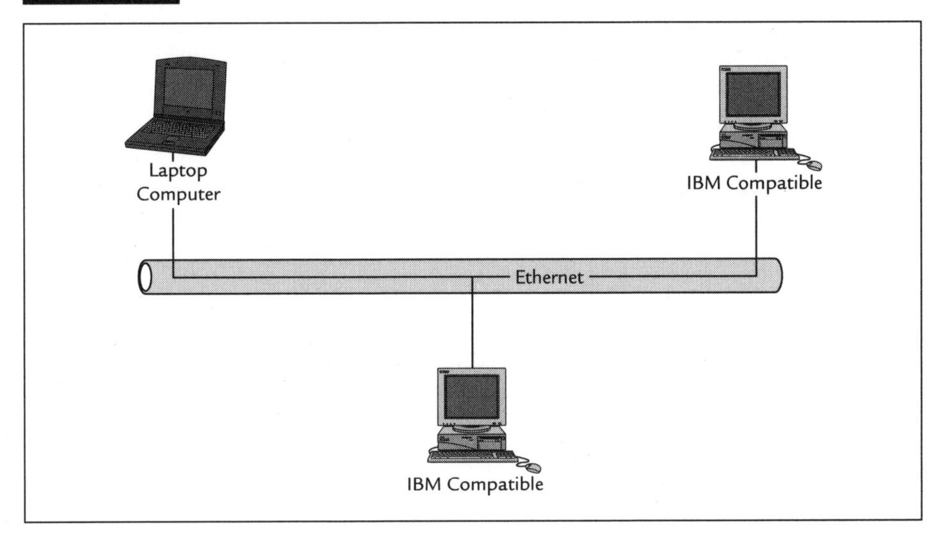

FIGURE 2.6

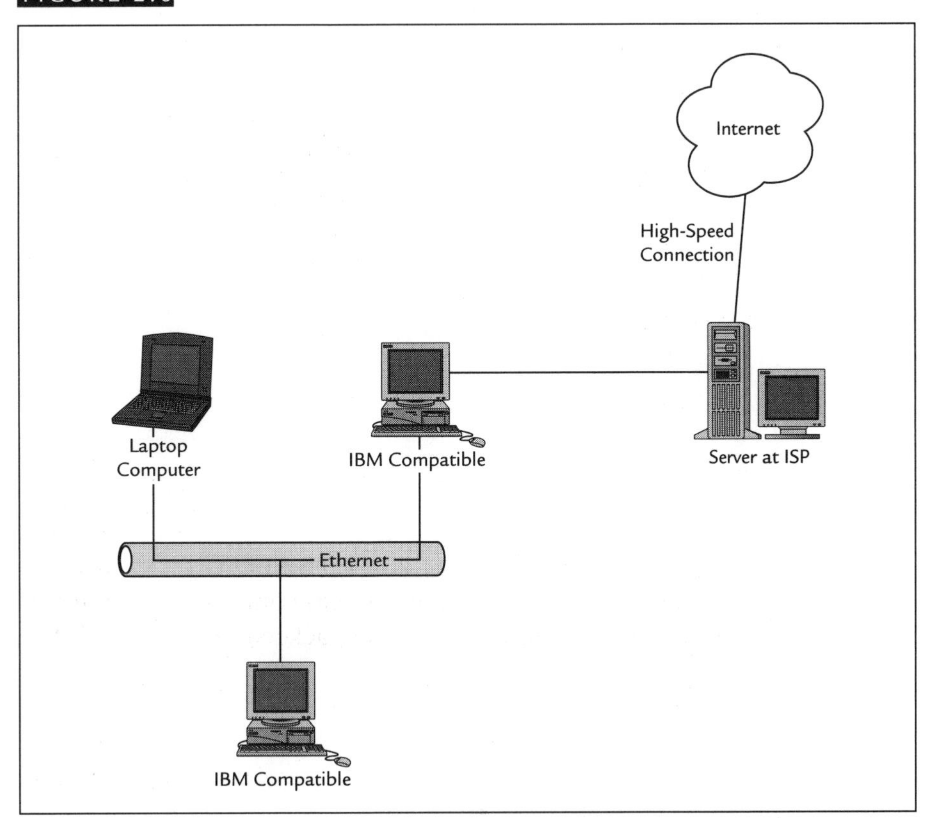

Internet. This computer is exposed to the Internet and is the access point for hackers to enter your private network. Remember the example of the laptop from work? In this example the laptop could be from your office. Data that was protected at work is now potentially exposed through your personal connection to the Internet.

In our diagrams you may have noticed that there are no "Servers." You don't need a server for a network. The old days of having a file server and a print server are gone. Any PC on the network can do these tasks. Today you can set up what is known as a peer-to-peer network. We will cover all of these components in a later chapter. One of the nice features of a home network (OK, any network) is that you can combine any type of operating system. We can mix Unix, Win95, Win95, OS/2 (Yes OS/2), and even Macs all on the same network.

2.3 Connection Types (You Can't Get High on POTS)

Both business and personal computers may be connected through various types of technologies. Each option may have associated security risks and both software and hardware requirements. In later chapters, we will address security prevention based on the type of connection you are using. For now, let's cover some of these connection types in order to understand the technology and how they connect us to the Internet.

2.3.1 Dial-Up

Let's start off with dial-up. Most dial-up connections are effectuated via a system known as POTS. Plain old telephone service (or POTS[5]) is how you connect to an ISP. You unplug your phone; place the phone cable into your modem and "dial-up." If your speaker is on you hear a bunch of screeches and noises, and then you are ON. At this point you have connected to the Internet. Due to the design of POTS it is difficult to get high speeds from a dial-up connection.

As we mentioned, modems are used on each end of the connection that takes a computer digital signal, converts it to analog, and at the receiving end converts it back to digital. This is accomplished by modems that can be internal to the PC or external. Today most computers are shipped with a 56k modem built into the computer. Using software from the O/S or from an ISP you can be connected to the Internet about 10 minutes after taking the computer out of the box.

5. For more information about POTS see http://www.howstuffworks.com/telephone.htm

2.3.2 ISDN

Integrated Services Digital Network (ISDN) is a set of standards for digital data transmission over ordinary telephone (POTS) copper wire. The ISDN, which requires a special adapter installed at both ends of the connection, acts similarly to a dial-up service in the sense that a dial-up number is used to find (dial) the service provider.

There are several levels of service available from your local phone company (FYI—ISDN is not available everywhere). The two most common levels of service are:

- Basic rate interface—BRI is targeted for homes and small businesses; and
- primary rate interface—PRI is for larger users and businesses.

The ISDN is implemented via a set of channels. These are designated by letters for the type of channel, B for data and D for control. Both rates include a number of B-channels and D-channels. Each B-channel carries data, voice, and other services. Each D-channel carries control information. The basic rate interface includes two 64 kbps B-channels and one 16 kbps D-channel. A basic rate user can have up to 128 kbps service. The primary rate includes 23 B-channels and one 64 kpbs D-channel in the US. One nice feature of ISDN is that you can use some of the channels for voice as well as for data.

In Figure 2.7 the computer will dial-up a service provider via an ISDN modem. The modem will dial another modem via the public switch telephone network. The other modem will answer and establish a connection. Once the connection[6] is established then the computer can access the Internet.

FIGURE 2.7

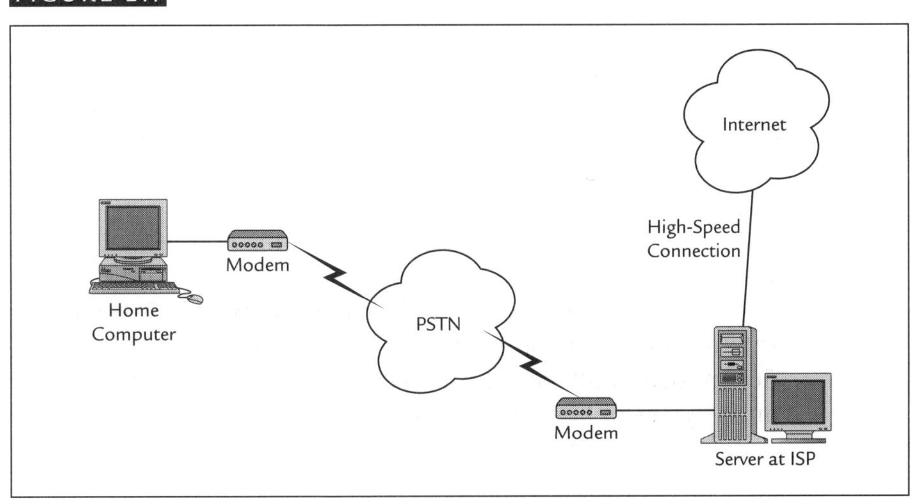

6. Note: Authentication and authorization may be needed.

2.3.3 DSL

Digital subscriber line (DSL) is a high-speed network connection using the same wires as a regular telephone line (remember POTS). The speed is typically higher than the dial-up connection. The DSL can use the same wiring as your typical phone circuit. Many companies that offer DSL will provide a DSL modem with the installation. Actually the modem is known as a transceiver. This (modem) transceiver can connect to a customer's computer via many different methods. One method is to connect the computer to the modem via a USB port[7]. Another method is to connect the mode to an Ethernet Card[8] in the computer.

FIGURE 2.8

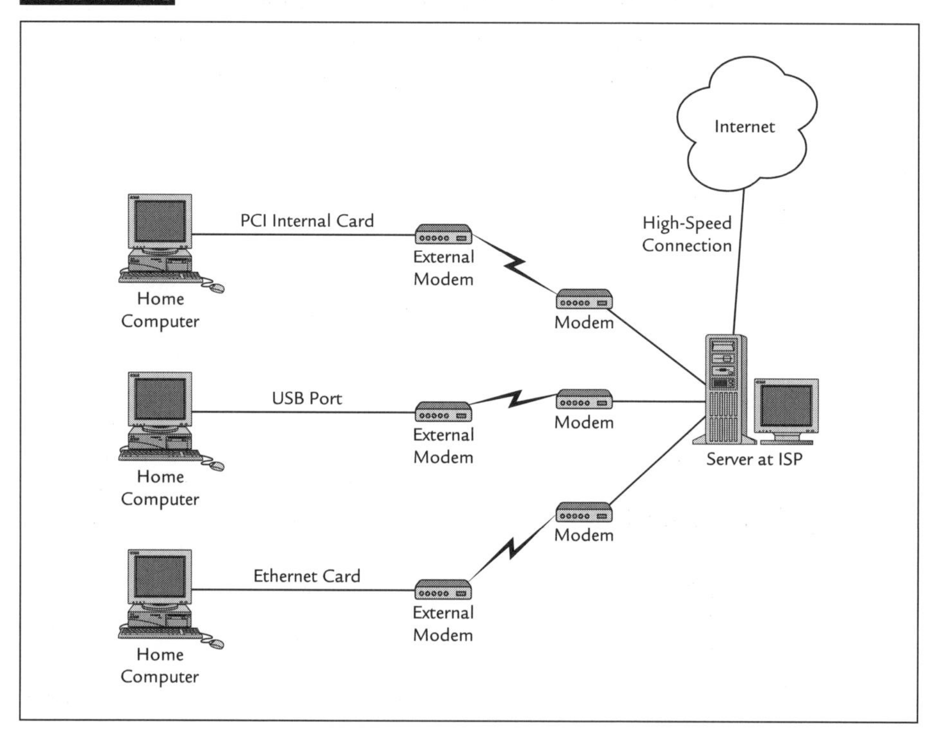

7. Universal serial bus (USB) is a connectivity specification developed by the USB Promoter Group. The USB is targeted for peripherals connecting outside the computer in order to eliminate the hassle of opening the computer case for installing cards needed for certain devices. For more information see: http://developer.intel.com/technology/usb/

8. An Ethernet local area network (LAN) technology is a specification from an IEEE standard, 802.3/ (Institute of Electrical and Electronic Engineers — IEEE). Originally developed by Xerox, DEC and Intel, an Ethernet LAN typically uses coaxial cable or twisted pair wires.

In Figure 2.8 you will see three ways to connect DSL directly to a computer. In the first, you see the modem connecting directly to the PCI card. This is a special card that connects directly into the PC. A cable connects the card to the modem and then the modem dials the ISP. In the second example a USB port is used. A cable is connected from the USB port on the computer to the modem. In the last example the modem connects directly to an Ethernet NIC (network interface card) in the computer.

Finally, there is the scenario where you can connect the modem directly to your home network. In the example given in Figure 2.9 the modem is connected via Ethernet to a "Home Router." The router will then route the TCP traffic to and from the home computers. This way any computer on the "home" network will be able to access the Internet.

FIGURE 2.9

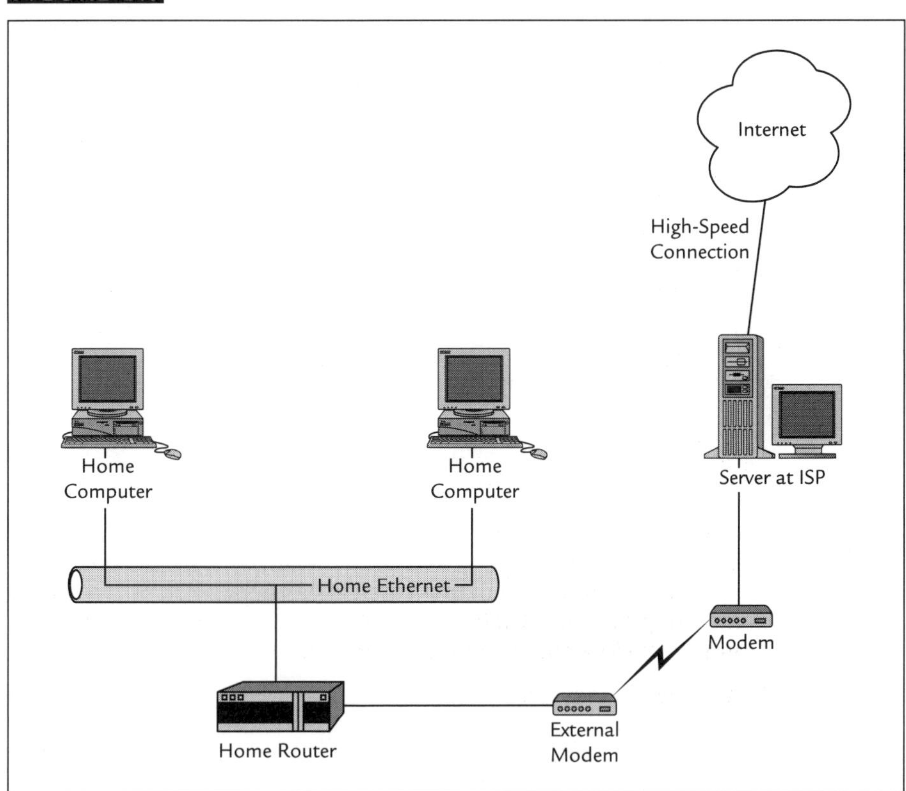

2.3.4 Cable Modem

Cable networks for TV access began in North America more than 30 years ago. Initially cable was used to provide TV access to locations that had difficulty in receiving TV signals transmitted via airwave transmission towers. Cable companies were created based on licensing for a specific geographic area and would sell access based on some type of subscription service, normally involving a monthly charge. Soon cable companies began offering content and not just a rebroadcast of the major network and their material. And the next thing you know old Jed is now on TNT and Ted Turner is a billionaire. (Get the joke, Jed, Ted—Beverly Hillbillies?) In order for this process to work, cables were installed (dig up dirt and put in cable) to each house. This is what was done at my house. The cable companies discovered that they could offer Internet services via the same cable that was being dropped into each house. Most cool. So faster than Ellie Mae's cat swimming in a cement pond, cable Internet modems were created and the cable companies had a new service. The cable modem is a box (looks like a box to me) at the user end of a cable that allows a computer to be connected to the Internet through an existing TV cable connection. This box is connected to the existing cable that comes into the house. Remember old POTS? Well the cable modem works in a similar manner to a standard modem in that it takes a digital signal from the computer and converts it for transmission over the cable network.

Following the steps as illustrated by Figure 2.10, starting on #1, you see that your home computer is tied to a "home network." The computer is tied to this home network via #2, a NIC card.[9] The cable[10] modem, #3, connects directly to the home network via an Ethernet cable (more on this later). Somewhere in this connection is a splitter[11] box, #4. The splitter sends one signal to the cable modem and the other to the TV sets in the house, #5. From the house the cable connects to the cable company, #6. From there it connects to the Internet #7.

This book is primarily concerned with security and protecting your PC. There are many discussions on the speed differences between the various Internet connections that we have talked about and touched on only

9. Network Interface Card.
10. The cable modem demodulates the incoming signal and translates it back into IP packets the computer can understand.
11. The cable's bandwidth is wide enough to let users watch television and maintain an Internet connection. A splitter in each house sends one signal to the TV set and another to the computer's cable modem.

briefly here—if you want to know more about the speeds of the various connections check out the following URLs:

1. http://coverage.cnet.com/Content/Features/Techno/Cablemodems/ss06.html
2. http://www.vicomtech.com/knowledge/reference/cable.modems.html#1
3. http://www.pcworld.com/hereshow/article/0,aid,17150,00.asp

FIGURE 2.10

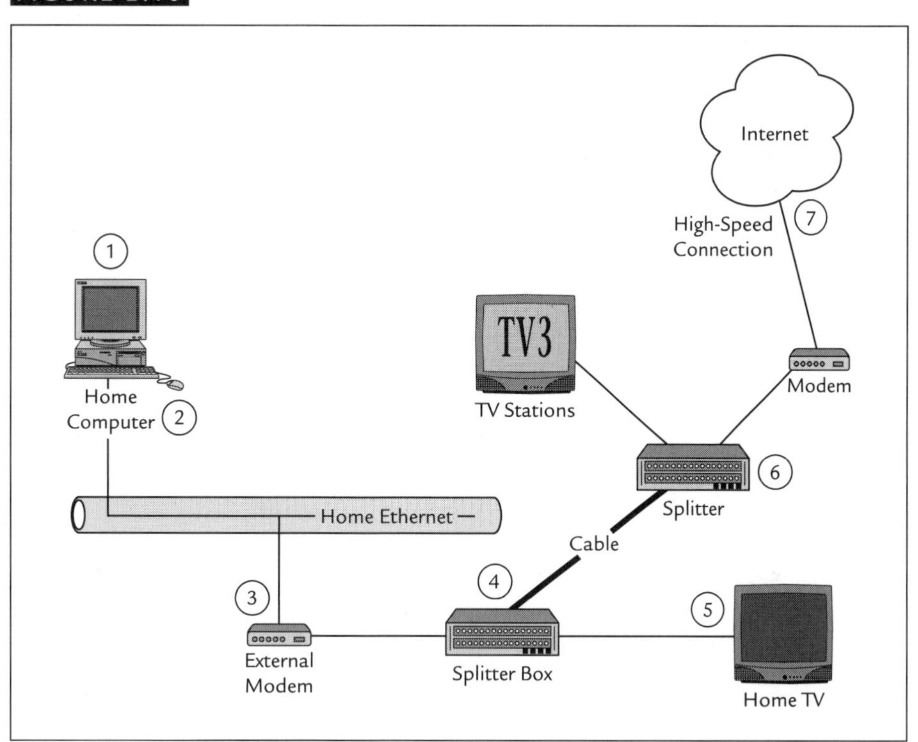

CHAPTER 3

Connecting Your Home Network to the Internet

This chapter tells you how to set up and configure a secure home network. There are many references to TCP, IP, DNS, and DHCP. If you need to know how TCP/IP works and/or want a refresher review then please read the TCP/IP reference chapter (Appendix 2) before continuing.

In the diagram in Figure 3.1 you see an Internet connection being routed into the house. Once in the house you may hook it up to a hub. From the hub you connect to all of the other computers in the house.

3.1 Connection Types

Today we have two choices for connectivity, physical cable and wireless. The two most popular types of physical network cabling are twisted-pair[1] and thin coax.[2] The 10BaseT cabling looks like ordinary telephone wire, except that it has eight wires inside instead of four. Thin coax looks like the copper coaxial cabling that's often used to connect a VCR to a TV set.

The UTP cable looks much like telephone line and the UTP network wires run out from a central hub like the spokes of a wheel. From a hub to each

1. 10BaseT

2. 10Base2

FIGURE 3.1

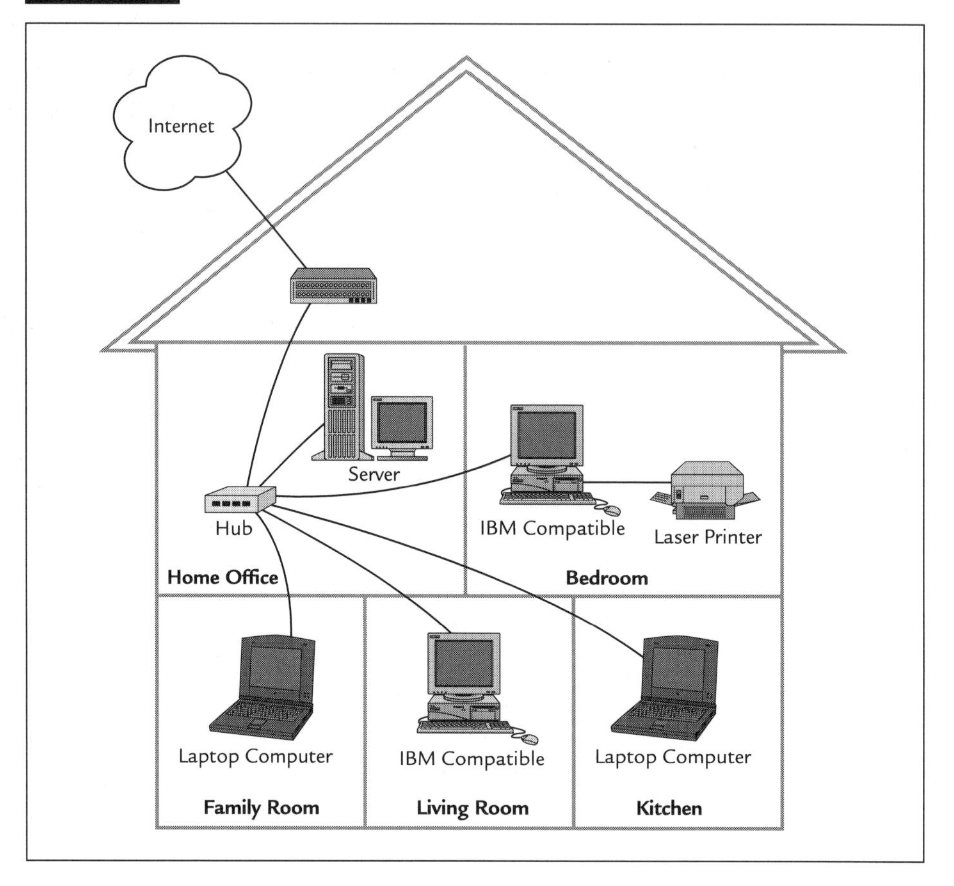

computer you will need RJ-45 connectors. These cables can be purchased from many difference vendors—check out www.microwarehouse.com. There is also a cable type known as Thin Ethernet, a cable that looks similar to cable TV wire. We will focus on UTP cables in this book.

3.2 Network Interface Cards

A networked computer is connected to the network cabling with a network interface card, (also called a NIC,[3] "nick," or network adapter). The brand of card isn't important, but make sure each one works with your operating sys-

3. Network Interface Card — NIC

tem. Windows 95, 98, and 2000 have an auto detection system that will detect and set up your card for you. Here are some vendors to consider:

- EtherFast 10/100 Card w/Wake—Linksys http://www.linksys.com/
- DFE-530TX Plus 32-bit 10/100 PCI—D-Link Systems http://www.3com.com/
- Etherlink 10/100 PCI NIC 3Com http://www.3com.com/
- Fast EtherLink XL PCI—3Com http://www.3com.com/
- Pro/100 S Desktop Adapter—Intel http:// www.intel.com
- Netgear FA311TX PCI 10/100—Netgear Inc. http://www.netgear.com
- EZ Card 10/100 100Base-TX—SMC, Inc. http://www.smc.com/
- EZNet 10/100Base-TX PCI Card,—SMC, Inc. http://www.smc.com/

Network cards come in three basic types: ISA,[4] PCI,[5] and PCMCIA.[6] Each type is typically plug and play. Most of today's computers use either PCI or PCMCIA cards, but you may still find some ISA cards out in the marketplace. Make sure that the card you choose also has the correct cable type connector, that is, UTP or thin Ethernet. Many cards are manufactured with a dual cable configuration.

When you purchase your Ethernet card, read the installation instructions for your particular computer type and card type. This site, http://www.onecomputerguy.com/networking/tcpip.htm, has some great screen shots that show how to setup a network card.

Before we set up your network we will still need to review some more of the components that you may need in your network. These components include:

a. Setting up the NIC;

b. Router;

c. Hub;

d. Router; and

e. Personal firewalls.

4. ISA is a standard system bus based on the IBM AT architecture.

5. PCI, a high-speed system bus that connects between a microprocessor and attached devices, is installed in most new desktop computers.

6. A PCMCIA card is a credit card-sized device that connects to a notebook, laptop or PC computer. This card can be an Ethernet Card, Token Ring, Memory Card, hard drive, and more.

3.3 Setting Up the NIC

The TCP/IP protocol is the one you will be using to access the Internet. In Chapter 1 we discussed the origins of TCP/IP. Every computer on the Internet has a TCP/IP address. Before you try to set up you home network, read Appendix 2, TCP/IP Reference.

One important consideration to understand is that each entity on the Internet has a registered address. These addresses are unique for each computer. So you may ask, "do I need one of these registered addresses for my home computers?" The answer depends on how you set up your home network. Figure 3.2 provides an example.

In this example you have two registered addresses from the service provider. In each machine you will need to set up the following:

- Registered IP address (this is assigned you to you by the service provider);
- Default gateway: (also assigned by the service provider); and
- DNS (also assigned by the service provider).

Once this is set up then you are ready to roll.

FIGURE 3.2

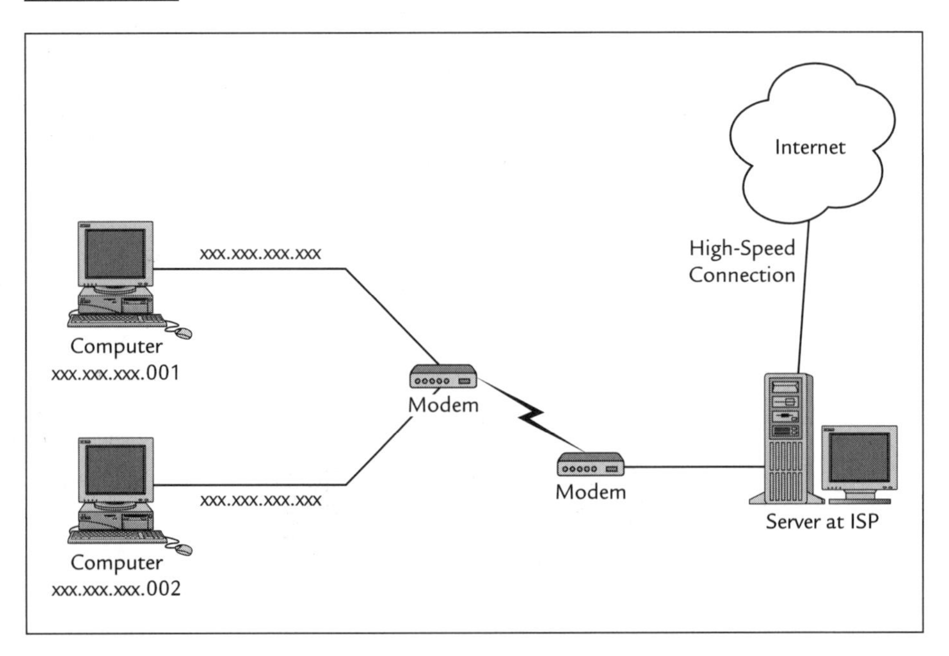

There is a problem with this configuration however. What do you do when you have a third computer that you want to add to your home network and you need to go back to the service provider and get another address.

In the example given in Figure 3.3, NIC has a registered address and the other does not. The home network uses any address that you want to use (keeping to the IP addressing rules). Now you only need one address from the service provider and you can add as many computers as you like to your home network, with all of them using just one address.

The next item we need to discuss is the HUB.

3.4 HUB

The network hub is an interconnection device that provides an electrical circuit to other network devices. A hub can provide all of the connection to a network or can connect to other hubs.

FIGURE 3.3

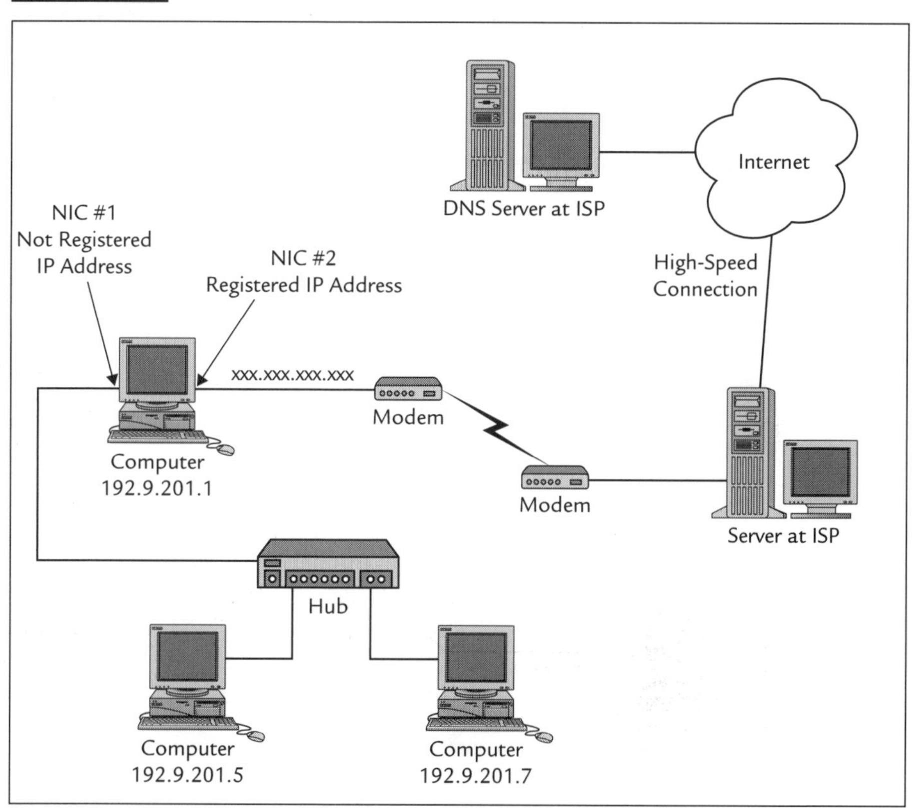

One concept that we have not spent much time on is the process by which Ethernet actually communicates on the network. Called carrier sense multiple access/collision detect (or CSMA/CD for short), this protocol provides carrier transmission access to Ethernet networks. However, this is not the protocol for TCP/IP. Review the OSI reference model in Appendix 2. Ethernet needs to connect on a physical level before IP can communicate. In the example given in Figure 3.4, three computers and the hub, you see the physical connection of our computers. All computers connect to the hub and can talk to each other at the physical layer.

As shown in Figure 3.5, you can connect many hubs together to make a large network. Here is a list of hub vendors and hubs for you to check out:

- Etherfast 16-Port 10/100 Desktop—Linksys http://www.linksys.com/
- EtherFast 8-Port 10/100 Desktop—Linksys http://www.linksys.com/

FIGURE 3.4

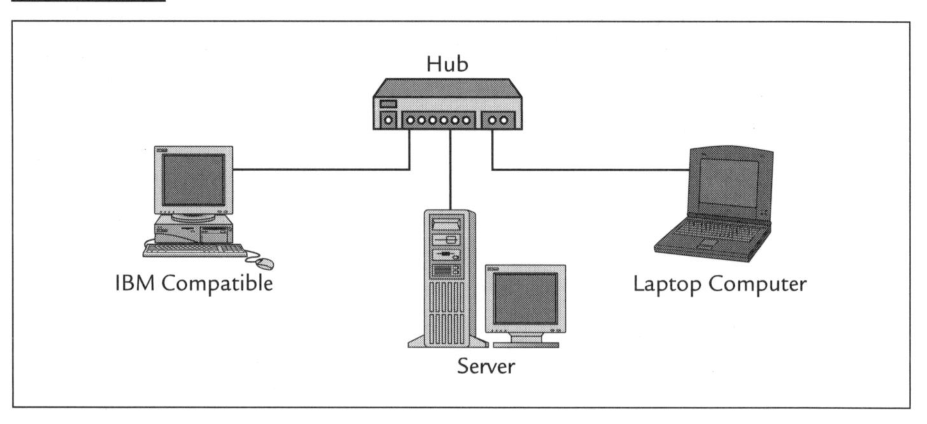

FIGURE 3.5

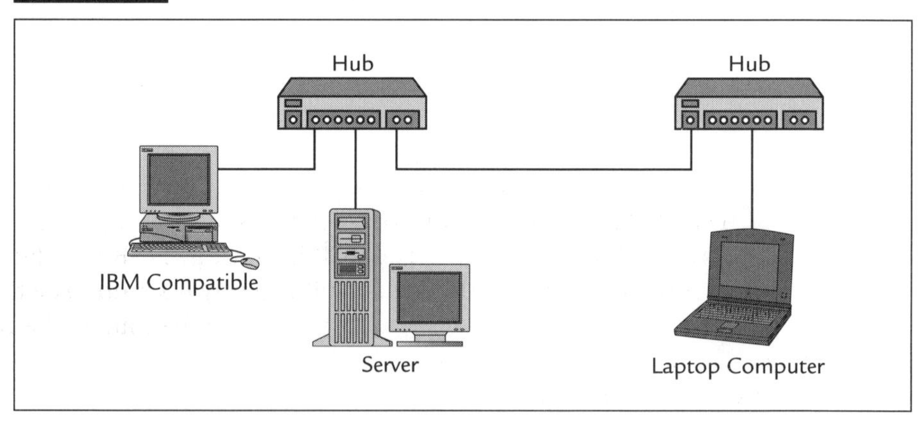

- EtherFast 24-Port 10/100—Linksys http://www.linksys.com/
- DS516 16-Port Auto 10/100—Netgear Inc. http://www.netgear.com
- Netgear EN104TP 4 Port 10BT—Netgear Inc. http://www.netgear.com
- DS108 8-Port Auto 10/100 Hub—Netgear Inc. http://www.netgear.com
- 8-Port 10/100 Dual Speed—SMC, Inc. http://www.smc.com/

3.5 Routers

At any one point in time there are millions of packets on the Internet. In order for a packet to get from one point to another it will need to be routed. On the Internet, a router is hardware and/or software that determines the next network point to which a packet should be forwarded toward its destination. The router may be connected to many different networks and decides which way to route each packet based on the header information in the packet. Most routers will maintain a table of the available routes and the status of those routes. In the example provided in Table 3.1, this router will have three networks that it will support—Network1, Network2, and Network3. The router will have three interface cards, each card pointing to a particular network. The router will also keep a table (Table 3.1) of the network name and address and the route to the Network.

TABLE 3.1

Network Name	Interface Card #	IP Network Name
Network 1	1	192.9.200.X
Network 2	2	192.9.202.X
Network 3	3	192.9.201.X

Figure 3.6 shows the steps for PC-B(192.9.200.3) to send a packet to PC-D (192.9.201.4)—PC-B will attempt to resolve the address for PC-D on its own network (192.9.200.X). The TCP/IP stack in PC-B will determine that PC-D is not on its network. The default gateway is set up to be the router, at address 192.9.200.1. Then the packet is sent to the router. The router looks up the target network in the IP destination part of the IP header. The router then sends the packet to the network on Internet card #3.

FIGURE 3.6

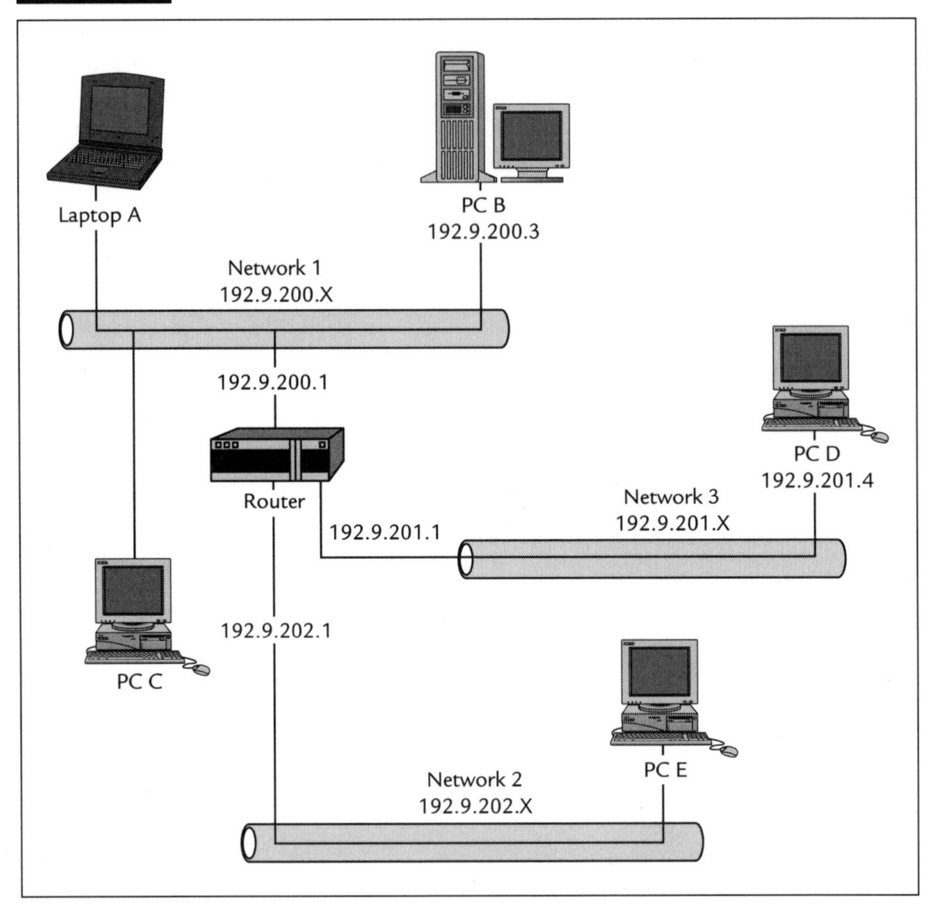

Routing is a function associated with the network layer (layer 3) in the standard model of network programming. Take a look at the OSI[7] model in Table 3.2.

Remember that the IP address (xxx.xxx.xxx.xxx) is maintained in the IP part of the TCP/IP protocol and thus routing also occurs at this level.

There are books and URLs on the complexities of routing. For the purposes of this book it was necessary to cover only the basics.

Many routers have another feature that we will be using later on: network address translation (NAT). The Internet Engineering Task Force (IETF) Request for Comments RFC1361 defines NAT. The IETF defined this set of

7. Review the OSI reference model in Appendix 2, TCP/IP Reference.

TABLE 3.2

Protocol Implementation

<table>
<tr><td></td><td>DARPA Layer</td><td colspan="3"></td><td>OSI</td></tr>
<tr><td rowspan="3"></td><td rowspan="3">Process/
Application</td><td colspan="2" rowspan="3">FTP
SMTP
TELNET
RFC: 959,821,854</td><td rowspan="3">TFTP
NFS
SNMP
RFC: 783,1094</td><td>Application</td></tr>
<tr><td>Presentation</td></tr>
<tr><td>Session</td></tr>
<tr><td></td><td>Transport</td><td colspan="2">Transmission Control
Protocol (TCP)
RFC793</td><td>User Datagram
Protocol (UDP)
RFC 768</td><td>Transport</td></tr>
<tr><td>Routing
Layer 3</td><td>Internet</td><td>(ARP) Address
Resolution
RFC826,903</td><td>(IP)
Internet</td><td>Internet Control
Message Protocol
RFC792</td><td>Network</td></tr>
<tr><td rowspan="2"></td><td rowspan="2">Network
Interface</td><td colspan="3">Network Interface Cards:
Ethernet, Token Ring
RFC894 RFC 1042</td><td>Data Link</td></tr>
<tr><td colspan="3">Transmission Media:
Twisted Pair, Coax, Fiber, Wireless, etc.</td><td>Physical</td></tr>
</table>

standards that lets an Internet-connected (in this case a registered IP address) host act as an Internet gateway for internal LAN clients by translating any client's internal network IP addresses into the appropriate address on the NAT-enabled gateway device. Remember that we discussed registered addresses. If you don't remember then put that beer down and go back and read the TCP/IP reference chapter (Appendix 2). Every device on the Internet has a registered address, but not every computer that communicates to the Internet has a registered address. So how does this work? We use NAT technology. The NAT technology protects internal client IP addresses and makes them inaccessible to registered Internet hosts. To the end-user NAT is transparent. There is nothing to set up or configure and no special software to purchase. The network administrator has a bit of work to do, but with DHCP the average user won't care that they don't have a registered address.

FIGURE 3.7

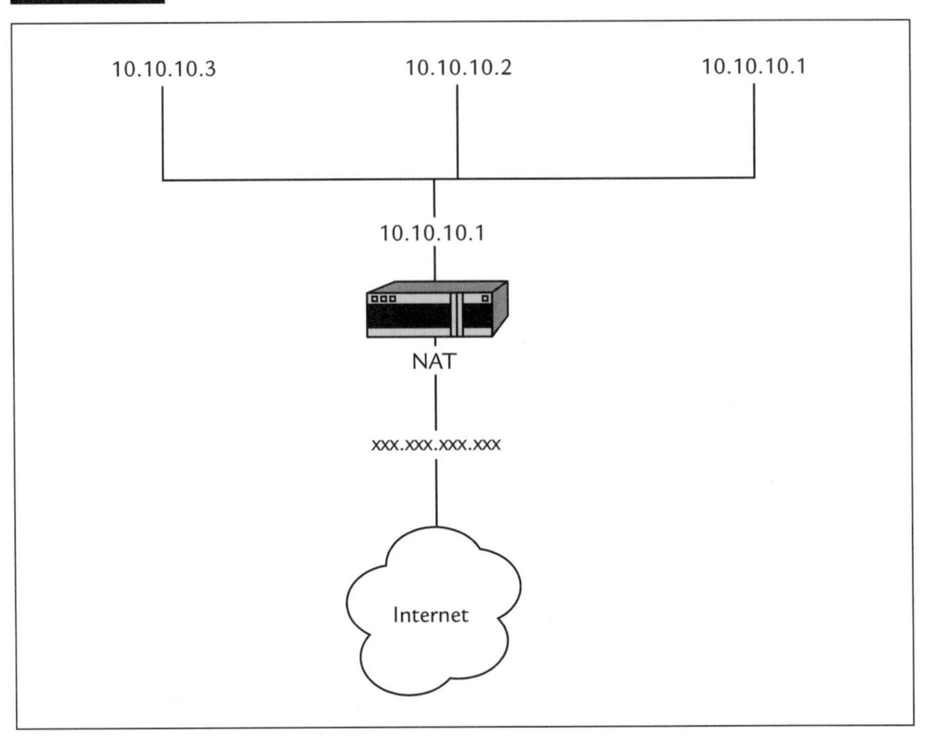

In Figure 3.7 you see three addresses, 10.10.10.1, 2, and 3. These are known as 10-Net[8] addresses. (We talk about this in the TCP/IP Appendix (2)[9].) The addresses are all linked to a single registered address on the Internet (xxx.xxx.xxx.xxx is not a legal address—this is just an example). The NAT would keep track of the IP address and the TCP port of each address as a transaction is implemented over the router. This process solves several problems for us:

- If we have 10,000 users then we don't need to purchase 10,000 registered addresses. This can save a bunch of cash.
- We now have only one access point to the big bad Internet and we can control the input and output of each packet if necessary.
- NAT can also be used as a security feature—for example, if someone tries to access your router from a 10-net address, then you know it's bogus.

8. http://info.internet.isi.edu/in-notes/rfc/files/rfc1918.txt
9. Guess what — tired of seeing "see the TCP/IP reference chapter" footnotes—why don't you read that chapter?

In addition, NAT is a standard feature of the Windows 2000 server's routing and remote access service (RRAS) and the Win2K Professional's Internet Connection Sharing (ICS) component. For more information on NAT check out http://www.ietf.org/html.charters/nat-charter.html.

3.6 What about Networking my MAC?

Macintoshes include built-in networking capabilities, so if you like you can create a Mac-only network by simply using an Apple LocalTalk cable between computers and setting a few Share options in the System menu. But what about Ethernet ? Obtain a transceiver. Or you can even go wireless—Check out http://www.Farallon.com/news/01_01_08_symmac.html, and Farallon has Ethernet transceivers for MACs (http://www.Farallon.com/products/ether/trans/emtrans.html). Then configure your MAC for an IP address and you're on your way.

3.7 Personal Firewalls

So far we have discussed the various components of a network. In Chapter 5 we will be putting all of these components together to build "secure" home networks. One of the components we will be using is known as a "Personal Firewall." So before we get too far into our discussion—what is a firewall?

A firewall is a physical structure that is designed to keep a fire from spreading. Cars have firewalls and buildings also have firewalls. Internet firewalls, the object of this discussion, are intended to keep the bad dudes out of your computers. Most large corporations will have a DMZ with a firewall or two. These firewalls will keep unwanted traffic out of the corporate network and away from your corporate-connected computer. Today the face of the Internet network is changing. At one point in time the corporate computer was protected behind the corporate Maginot[10] line of defense. The Internet network is dynamic and changing with each new product development. The corporate as well as the home computer is linking together (like *Colossus: The Forbin Project*) and communicating peer to peer. Take a look at Ray Ozzie's Groove.[11] With all of this great new technology come networks that can access many different points. Now with the advent

10. http://www.ifrance.com/letunnel/maginot-e.html

11. http://www.groove.net/

of cable, DSL, and ISDN you can connect to the Internet at speeds almost as fast as your corporate network does. At the same time, connecting to the Internet without the defense of your corporate firewall is much like the Germans of WWII finding the weaknesses in the Maginot line—or in this case—just going around the defenses. As soon as you take your computer from the safety of your corporate network and connect it to the naked ISP service that you have at home then you are at risk.

When first introduced, personal firewalls were marketed to the broadband (DSK, cable modems) consumer market to protect individuals with broadband Internet access. Today more and more companies are arming their users with personal firewalls. There is a risk not only at home, but also on the road, because many hotels are starting to provide high-speed access to their rooms. This is a great service offering and one that I use when I travel. The problem with this is that you expose your computer to the hotel's untrusted Intranet. This hotel Intranet then connects to the Internet. You are potentially exposed at two points, the Internet itself and the hotel's service network.

Now you say, I use a VPN to connect to my corporate network, so my data is safe. Sorry Charlie, incorrect. Yes, the data you may be sending to your company is encrypted, but your computer itself is open to attack.

Here is an example: Your corporate computer is connected to the Internet via a cable modem from your house. You are using VPN software to communicate to your corporate network, and so all is fine. All of this data is encrypted, password, attachments, and so on. But you have file sharing turned on, and you have shared a directory that is off of the secret corporate announcements. Now a hacker can access this file share and take your information. Another example of this is where a Trojan horse has been placed on your system—in this case you have turned your computer into a server for the hacker to connect to and extract the data. As you can see, the VPN will not protect your computer from an unprotected network connection. In a worst-case scenario, the hacker may be able to activate the VPN and actually connect directly to the corporate network. Now the hacker is using your computer to do more hacking, which is not cool.

Personal firewall products such as those from ZoneAlarm[12] and BlackIce[13] are targeted specifically at protecting the isolated computer. This computer can be at work, at home, or on the road. These products provide personal policy control mechanism event logging, and some type of alert system.

12. http://www.zonelabs.com/index.html

13. http://www.networkice.com/

> Warning:
>
> This is one of those disclaimer notes — please do not install any product on your corporate computer without talking to your network security department. Why?
>
> 1. Always follow your corporate guidelines for software management and installations.
> 2. Some personal firewalls can interfere with VPN software.
>
> If your company does not have a policy on personal firewalls, then ask them to write one.

The trade magazines have been talking about the new ISP. This one will offer firewall services for you and your home computer. At this point the authors are skeptical of this approach. On paper this looks good and may work fine for when your computer is at home, but when you leave and take the PC on the road, then who will protect your computing assets? The answer is YOU.

As our dependence on the Internet and computers grows, so will the personal consequences of a security breach. Whether to protect your personal information from theft or to keep your PC from being hijacked by a hacker, installing a personal firewall is now a required step to keep your data safe.

More information if you are interested:

http://www.webattack.com/shareware/security/swfirewall.shtml
http://www.practicallynetworked.com/networking/wireless_chart.htm
http://www.robertgraham.com/pubs/sniffing-faq.html#software-windows
http://Network-Tools.com/
http://www.geektools.com/cgi-bin/proxy.cgi
http://grc.com/su-firewalls.htm

CHAPTER 4

Securing Your DSL, Cable Modem, and Dial-Up Connection

In this chapter we will be looking at various mechanisms to protect your computer. We will be looking at DSL, cable modem and dial-up connections to the Internet. We will also show you how to set up and use a personal firewall.

4.1 Virus Review

At this point you may have noticed that we have not spent much time on viruses. There are many resources and books on this subject but we cannot emphasize enough the importance of having virus software on your computers. Many of the new viruses today (such as the "I love you" and "Anna Kournikova" viruses) spread along with normal messaging traffic. As a result many firewalls will not detect this type of virus. So please remember that firewalls are not a replacement for good virus software; you must use the software.

4.2 Law

Another issue that someone always likes to bring up is "The Law." As the authors are not lawyers, it is up to you to do your own research. With that said, here is some reading material:

- FindLaw http://www.findlaw.com/01topics/10cyberspace/index.html
- Supreme Court lets stand decision freeing Internet providers from liability for e-mail content http://www.cnn.com/2000/LAW/05/01/scotus.defamation.ap/
- Control of arms exports and imports http://www4.law.cornell.edu/uscode/22/2778.html

4.3 Software

As part of your defenses against the bad dudes, you will need to keep your software updated. Microsoft has been very good about keeping security patches for their software updated and available. Check out http://www.microsoft.com/security/ for details. For now, here are some URLs for Outlook patches:

- Auto-run patch for Outlook 97 http://officeupdate.microsoft.com/downloadDetails/O97attch.htm
- Auto-run patch for Outlook 98 http://officeupdate.microsoft.com/downloadDetails/Out98sec.htm
- Auto-run patch for Outlook 2000 http://officeupdate.microsoft.com/2000/downloadDetails/Out2ksec.htm

4.4 Attacks against You and Your Pets

Let's review the various attacks that your home computer could undergo (your corporate computer can also experience these attacks). After we look at the various attacks then we will discuss solutions and tools that can help protect your computer. Let's start by reviewing the issues and then we will build our toolbox. (Future references to this list are known as the **List of Death**—sorry for the dramatics.)

- Virus
- Trojans
- E-mail virus
- Corrupted IP packets
- Port scanner attacks
- Attacking shared printers

- Attacking shared files
- Taking control of your PC—back orifice
- Telent attacks
- Spider attacks
- DOS attacks (denial of service)
- spam
- Social attacks
  - The network police—give me your password and your credit card number.
  - A social intrusion is when a hacker poses as an employee, authority figure, or friend in an attempt to acquire sensitive information about you and your systems. Perhaps the most common social intrusion is that of someone posing as a system administrator and asking for your password.

A part of our toolbox is to review good security practices. Then we will look at the various scenarios that can be used to protect our computers. Let's start with good security practices.

4.5 Good Security Practices

Here are a few examples of good security practices:

- Take the time to upgrade your software and operating system on a regular basis. Many older versions of software, including Web browsers, have known security issues. Patches and fixes are typically included with a new or updated software release. Go out to your software vendor and check out the latest release.
- Don't e-mail anything that you would not want to share with anyone. Never e-mail sensitive information such as passwords, credit card information, and so on, to people unless you have software installed that can encrypt your e-mail.
- Be careful with each Web site you visit. Never submit sensitive information via a Web page unless the Web site is secure. As SSL is the mechanism that allows you to send information over a secure line. Look for the small key icon on the bottom of your browser (Internet Explorer 3.02 or better) or a closed "lock" (Netscape 3.0 or better).

- Try to protect your network addresses. Do not reveal your cable modem, DSL, or ISP connection's IP address or other system networking information to anyone. Your telephone company and Internet service provider should already have this information. So if someone calls asking for this information, tell him or her to go jump in the lake.
- If you use "chat rooms" or IRC sessions, be careful with any information you share with strangers. Hackers are notorious for "address harvesting" from chat rooms and other interactive areas.
- If you have a DSL or cable modem connection, turn your computer off when not using it. These "always on" connections are particularly vulnerable because they provide more opportunities for hackers to find your computer.
- Be careful of files e-mailed to you from people you do not know. One common way of getting viruses, as well as inadvertent installations of software that allow intruders easy access to your system, is to embed the software into some cute dancing dog executable or some other e-mail attachment. While you are laughing at the activity of some on-screen cartoon, hackers are opening up your system.
- Be sure and change your passwords regularly. Also, use passwords that are not easy to figure out. The most difficult passwords to crack are those with upper- and lowercase letters, numbers, and a symbol such as % or #.

All of this stuff is well and good, but how do you protect yourself from the **List of Death**? Do you want the simple answer, or do you want the right answer? Let's answer both—the simple answer—"Nothing guarantees protection." There is no one product, solution, magic dust, or tool to protect your computer from the **List of Death**. (Imagine it is Darth Vader saying that every time you read it.) The real answer is "It is a combination of tools, approaches, and magic dust" (FYI—the magic dust is not legal in this country).

4.6 The Approach

We will be looking at several different scenarios. Each of these will offer some insight into how you can create your own unique solution. Our approach will include the following factors:

- Software—Personal firewalls;
- A computer (good start, huh?);

- Tools—routers, gateways; and
- And as we mentioned—good security practices.

The personal firewall is the technology that we will discuss in great depth in Chapter 5. For now, let's go into a bit more detail. Firewalls provide the technology needed to protect your computer from the bad dudes on the Internet, your corporate Intranet, or any network. As we have shown you, attacks can come any place to which your computer is connected.

Although a personal firewall won't get you a new life or a new wife, or keep you from doing something stupid, it will do the following things for you.

A firewall, if configured properly, can prevent an unauthorized user from accessing your PC via a network. Some software may even block a Trojan horse program.

So how does this magic program work? When you're connected to the Internet, you're sending and receiving information in small units called packets. You should remember this discussion from Chapter 3. A packet contains the addresses of the sender and the recipient along with a piece of data, a request, a command, or almost anything having to do with your connection to the Internet. A personal firewall examines (tests) each data packet sent to or from your computer to see if it meets a set of criteria. If the packet passes this test, then the packet is then allowed to move on to your computer.

The criteria a firewall uses for passing packets along depend on the kind of firewall you use. The most common type you'll find for home and small business use is called an application gateway firewall—FYI, test the firewall after it is installed—check out this URL http://security2.norton.com/us/intro.asp?venid=sym&langid=us.

An application gateway, often called a proxy, acts like a customs officer for data. When I flew from Jakarta to Los Angeles, in the customs area at the airport there was a cute Beagle dog. Just as this little dog is trained to sniff for fruits and vegetables, your computer also has a short customs dude installed to look at the packets as they are sent into the computer. Mr. Customs filters the packets based on the IP address and even content. If Mr. Customs finds some illegal packets, the packets are rejected or the address from where the packets were sent is locked out. As we have stated before, most large corporations have some type of firewall that sits between the Internet and the trusted corporate network. Let's look at some of the protection that a personal firewall can provide:

- Alert you to a Trojan horse trying to operate on your computer. This is accomplished by providing information about what outbound ports are active on your computer;

- Hide the open ports on your computer and/or network;
- Hide the shares that are open on your computer or network;
- IP address blocking;
- A firewall can render your computer invisible to the Internet and potential intruders; if you can't be seen, you can't be attacked;
- E-mail attachment protection—like stopping the love bug virus; and
- Cookie controls—alerts you to cookies being set in your computer.

We will now review several home networking examples. We will use the following format:

- Scenario Name
- Potential Use
- Exposures
- Potential Security Solution
- Hardware
- Software

The *Scenario Name* will be a simple descript of what the scenario is about. The *Potential Use* will describe the area of impact to your computer or home network computer. The *Exposures* will describe what can happen to you and how the bad dudes can hack into your computer. The *Potential Security Solution* will show one possible solution you can use to protect your computer and/or network. The *Hardware* needed will describe the basic peripherals that you may need to add on to your computer. The *Software* will describe any software that will need to be installed and/or configured for your computer.

4.6.1 Scenario One

Scenario Name: Single computer, no home network—dial up to a service provider.

The example in Figure 4.1, a single computer connecting to the service provider, is one of the simplest. Your exposure is limited to a single access point to the Internet.

Potential Use: Dial-up speed access to the Internet (dial-up via a modem).

Exposures: Virus, port scanning, share attacks, DOS.

Potential Security Solution: Virus software and personal firewall.

Hardware: Modem must be installed in or attached to your computer. Most new computers today are shipped with a modem.

Software: Many service providers will send you the software needed to set up and configure the modem and dial-up components of your computer. Built into Windows 95, 98, and 2000 (as well as NT) are dial-up programs that you can use to connect your computer to an ISP. These are simple to use and configure. (See dial-up configurations at the end of this chapter.)

4.6.2 Scenario Two

Scenario Name: Single computer, no home network—via a DSL or cable modem connection.

Again, Figure 4.1, single computer connecting to the service provider, is one of the simplest. Your exposure is limited to a single access point to the Internet.

Potential Use: High-speed access to the Internet (DSL or cable modem).

Exposures: Virus, port scanning, share attacks, DOS.

Potential Security Solution: Virus software and personal firewall.

FIGURE 4.1

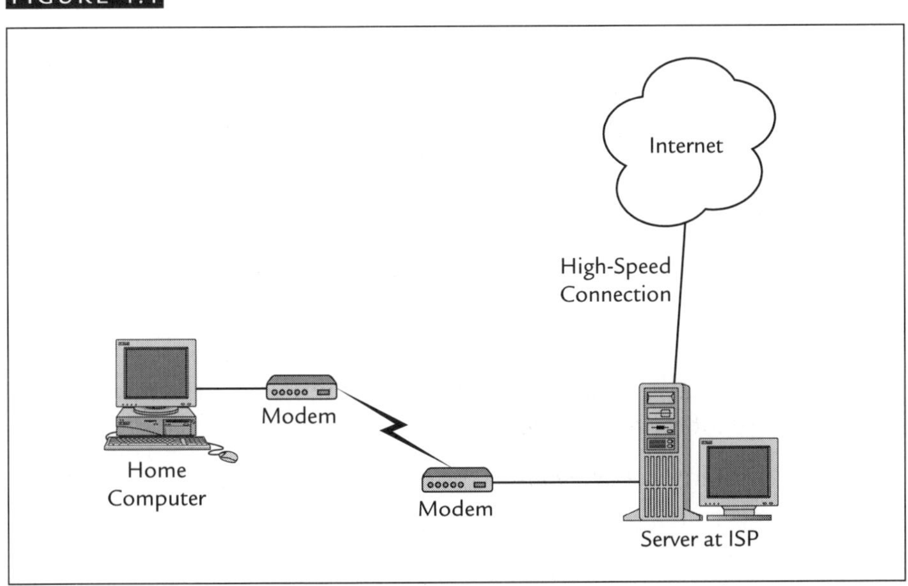

Hardware: Cable modem and Ethernet card. (In some cases the USB port can be used. See your ISP for information.)

Software: Ethernet card drivers and TCP/IP configurations.

4.6.3 Scenario Three

Scenario Name: Home network, multiple computers.

In Figure 4.2 you have several computers connecting to an ISP via a single registered address.

Potential Use: High-speed access to the Internet (dial-up, DSL, or cable modem), network at home.

Exposures: Virus, port scanning, share attacks, DOS. The total home network is exposed.

FIGURE 4.2

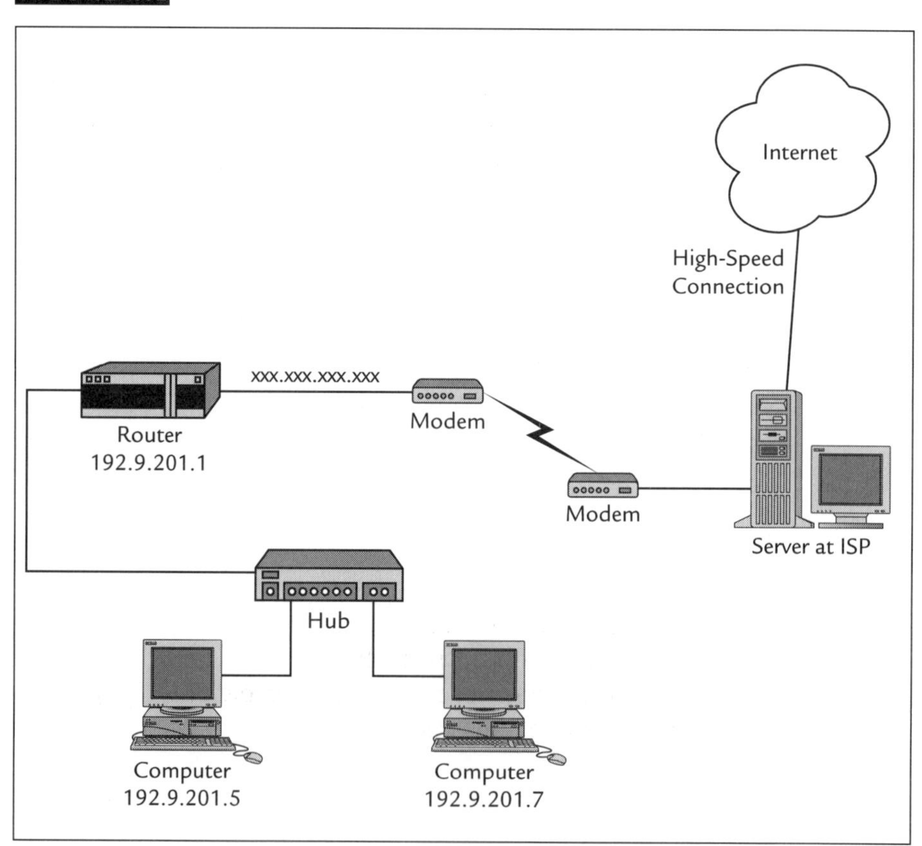

Potential Security Solution: Router, virus software and personal firewall.

Hardware: Cable modem and Ethernet card (in some cases the USB port can be used See your ISP for information), router, and a hub.

Software: Ethernet Card drivers and TCP/IP configurations.

This solution shows the router as an intercept point for all traffic into the home network.

Let's review some of the configuration information for this scenario:

In this example we are using a LinkSys router. This particular router has several nice features:

- DHCP;
- ability to block ports;
- ability to redirect ports;
- ability to log traffic in and out of the router; and
- more.

This particular product can be configured via a browser. Note: Contact Linksys with any questions, and please read the instructions before trying this at home. Linksys has a great URL with all of the user guides, so if you have lost your instructions then go and download another: http://www.linksys.com/products/userguide.asp.

I helped a friend of mine to set up her Linskys Router. Being a good IT type person we followed the directions. As mentioned before Linksys provides exacting directions. The problem we had was the ISP (an unnamed cable company) provided incorrect addresses for the default gateway and DNS. So here is what we did:

1. Confirmed that the router was working. We were able to open and display the Web page for the router. All was good.
2. We called the ISP and said, "Our stuff is not working." This is where things went really bad.
3. Called Linskys to confirm our suspicions. They talked to us—without condemnation.

(continued on next page)

(continued from previous page)

The issue was that the ISP would not support any configuration other than what was setup by the ISP installation service rep. We were reminded that the ISP will not support routers, home networks, video games, coffee pots, or firewalls. I called Linskys and talked with them, and they came to the same conclusion that I had: We had incorrect information from the ISP. So we hung up the phone and called the ISP once again . . . getting a different service rep. We told the rep that "everything is fine and nothing is broke, but we would like to confirm the following assigned addresses":

- Assigned IP address;
- Subnet mask;
- Primary DNS Address;
- Secondary DNS Address;
- Default Gateway;
- Subdomain Address;
- POP3 Gateway Address;
- SMTP Gateway Address;
- News Server Gateway.

We obtained the correct information and now all is well and working.

Let's discuss how to configure your TCP/IP settings (here are the assumptions):

- Static address for the router from the ISP;
- DHCP for the client computers;
- DNS settings to be placed into the router for DHCP assignment to the end computers; and
- Default gateway assigned.

Let's assume that the IP address is a static address that has been assigned from the service provider. This address (xxx.xxx.xxx.xxx) will be a unique address that is assigned only to you and your computer. In our example we will not be using that address for a computer. We will assign it to a router.

Figure 4.3 gives an example of setting that address for our Linksys router.

FIGURE 4.3

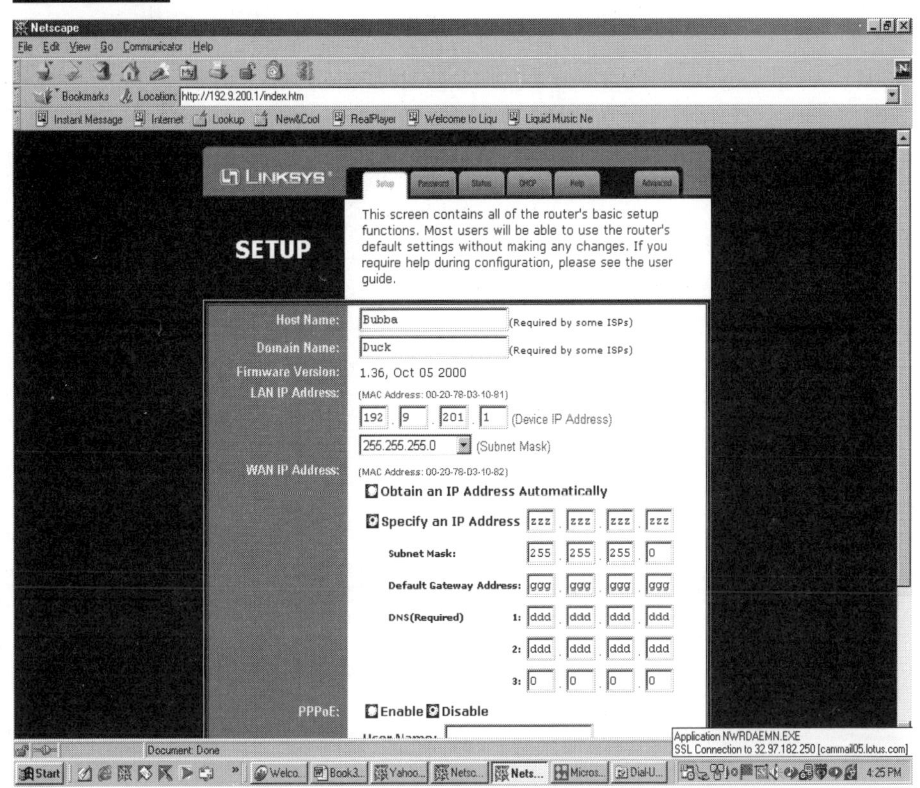

The LAN address will be the connection for this router to the home network. If you were to have more than one router then each router would have a unique IP address. This address is yours to select at your leisure. The default address that the Linksys router is shipped with is 192.168.1.1.

So let's stop and test your understanding of TCP/IP:

Question 1. Are 192.168.1.1 and 192.9.200.1 on the same IP network?
Question 2. Are 192.168.1.1 and 192.168.2.1 on the same IP network?
Question 3. Are 192.168.1.1 and 192.168.1.800 on the same IP network?
Question 4. Are 192.168.1.1 and 192.168.1.3 on the same IP network?

Answers: Answer Q1. No (Review Appendix 2)
Answer Q2. No (Ditto)
Answer Q3. No (Again)—Note: xxx.xxx.xxx.800 is not a valid address.
Answer Q4. Yes (And again, see Appendix 2).

Why is this important? In order for your IP devices to talk they need to be on the same network and/or be able to find a router on the same network in order to get "out" to the Internet. Get it? If not read the chapter on TCP again, and take the time to understand the ARP concept.

Next, fill out the IP address that was given to you by your ISP. Here is the information you will need. Fill in the dialog box. As shown, we used a simple code to match each item in the example:

1. IP address (zzz.zzz.zzz.zzz);
2. Subnet mask (255.255.255.0—this is an example only. If it very possible that you will get a different subnet make);
3. Default gateway address (ggg.ggg.ggg.ggg); and
4. DNS address (1 or 2) (ddd.ddd.ddd.ddd).

Now the router is configured. We are all set and ready to go, right? Doh! We forgot to configure the TCP/IP for each computer. At this point I must apologize: We will cover one more time the fact that you cannot put the computers on different IP addresses. Again here is the example: 192.9.201.5 and 192.9.201.7 are on the same IP network. Okay, I know you understand this now.

Let's configure one of the computers (you can just duplicate these steps for the next computer).

In this example we will manually set the address into the computer. I actually use DHCP from the Linksys router in my own network. We will show you how to set up DHCP later.

The example given here in the figures is for Windows 95 and 98. Windows 2000 and NT are a bit different, but most of the setting types are the same (example: IP address and default gateway).

Now, first open up the control panel and select Network (see Figure 4.4).

Double click on the Network Icon (see Figure 4.5). This will bring up a dialog box that will have three tabs on it. These tabs are for Configuration, Identification, and Access Control. Select the Configuration tab.

Once on this tab, if necessary scroll down and then select where the TCP/IP is bound to your network adapter. As shown in Figure 4.6, it will have a name something like this TCP/IP –> Your Network adapter.

Select the properties button. Select the IP Address tab and fill out the fields. In the example shown in Figure 4.7 we are using 192.9.201.5 and a subnet mask of 255.255.255. 0.

Next select the Gateway tab. The Gateway address will be the address of the router. Enter the address of 192.9.201.1 as shown in Figure 4.8 and press the add button.

FIGURE 4.4

FIGURE 4.5

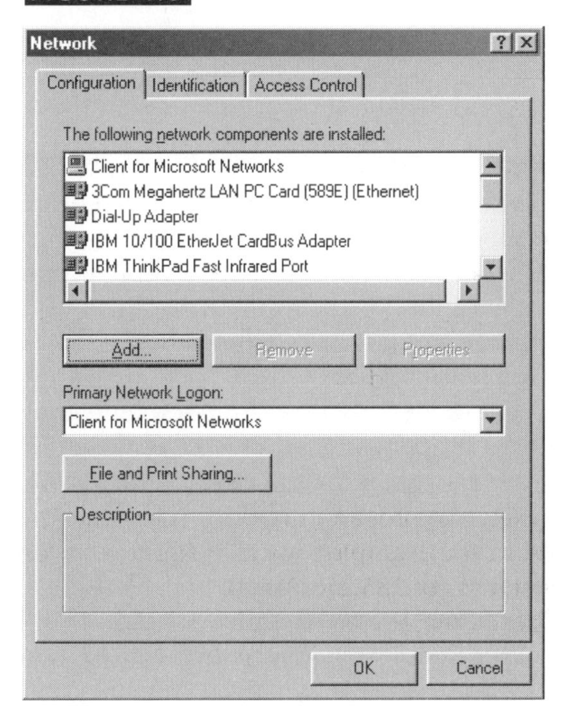

FIGURE 4.6

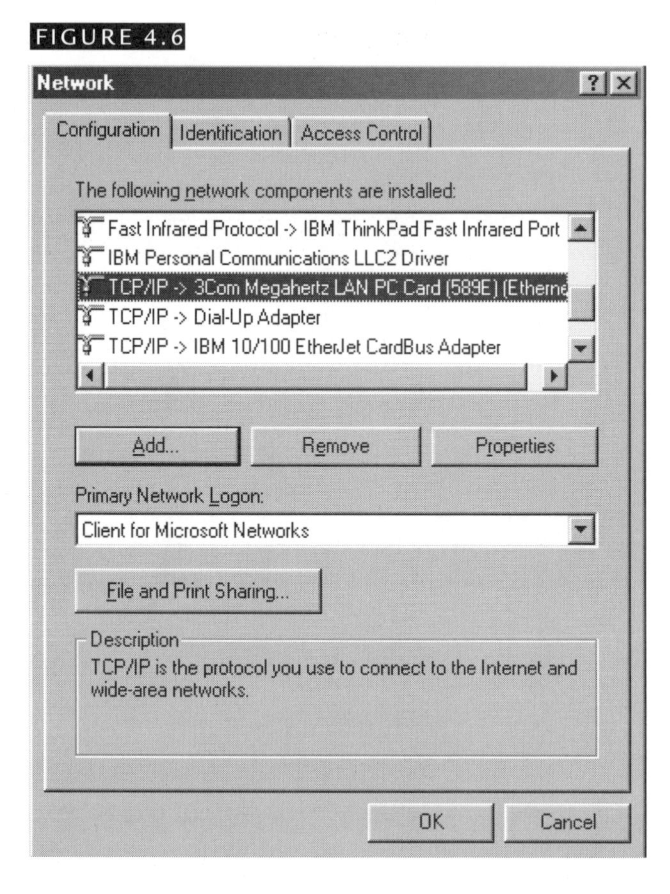

This is where things can get a bit confusing. Next select the DNS tab. Remember the DNS is the mechanism that translates domain names (and URLs) to IP addresses. Example, what if you wanted to open the URL http://www.lotus.com? In most cases you would use the DNS server from the service provider. Here is how it works:

You type http://www.lotus.com into a browser. Your computer looks up the name of the DNS server from the configuration settings in your network settings. The computer sends a request to the DNS server that says "Yo, Mr. DNS server, what is the IP Address for www.lotus.com?" The DNS server for the ISP returns the following: "Hello, Mr. Computer, the address is 129.42.242.50, thank you and have a happy day."

So now you see the importance of having a DNS server. Next fill out the dialog for the DNS search order.

In the DNS Server Search Order field as shown in Figure 4.9 add the DNS addresses that have been provided to you from your ISP.

FIGURE 4.7

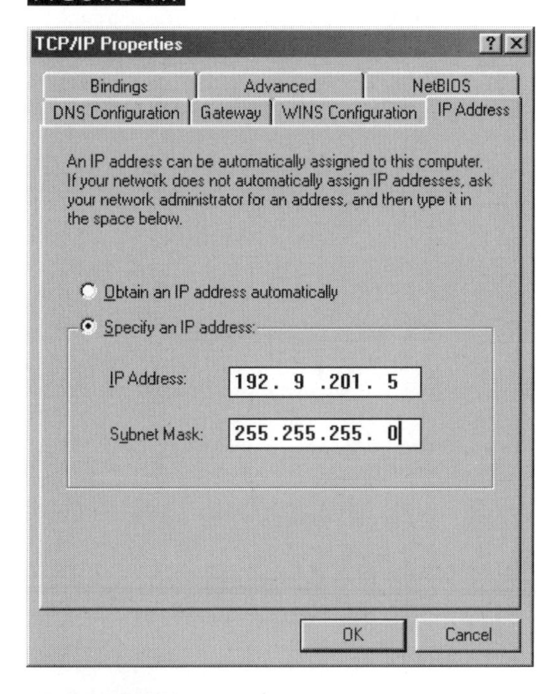

FIGURE 4.8

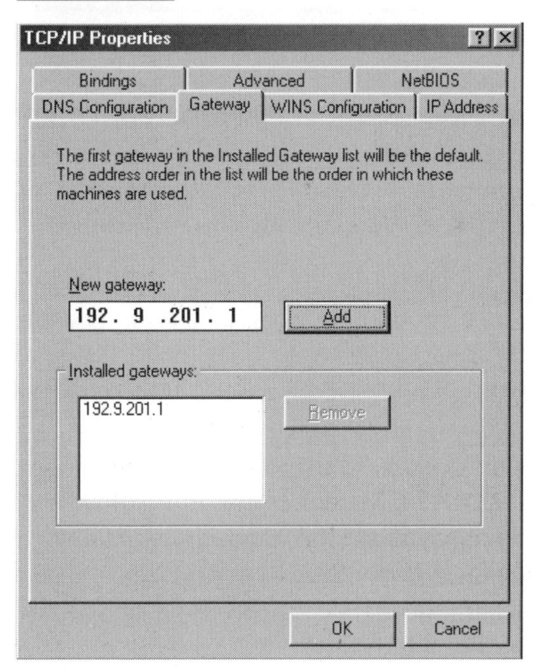

FIGURE 4.9

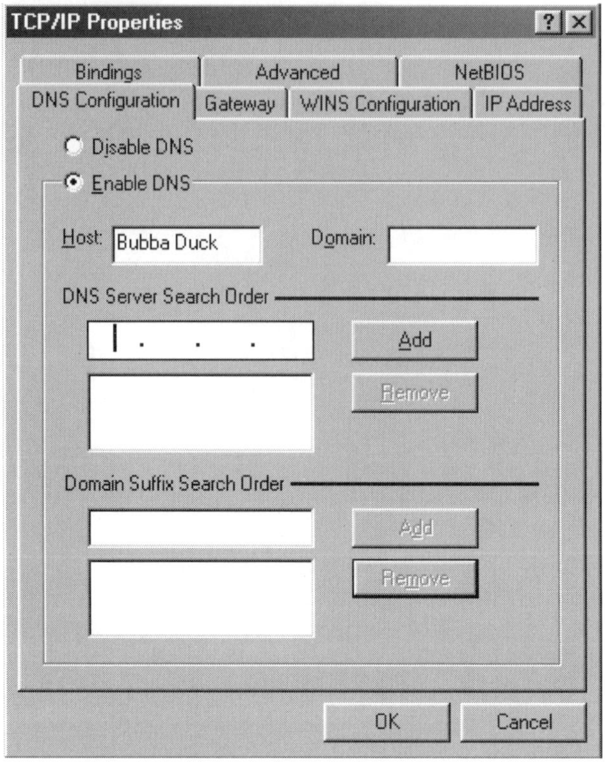

That is it; now repeat this task for each computer on your Network. At this point you may be a bit confused. Okay, using Figure 4.10, let's connect to a Web site. We will show you each connection as we go.

1. At the computer browser type http://www.lotus.com.
2. The computer will send a series of packets to the hub. The hub for the most part is not very intelligent. It just moves packets around on the wires. It is up to the IP to actually route the packets.
3. The computer looks in its local tables to see if it can translate, for example, lotus.com into an address. In the computer's local tables it finds that the DNS server is not on the local network.
4. The computer then looks up the address of the default gateway. The request (IP Traffic) is not routed to this address—or the Linksys router. The traffic is now sent to the router and the route looks at the destination of the traffic. In this case, again, it is not on its local network. The

FIGURE 4.10

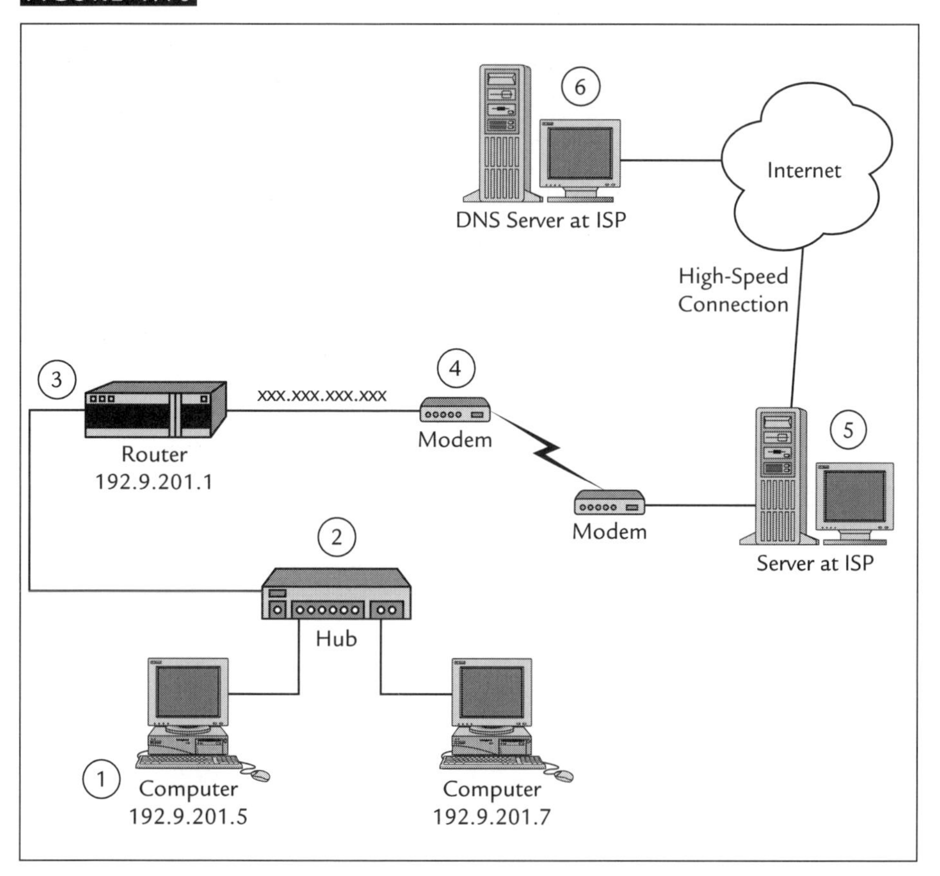

router also has an address for its default gateway and then routes the traffic to another location, which may be another router.

5. The traffic is now at the ISP and it looks to see where the DNS server really is. Traffic is routed to the DNS server.
6. If the DNS server can resolve the address that it was sent then it will return an address back to the requesting computer. At this point the browser attempts to contact the site following the same steps and path that it used to get the DNS address.

These steps shown are the same for either a static IP address or a dynamic address. What if I want to set up a dynamic host configuration protocol (DHCP) from my Linksys router for my home computers? This is very easy. Again you need to make some changes in the Linksys router and the computers.

Use the example in Figure 4.11 to set up your DHCP for your home computers.

Select the DHCP tab and then fill out the starting address that the DHCP service will use to assign addresses. Make sure it is one more than the address that you will be using for the address of the Linksys router itself. In this example we show 192.9.201.2 as the first address and then 10 additional addresses can be assigned if needed.

Go back to the Network settings in your control panel of your computer.

As shown in Figure 4.12, select "Obtain an IP address automatically." That's it, nothing more to do. Why? When DHCP is configured for a router, at least for Linksys, the router will send the DNS information computer along with the DNS server addresses. Most cool!

4.6.4 Scenario Four

Scenario Name: Home Network, multiple computers. Using a PC as a router and firewall. In this example you have several computers connecting to an ISP via a single registered address.

Potential Use: High-speed access to the Internet (dial-up, DSL, or cable modem), network at home.

FIGURE 4.11

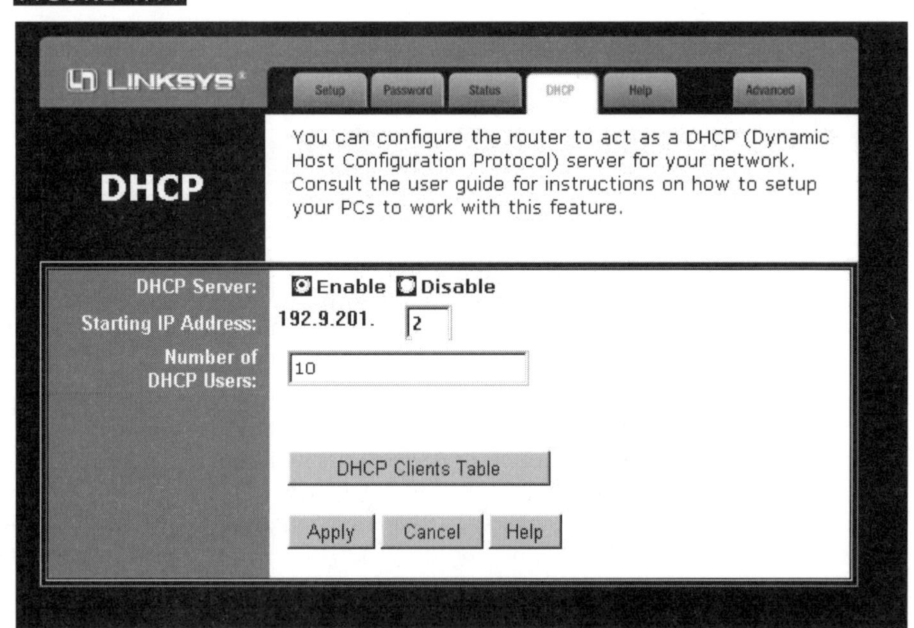

FIGURE 4.12

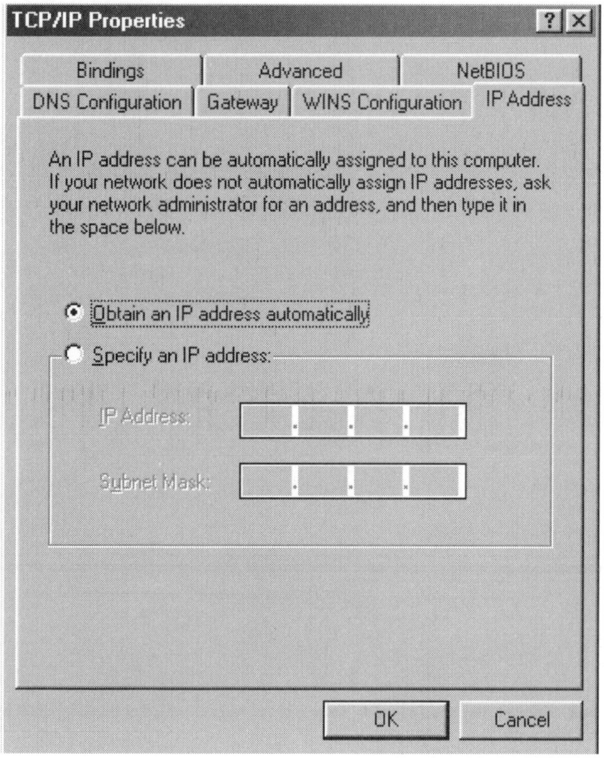

Exposures: Virus, port scanning, share attacks, DOS. The total home network is exposed.

Potential Security Solution: PC, virus software, and personal firewall.

Hardware: Cable modem and (2) Ethernet cards, (in some cases the USB port can be used, see your ISP for information), PC, and a hub.

Software: Ethernet Card drivers and TCP/IP configurations.

This solution shows the PC as an intercept point for all traffic into the home network.

The only difference in the example as shown here in Figure 4.13 and the router example is that you are using a PC as the intercept point for all traffic in and out of the home network. One big advantage of this solution is that you can install firewall software on the routing PC. In this case you may not need personal firewall software on every computer in the home network. Windows NT and 2000 support this type of configuration. In this

FIGURE 4.13

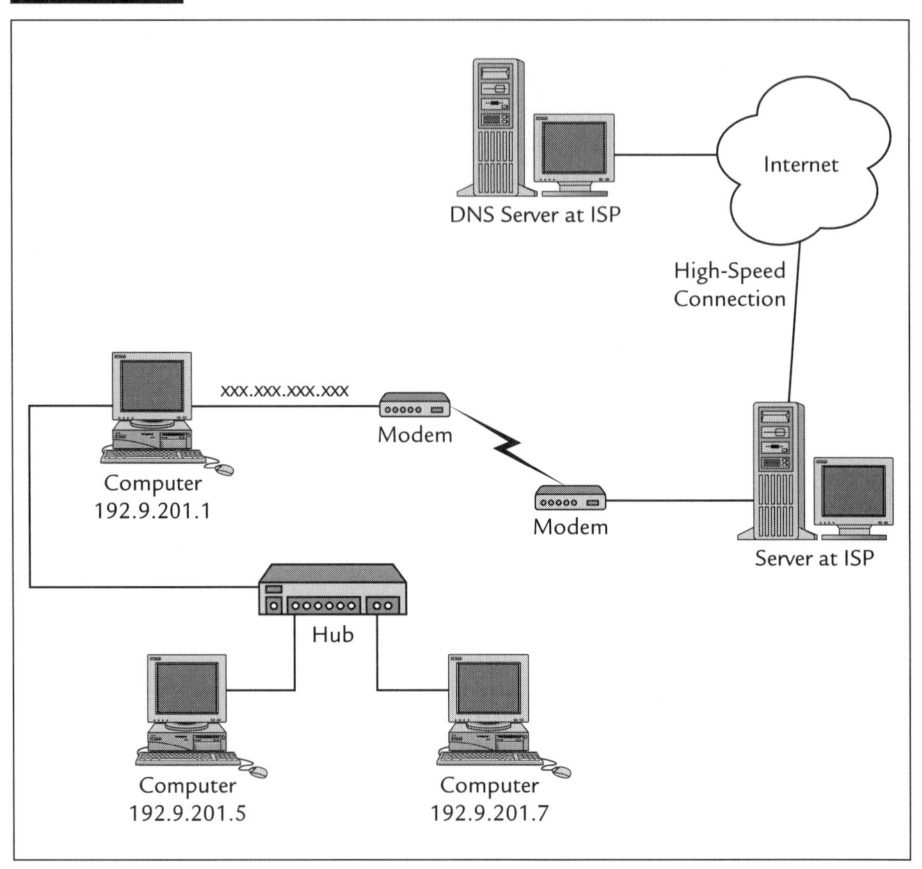

scenario you would install two NIC cards, one for the assigned IP address that will connect to the Internet via the ISP and one for the Internet (trusted) network.

4.7 A Quick Overview of a Wireless Home Network

A wireless LAN is just that—wireless. Computers and routers will connect to each other via a set protocol and via a radio frequency circuit. Much like TV or your cell phone, your home network can connect computers together without wires. This protocol, known as IEEE 802.11, was completed in 1997 for wireless LANs (WLANs) and became a significant development resulting from wireless networking technologies. This standard, developed to maximize interoperability between differing brands of wireless LANs, can work with standard Ethernet, via a bridge or access point (AP). Wireless Ethernet uses a carrier sense multiple access with collision avoidance (CSMA/CA) scheme, whereas standard Ethernet uses a carrier sense multiple access with collision detection (CSMA/CD) scheme.

One of the biggest advantages of the 802.11 standard is that products from different vendors can interoperate with each other. This means that you can purchase a wireless LAN card from one vendor and a wireless LAN card from another vendor and they can communicate with each other, independent of the brand name of the card.

The next iteration of the standard was the 802.11b release. The 802.11b standard allows for encrypted communication between clients and access points via wired equivalent privacy (WEP). Wired equivalent privacy is an optional RC-4-based, 40-bit encryption mechanism that encrypts the data portion of the packet.

There are many vendors that offer wireless devices. Here are some from Linksys:

BEFW11P1—EtherFast Wireless AP + Cable/DSL Router w/PrintServer
BEFW11S4—EtherFast Wireless AP + Cable/DSL Router w/4-Port Switch
WAP11—Instant Wireless Network Access Point
WDT11—Instant Wireless PCI Adapter
WPC11—Instant Wireless Network PC Card
WUSB11—Instant Wireless USB Network Adapter

There are several specifications to look for when you are shopping for wireless Ethernet.

4.8 Network Card for the PC

- 11 Mbps high-speed transfer rate
- Compatible with Windows 95, 98, 2000, NT, and Millennium
- Plug-and-play operation provides easy setup
- Works with all standard Internet applications
- Interoperable with IEEE 802.11b (DSSS)
- 40-Bit WEP encryption protocol

4.9 The Access Point

- High-speed transfer rate of up to 11 Mbps
- Interoperable with IEEE 802.11b (DSSS)
- Provides roaming and load balancing
- Check the number of users the AP can support (32 + is good)
- Long operating range—example: 120 m (indoor) and 300 m (outdoor)
- Hardware-wired equivalent privacy (WEP)
- Works with all standard Internet applications

Also check out the range—an example follows.

4.10 Operating Range

- Indoor:
  - 50M (164 ft) @ 11 Mbps
  - 80M (262 ft) @ 5.5 Mbps
  - 120M (393 ft) @ 2 Mbps
  - 150M (492 ft) @ 1 Mbps
- Outdoor:
  - 250M (820 ft) @ 11 Mbps
  - 350M (1148 ft) @ 5.5 Mbps
  - 400M (1312 ft) @ 2 Mbps
  - 500M (1640 ft) @ 1 Mbps

An example of a home configuration using wireless technology is shown in Figure 4.14.

FIGURE 4.14

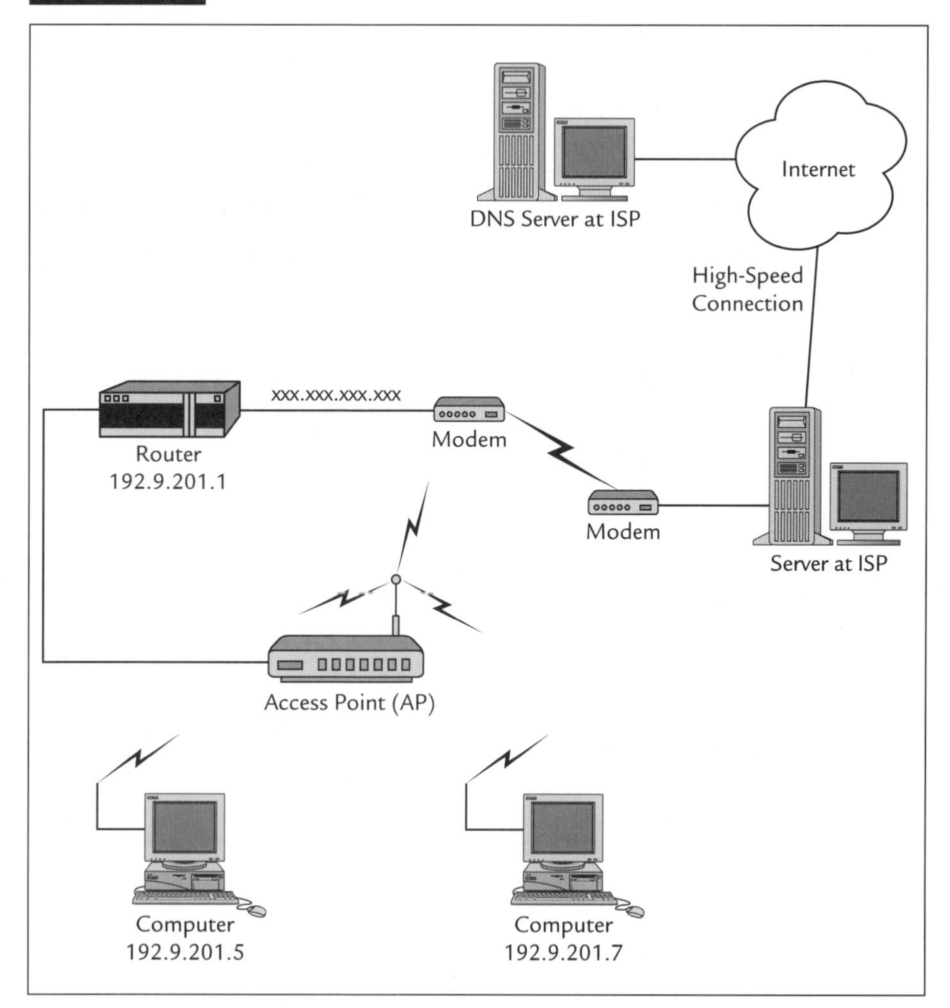

4.11 Dial-Up Configuration Settings

Before you start this process check the following:

- If you have a corporate computer, do not make any changes before talking with your help desk.
- You have a working ISP connection. Then you don't need to be here.
- If you are not sure about your dial-up connection and its requirements, then contact you ISP for help.

- If you are really lost, then go to bed.

This section if provided as a reference so you can set up a dial-up connection to your ISP. Here is where you can look at the dial-up properties for Windows 98. At the desktop double-click on "My Computer." This will open up the screen shown in Figure 4.15.

Double click on Dial-Up Networking. In the Dial-Up Networking dialog box double cliock "Make a New Connection" as shown in Figure 4.16.

The dialog box in Figure 4.17 will display "Make New Connection."

In the Name box type in the name of your ISP—I have used "My ISP" (is that original or what?).

As shown in Figure 4.18 fill in the phone number information.

Now you are finished—press the Finish button as shown in Figure 4.19 and you are done (almost).

It is here that you need to talk with your service to obtain the following information:

Is a static address supplied?
If yes, then will the ISP automatically provide default gateway and DNS settings?

FIGURE 4.15

FIGURE 4.16

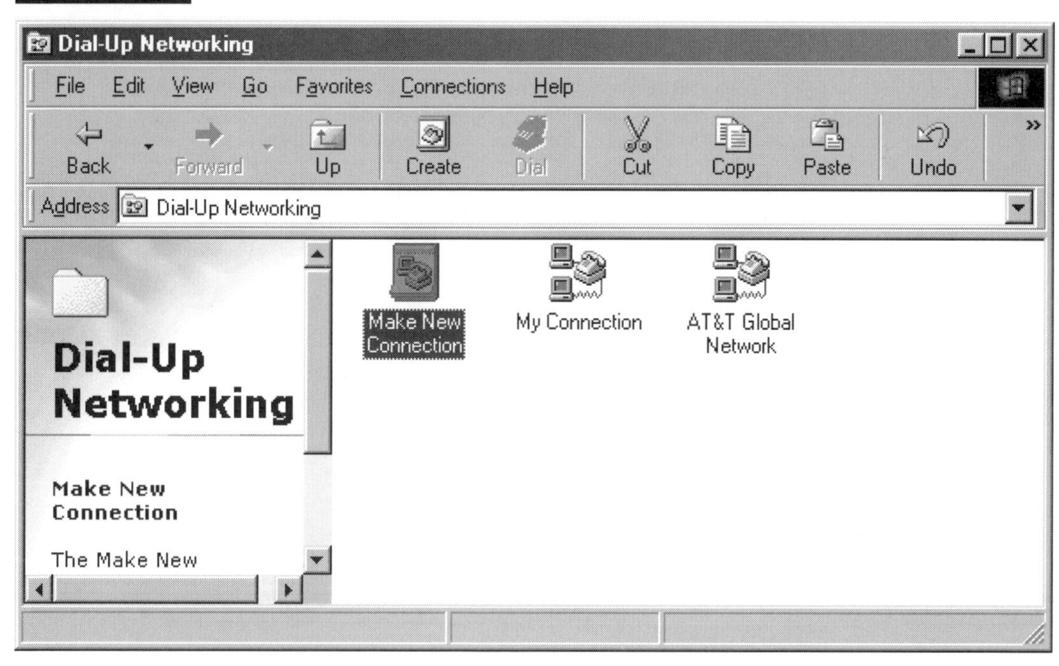

FIGURE 4.17

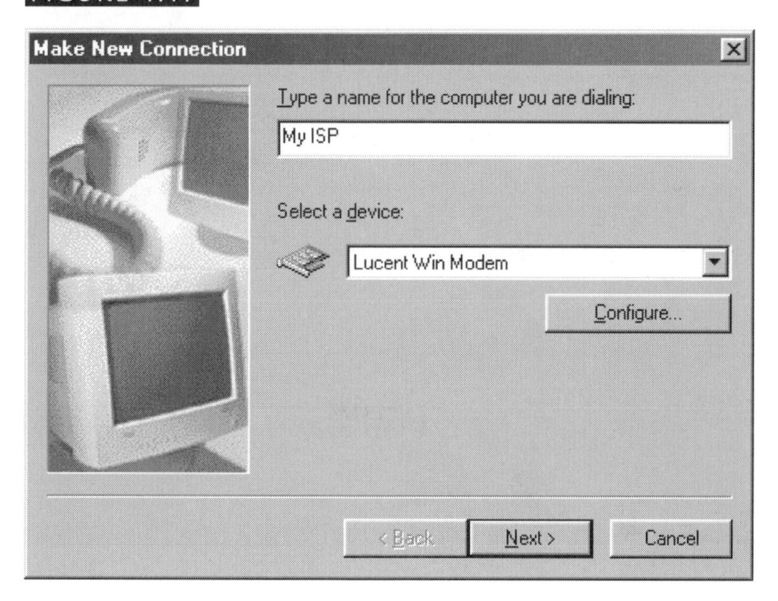

FIGURE 4.18

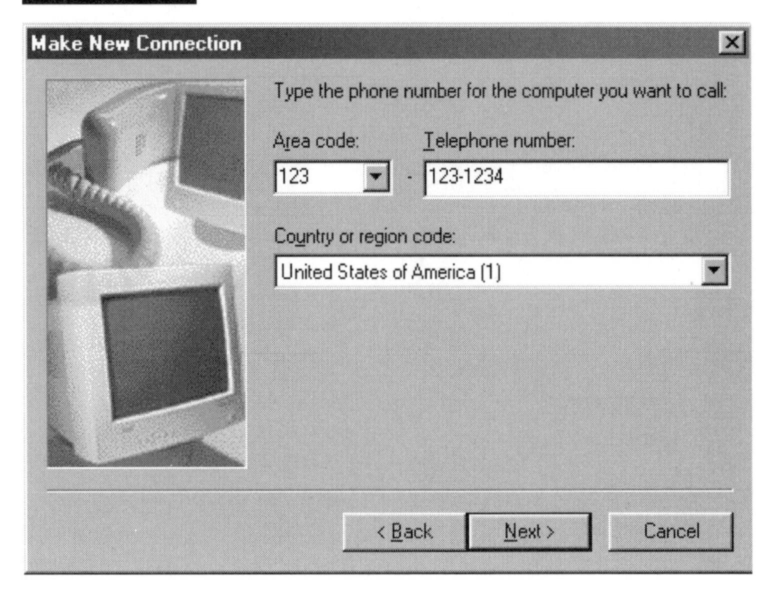

FIGURE 4.19

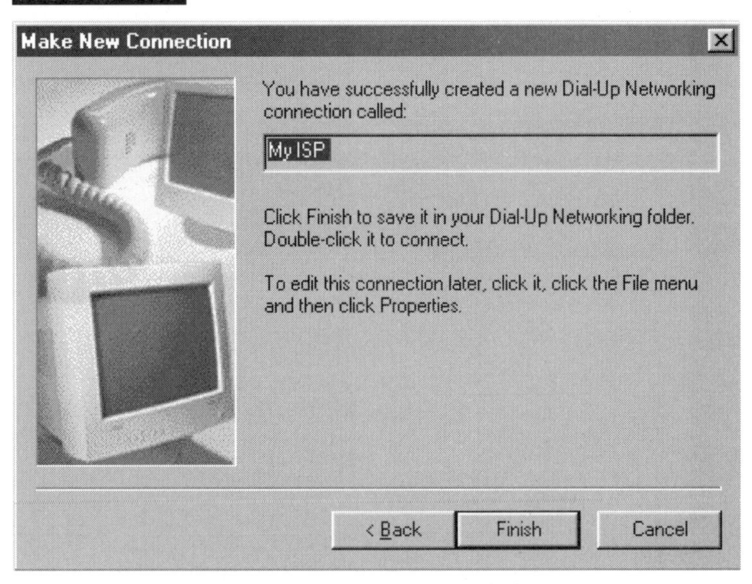

If the ISP provides a static address then fill out these dialog boxes:

Open the Dial-Up Network Icon. Double click the ICON for the dial-up service that you created. In Figure 4.20 it is My ISP.

FIGURE 4.20

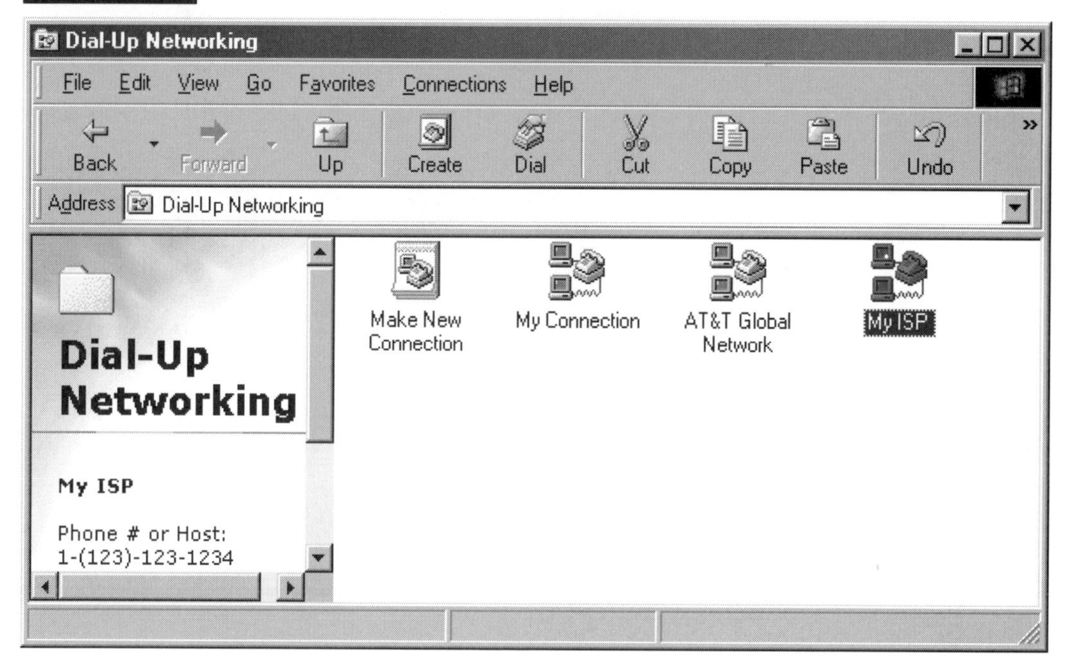

Enter the user name that you are using and the password (see ISP for this information).

At this point you will connect to your service provider and you are on the Internet.

Say you need to edit the TCP/IP configuration for this dial-up connection. Using the same example as shown in Figure 4.20, select My ISP, but this time click on your right mouse button. Select the Properties selection and a new dialog box will be shown as seen in Figure 4.21. Select the Server Types tab.

Now select the TCP/IP Settings button (as shown in Figure 4.22). This will bring up a new dialog box for TCP/IP.

The TCP/IP settings (as illustrated by Figure 4.23) are used to configure your TCP/IP settings for the dial-up session only. Please contact your ISP before making any changes. If your service provider does not automatically update these settings then you will need to make the changes yourself.

FIGURE 4.21

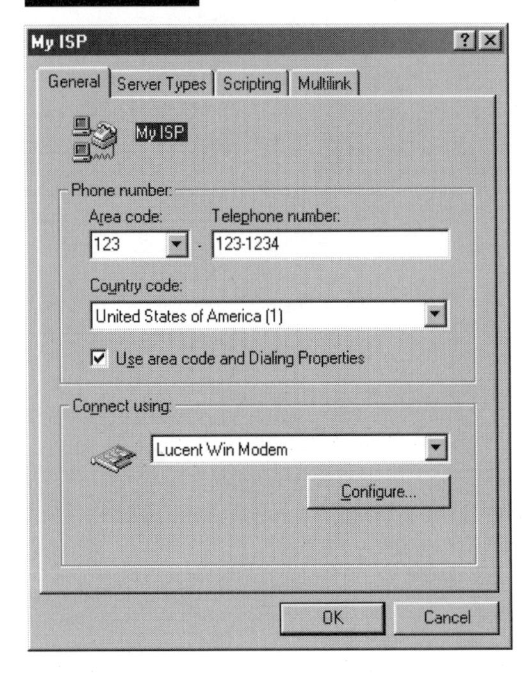

FIGURE 4.22

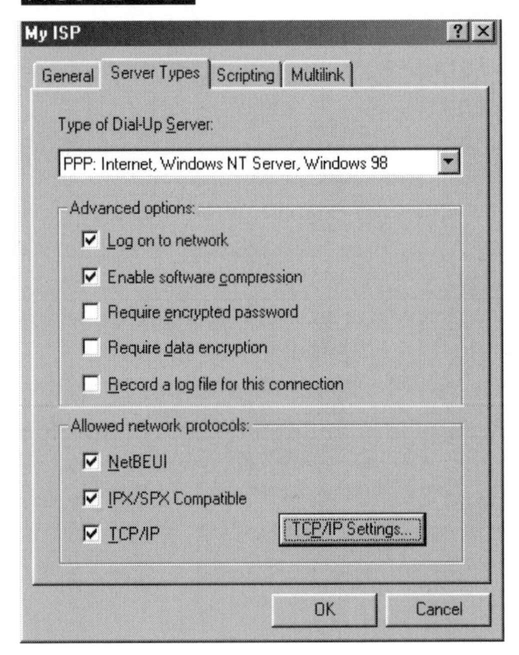

FIGURE 4.23

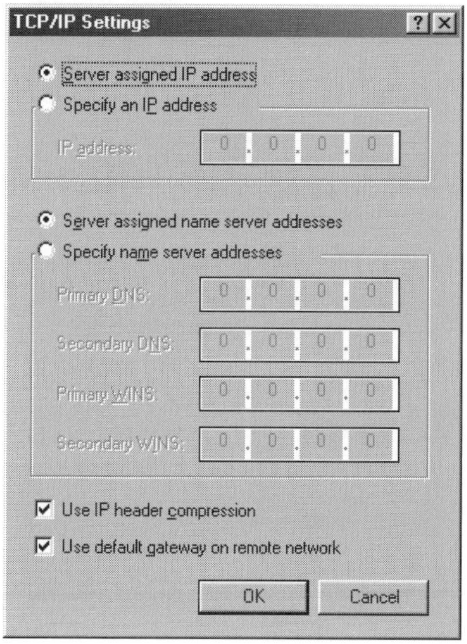

4.12 WinIPCfg

One question that comes up after you install a home network is how do I check to see what address has been assigned to my computer?

There are two basic tools you can use. If you are using Windows 95 or Windows 98 use a tool known as WinIpcfg. Here is how it works: As shown in Figure 4.24 at the start menu select Run. Type Winipcfg and select OK.

As shown in Figure 4.25, the window will display the IP address that has been assigned to your computer. Here you will see the IP address, subnet mask, and the default gateway. Select More Info>>>.

As shown in Figure 4.26, now you will see the DNS servers that have been assigned and information about how long the DHCP lease has been in effect. You can also reset one or more IP addresses. The **Release** or **Renew** buttons release or renew, respectively, one IP address. If you want to release or renew all IP addresses click **Release All** or **Renew All**. When one of these buttons is clicked, a new IP address is obtained from either the DHCP service or as a result of the computer assigning itself an automatic private IP address.

FIGURE 4.24

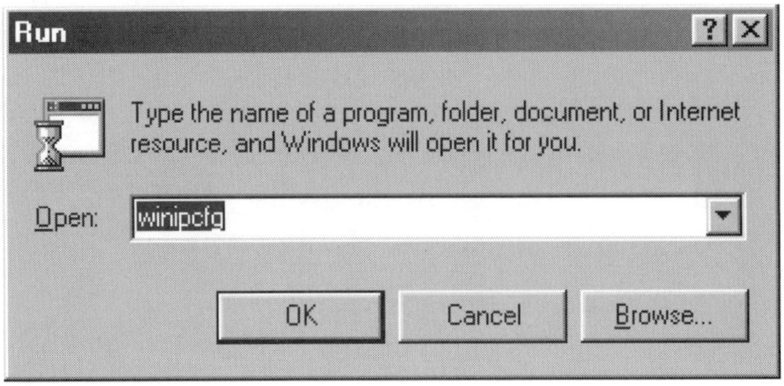

Run

Type the name of a program, folder, document, or Internet resource, and Windows will open it for you.

Open: winipcfg

OK Cancel Browse...

FIGURE 4.25

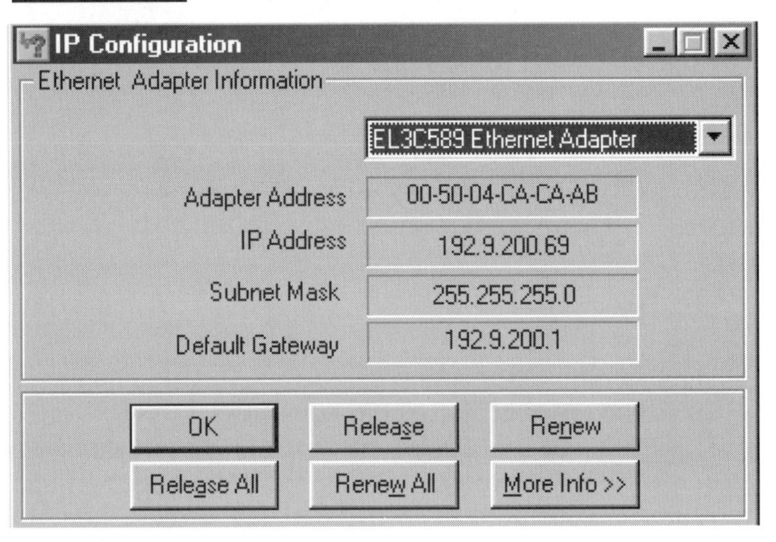

FIGURE 4.26

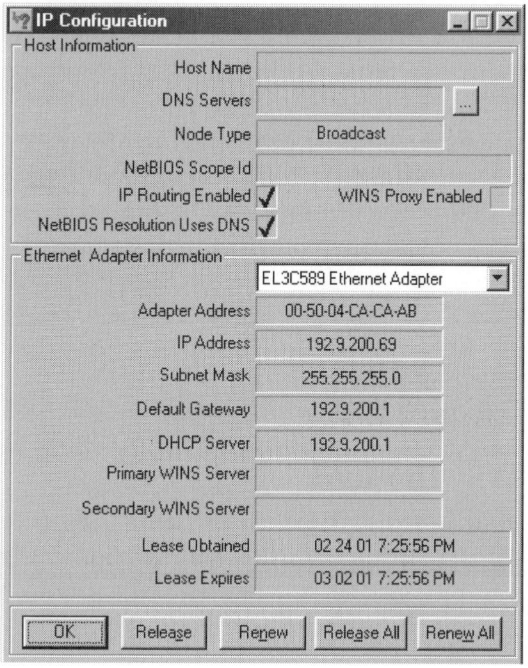

4.13 IPConfig

On NT and Windows 2000 you use Iconic. The IPCONFIG.EXE is a utility included with Windows NT Workstation and Server. The purpose of this utility is to provide the user with diagnostic information related to TCP/IP network configuration. The IPCONFIG also accepts various dynamic host configuration protocol (DHCP) commands, allowing a system to update or release its TCP/IP network configuration. Here is how to use Iconic:

IPCONFIG [/? | /all | /release [adapter] | /renew [adapter]]

/? Display this help message.
/all Display full configuration information.
/release Releases the IP address for the specified adapter.
/renew Renews the IP address for the specified adapter.

With no parameters, IPCONFIG will display only the IP address, subnet mask, and default gateway for each adapter bound to TCP/IP. With the /all switch, IPCONFIG will display all the current TCP/IP configuration values including the IP address, subnet mask, default gateway, and WINS and DNS configuration.

At this point in our discussion about messaging security we are going to talk about two types of mail, junk mail and spam mail. I actually separate junk mail from spam mail. The difference I think is in the premediation of the type of mail—with junk mail merely junk. Spam mail occurs typically because someone has added you to some type of mailing list (automatic in most cases) that is sending you messages without your permission. In many cases, but not all, junk mail comes to you with your permission.

4.14 Junk and Spam

4.14.1 The Junk

Let's start our discussion of unwanted mail with junk mail. This type of mail can actually arrive in your e-mail box due to some action on your part. For example, last week you went to a site and registered to access some information about the site, or you filled out an information card to receive a free magazine. Now you are receiving e-mail and some of this is e-mail you want so it is NOT junk, but rather stuff—yes, the stuff you want to read. (I would make this a comedy routine, but someone got to it about 20 years earlier.) So far, so good. After a while that stuff starts to add up and the next thing you know, you have junk mail. You have added yourself to 100s of e-mail lists. I had one that showed up the other day that I had forgotten about because they went off-line for about a year and then started back up. Most of the companies you have been doing business with will typically include a URL that allows you to remove your address from their distribution system and these reputable companies will then remove you from the list. Now you say "I don't see the problem." Well, hold those horses for a minute and keep reading.

At this point you are receiving a little bit of junk mail, but it's OK because you asked for it. A subscription here, a catalog update there, a job posting here. Let's say that adds up to 20 pieces of junk mail a day, not much. Now let's add a bit more and, to magnify our problem, let's start this at the end of November. This is Christmas time, we are all happy, we will be taking some time off to eat, get drunk, check out some questionable Internet sites, and then send that really good-looking person down the hall an electronic Christmas card. Here is what you do: Go to some great URL and find that e-card, then send it to your new buddies. That card may have an attachment, a Christmas tree that is animated and smiles at you, and when you look at the attachment you see that it is only maybe 500 kbytes. That is not very big, just half a Mbyte. So you send this to your buddy down the hall, he or she receives it, and of course loves it. Your new best friend now forwards it to another good buddy and then forwards it again. Finally someone forwards it outside of the company, and then finally it is forwarded back into the same company to another person. Now let's add some of this up, let's take two messages at half a Mbyte each, then add all of that junk mail that you are getting, then let's multiply it by two factors, one of which is the 10,000 employees at your company, the other is the holiday season. This adds up to a lot of messages and many of these messages are bigger than 500k, especially because some of these dumb nuts encrypted the message when they sent it out. The end result is that you have a clogged e-mail system with messages to and from known users or companies. To me this is junk mail, and to your company this should be classified as non-business use of the messaging environment. Later in this chapter we will discuss acceptable use policies and what should be in them.

4.14.2 The "Spam"

First off, let's provide a tribute to a wonderful meat product. The name SPAM is a registered trademark of Hormel Foods Corporation. Per the request of the Spam Web site we will be following the guidelines as specified in their URL,

http://www.spam.com/ci/ci_in.htm

The guidelines include use of the word spam in lower case when discussing the delivery of unsolicited commercial e-mail or UCE. Remember that the word SPAM is owned and trademarked by Hormel Foods. Go to your local grocer and purchase some, it's good and good for you.

With that said, we will continue. Here is what all of us have experienced: We happily log on to check our e-mail, and there are new messages waiting for us. This is exhilarating, we have mail, and this is most exciting. Someone really loves us, they really do. So with anticipation you look at the subject lines and you see the following:

- "Make money now"
- "Investment tips no one else knows"
- "Yes, these are the bodies you dream about"
- "Are you over 18 and would you like to be a model?"
- "Remember me, we met at. . . ."

Of course these are all valid and real messages and are all true; NOT! So after a while you start to see these messages pile up in your in-box, and you may try to reply to some of these messages. You may even try to ask to be removed from the senders' mailing lists. This does not always work; many times you will probably receive even more UCE.

There are several methods that spammers can use to get to you:

1. Purchase a list of names from various sources. Most reputable e-commerce companies that have your e-mail address will place some type of banner or disclaimer stating that they will not sell your address to an external vendor. But not all companies will offer this disclaimer.
2. If you take a list off of the Internet from anonymous sources. Examples:

   a. If you post an entry to an online service's or Internet bulletin board;
   b. Spend time in chat rooms on an online service; or
   c. Have a listing in an online directory service's service. Remember LDAP? Go to your favorite LDAP site and type in your last name.

Create a list of addresses based on a common suffix and a computed local part.

Some ISPs have spam and junk mail controls. Contact your local service provider and ask them if they offer this service.

CHAPTER 5

Physical Security and Insurance

The picture album many of us have stored on the top shelf of our closet is something of a mixed blessing. It makes us remember those events we would rather forget and lets us cherish the moments we wish to remember. A picture album[1] can take years to fill and countless dollars, all for a little nostalgia late one night, when we sit drinking a cup of coffee on the couch and thumbing through the album. But what if the album were to be lost or misplaced? Which would you lament the loss of: the album or the photos contained within?

The physical loss of a personal computer or laptop is costly, but the loss of the data stored on the computer can be devastating. Lost data can also be very expensive to replace. Personal computers (notably laptop) are easy targets. There have been several stories where presenters at security and computer conferences have had their computers stolen. Just turn around and "whoosh," their computer is gone. Laptops are prime targets for theft. Teams of thieves will work the airports, hunting for business travelers. (This happened to a good friend of mine.)

In this chapter we cover several devices that can be used to keep your computer secure using devices such as alarms, security enclosures, and alert systems as well as ensuring you have the right insurance policy. At the end of this chapter, a Security Checklist is provided to help ensure that you have covered the primary areas.

1. You may be among those who keep their album stored on their computer.

5.1 Where Are the Risks?

Security risks are most anywhere you keep your computer. I have seen several friends place their laptops in the back seat of their car. Think about it. What if someone took that laptop? What would it cost in time and resources to recover the damage? So bottom line, risks are everywhere from the home, office, hotel room, or car, to airports and airport restrooms—yes, even restrooms.

There are many products now available to prevent equipment and information loss. Some can be expensive and others are relatively inexpensive. The equipment you may need to secure your personal computer depends on your environment and what the computer is used for. We will start by discussing physical devices that can help thwart the bad dudes. First, here is a fact—if a bad dude really wants your laptop, then he or she will get it—no matter what you do. Now the good news, if you make it just a bit harder to rip-off your computer most of the bad dudes will skip your computer and go steal one that is easier to grab. Our job is to make it harder for the bad dudes to steal your computer. So let's see how we can keep the bad dudes at bay.

5.2 Theft-Prevention Devices

There are many theft-prevention[2] devices available on the market. (We will discuss the various devices and services in this chapter, and have some references for actual vendors in the reference chapter.) These devices include:

- Alarms;
- Antitheft devices;
- Security enclosures; and
- Automatic alert systems (If the computer is stolen then, once the thief uses it to connect to the Internet, it sends you the message, "Help—I have been stolen.").

5.2.1 Alarms

Alarms will not prevent the theft of equipment but usually act as a deterrent as well as to alert people in the vicinity that a computer has been tampered with. Alarms can be installed either external or internal to your equipment.

2. Please—if you are using a company supplied machine (laptop, computer), check with your company before using any of these alarm products. Always follow your corporate policies regarding company equipment and data.

These devices usually emit loud, piercing sounds if the equipment is moved or if the alarm is tampered with. Some alarms are equipped with keys to enable only authorized personnel to deactivate them. A cable alarm has a circuit built into the cable, so if the cable is cut it will sound an alarm.

The cable is attached to the computer and then armed.

5.2.2 Antitheft Devices

Antitheft devices can be used to prevent unauthorized access or removal of the equipment. Many of these devices use either adhesive-mounted pads or metal brackets to fasten the computer and other equipment to a desk or table. Anchors and cables enable you to attach your computer to a desk or tabletop. Cables are probably the most common physical security devices and, in many cases, the cheapest. Typically, steel cables are passed through a metal ring, which is attached to the equipment and a desk or table. Cables can prevent the bad dudes from quickly walking away with a piece of equipment. The cables can be cut, although not with ordinary tools. Additionally, there is a wide range of products; these include anchoring devices, security enclosures, security padlock cables, floppy drive locks, notebook kits, *case* locks and cable traps for mice, keyboards and other equipment.

5.2.3 Security Enclosures

Security enclosures are available for all types of PC equipment. Enclosures can also be cable locked to a desk or attached to a surface using special glues and/or bolts. Locking mechanisms can include padlocks, pick-resistant locks, and high-security locks. Many of these products include a no-theft hardware warranty. Check each vendor for coverage.

5.2.4 Automatic Alert System

This is software you actually have installed in your computer. If your PC is stolen then it will attempt to contact you (or a service) and tell you where it is should it be used to connect to the Internet.

5.2.5 Other Considerations

There are other considerations you should take into account when assessing how best to protect your PC. These can include protection against static electricity, power fluctuations, and loss of power.

Static electricity is quite common in today's modern buildings. Discharge of static electricity can cause loss of data, damage to delicate electronic parts installed inside the computer cabinet, and a malfunctioning computer.

Walking across a carpet can produce up to 30,000 V of static electricity. You can purchase products like chair mats that inhibit static electricity.

Power surges, brownouts, spikes, and power outages can result in loss of data and destruction of equipment. I have many times said very bad words when I lose power in the middle of updating my resume. You can purchase simple devices such as power bars especially designed to protect electronic equipment against power fluctuations. Many of these devices are cheap and easy to use. At the higher end of the cost spectrum you can purchase uninterruptible power supply (UPS) devices. These can be used in critical situations to prevent the loss of power.

5.3 Insurance

Often forgotten is insuring your computer and data. We know a laptop or home computer can be expensive. However, if your computer is being used for business the cost of the computer may be minimal compared to the data stored on that hard drive. So you may ask, "Do I need insurance?" Let's start with some simple questions:

- What would it cost to replace your computer?
- What should it cost to replace the data on your computer?
- Do you have a detailed inventory of your hardware and software?

And finally—

- Do you have insurance to replace that computer and its data?

Be sure you create an inventory of your hardware and software. Then put it in a safe place, such as a safe-deposit box.

Table 5.1 shows what you can create.

TABLE 5.1

Device Type	Quantity	Cost	Serial Number
Laptop—Brand X	1	$2500	S1234567
Printer—Brand Y	1	$300	S234567
Software Brand A	1	$700	Key—AB1234567
Network Hubs	2	$40	S1234 and S2345
Total Cost		**$3540**	

This record will serve two purposes: It will help you determine whether your existing insurance coverage is adequate if your equipment is stolen and it will allow you to provide important information to the police and your insurance company. Insurance companies treat this information (along with receipts) as proof of ownership. The police also use this data to track down stolen goods. Once you've inventoried your belongings, it's time to evaluate whether you have enough homeowner's or renter's insurance coverage. If your home setup consists of a single computer and printer valued at $5000 or less and they are used almost exclusively for personal purposes, then your existing policy is probably fine. In all cases contact your insurance company to determine what coverage you have. But don't just assume you have coverage: Check with your insurer. You also may want to purchase insurance that will cover the replacement cost of the computer and not the depreciated value.

Now if your computer setup exceeds $5000, or if you regularly use your computer for work, a standard homeowner's policy won't cover all your equipment. Specifically, if you operate a business out of your home or you regularly telecommute, your insurance company may deem your computer "business equipment," which isn't covered under a homeowner's or renter's policy. If the computer you have is a corporate computer, then ask your company what the policies are regarding insurance and what happens if the company-owned laptop is stolen.

After a bit of research I found that policies can differ from one insurer to another. See if your company will cover a traveling laptop. As we mentioned before, laptops can be stolen from airports and cars.[3] Not all policies will cover car or airport theft. Consumers who need extra coverage have two options: Get a floater on an existing homeowner's policy to cover all PC equipment or purchase a policy from a company that specializes in computer insurance. Note—specifically ask if both software and data are covered in any of these policies. Talk to your insurance agent and check out the plans offered by computer insurance companies to determine which type of policy would work best for you. In addition to the cost for this type of policy, other factors to consider include the comfort of dealing with a trusted insurance broker and the simplicity of buying a policy from a company that specializes in computer coverage.

Well-maintained records greatly increase your odds of recovering a stolen computer. The National Computer Exchange runs a Stolen Computer Registry, which law enforcement officials use to report and track

3. You might think that a laptop would be safe in a car trunk. I have seen many a computer get cooked in a trunk in the Texas sun and laptop screen crack from the Boston cold.

stolen PCs by serial number. Individual consumers can access the database to enter information about their stolen computer or to confirm that used equipment they're considering purchasing has not been stolen. Law enforcement officials also recommend labeling all home electronics with your name and address. Attaching permanent ID tags or etching personal information into the back of your equipment makes it harder for a thief to sell it. Marking your hardware also increases the odds of getting your property back if the police recover it.

5.4 PC Security Check List

1. Maintain detailed records. Do this for all your hardware and software, and include model and serial numbers.
2. Review your insurance coverage.
3. Be inconspicuous. If at all possible, avoid placing computer equipment near windows. Store your notebooks, digital cameras, and other smaller items out of sight.
4. Back up regularly. You can replace stolen hardware and software. You can't replace valuable business and personal files.
5. Make the thief's job difficult. For added security, buy a cabling or alarm system to make it that much harder for a burglar to hit and run successfully.
6. Finally, at the airport:
   a. When you're going through a metal detector, keep your laptop in your hand until the person in front of you has already cleared the scanner.
   b. Do not put your bag on the conveyor belt until you can follow it right through. Security stations are a common place for teams of thieves to work. One person (Mr. Metal) will set off the metal detector, holding up the line, while the other person grabs the laptop a hapless owner set down on the conveyor belt too early.
   c. Keep the laptop's serial number, model number, and record in a separate location. That will make it easier to recover if it's ever found.
   d. When you travel with your laptop, carry it in something that doesn't look like a laptop carrying case. A briefcase, a duffel bag, or a knapsack are all better choices and make you a less likely target.
   e. Look into encryption systems and other devices that make it difficult or impossible for thieves to use your laptop.

CHAPTER 6

Data Protection

Next on our list is data protection. One of the most effective methods of protecting your data is to encrypt the data on your laptop. A data encryption program or utility will encrypt the data so that if your system is stolen then the data cannot be read or used by the hacker (a.k.a. the bad dude who stole your computer).

In this chapter, we will review two methods to encrypt the data: Windows 2000 EFS and A vendor solution (GateKeeper™[1]). In the final section of this chapter, we will include information on how smart cards can be used to secure data and applications.

6.1 Windows 2000 EFS

Microsoft 2000 uses a system known as EFS or **Encrypting File System**. This system is the core file-encryption technology for storing Windows NT® file system (NTFS) files and directories encrypted on a Windows 2000 disk. The process is based on public key[2] technology and EFS is integrated into the

1. Special thanks to Dr. Phillip Jen (President and CEO, Armadillo Limited) for the information and demonstration of the Gatekeeper product, http://www.armadillo.com.hk
2. For a detailed description of public and private keys see *The Internet Security Guidebook,* Academic Press, Boston, USA.

Windows 2000 operating system. The Encrypting File System particularly addresses security concerns raised by tools available on other operating systems that let users access files from an NTFS volume without an access check.

The Encrypting File System allows users to store data securely on their personal computers by encrypting data in selected NTFS[3] files and folders. Because EFS is integrated with the file system, it is easy to manage, difficult to attack, and transparent to the user. This is very useful for securing data on computers that may be vulnerable to theft, such as mobile computers. The actual process of data encryption and decryption, using EFS, is transparent to the user. The user does not need to know or understand this process.

The EFS encryption of files is implemented using the following steps, where each file has a unique *file encryption key,* which is later used to decrypt the file's data:

- The file encryption key is encrypted—it is protected by the user's public key corresponding to the user's EFS certificate; and
- the public key of an authorized recovery agent also protects the file encryption key.

The EFS decryption of files works as follows:

- The file encryption key must first be decrypted when decrypting a file. The file encryption key is decrypted when the user has a private key that mathematically matches the public key.
- A recovery agent can also extract the encryption key. This is implemented by using the recovery agent's private key.
- Once the file encryption key is decrypted, either the user or the recovery agent can use it to decrypt the file data.

For more information about EFS, check out http://www.microsoft.com/TechNet/win2000/efsguide.asp

6.2 A Vendor Solution (Gatekeeper™)

The next product is one example of items you can use to encrypt the data on your PC. This one uses a smart card along with software to encrypt the data.[4]

3. Files and folders cannot be encrypted or decrypted on *F*ile *A*llocation *T*able (FAT) volumes.
4. Armadillo also offers a product known as VirtualGate—http://www.armadillo.com.hk/virtualgate.htm

Personal computers, operating and e-mail systems contain no effective protection against unauthorized access and theft of the user's confidential data stored on data disks or the hard drive. Confidential data can be read and stolen while your electronic mail can be accessed with damaging results. Although numerous protection devices and programs are available, these systems have proven to be unsafe, overly complicated, and/or not readily available to individual users outside the corporate environment. The GateKeeper is an encryption system designed for data security of individual users in a corporate and/or personal environment. By using 1024-bit RSA, RC4, or Triple-DES (3DES) encryption methods and the proven security of smart cards, the GateKeeper protects the integrity and confidentiality of the user's data files (documents, texts, spreadsheets, graphics, etc.), program files (stored on a data disk, hard drive, etc.), and/or messages transmitted through the Internet.

GateKeeper Internals:

- Physical lock. The smart card (more on smart cards at the end of this chapter) and the smart card reader control and protect your data like a physical lock and key. The entire system is accessible only after the correct smart card is inserted and the password given by the user. This hardware device is designed to further safeguard your computer from tampering and the unauthorized access of private files.
- File encryption. Once the files stored on your computer are encrypted by either 1024-bit RSA, RC4, or triple-DES (3DES), only the authorized user with the correct smart card and password can decrypt the information.
- E-mail encryption. The secure e-mail program utilizes principles similar to those used for file encryption functions. Only after the correct smart card and password are provided will the program allow the user to generate a specific encryption [key], thereby allowing the encryption and decryption of e-mail messages. The system's function is briefly outlined here:

1. A specific [key][5] is necessary to allow any encryption of e-mail messages. For example, user A wants to send a message to user B, and user B will generate a [key] specifically for user A.
2. User B will e-mail this [key] to user A prior to sending any e-mail messages, and it will be saved and stored by the user of the GateKeeper system.
3. This specifically generated [key] will be used when, and only when, user B wants to send an encrypted message to user A.

5. Subject to your security requirements, the forementioned [key] can be changed and/or regenerated at any time. This is a recommended safety precaution to ensure that your encrypted messages remain private and secure.

4. On the other hand, if user A wants to send an encrypted e-mail to user C, he or she must have a [key] generated by user C. Put simply, the [key] is specific to a particular message, depending upon the origin of the message.

After you have completed your work (e.g., text messages, document files, spreadsheets, programs, graphic files, etc.), you will be allowed to choose the specific type of encryption method to use for this particular file. Depending on your schedule and the importance of the file, you can choose the 1024-bit RSA[6] method for maximum protection, or RC4[7] and 3DES[8] for moderate protection. Simply click on the icon representing your choice of method, and your file will be encrypted and protected by GateKeeper.

Although no encryption software is unbreakable, GateKeeper is designed to provide maximum protection available for your personal or sensitive company files. A brief explanation of our encryption methods follows.

The larger the RSA encryption modulus, the greater the security for the user (e.g. 1024 bit > 64 bit). However, the operating time for encryption also depends very much on the size of the modulus. GateKeeper's 1024-bit RSA cryptosystem is designed to provide maximum security for users in a reasonable operation time. Please see http://www.rsasecurity.com/rsalabs/faq/3–1–1.html for more information.

6.3 Smart Cards

A smart card is a device the size of a credit card containing an integrated circuit that can be used to store a wide variety of applications. The integrated circuit in the smart card provides secure memory and hardware support for

6. RSA is a public-key cryptosystem that was developed by Ron Rivest, Adi Shamir, and Leonard Adleman in 1977. RSA is considered strong cryptography by the US government and requires approval from the US Bureau of Export Administration under the Department of Commerce. Currently, only 64-bit RSA encryption codes can be freely exported from the US. Armadillo acquired the usage of 1024-bit RSA only after lengthy negotiation with various governmental agencies and is under stringent restrictions as to locations of distribution.

7. RC4 is a variable key-size stream cipher with byte-oriented operartions, designed by Ron Rivest of RSA. The algorithm is based on the use of a random permutation. Please see http://www.rsasecurity.com/rsalabs/faq/3–6–3.html for more information.

8. Data Encryption Standard, developed by IBM and known as Lucifer, is widely used throughout the world. Please see http://www.rsasecurity.com/rsalabs/faq/3–2–1.html for more information.

security functions. Smart cards are known by different terms such as chip card, integrated circuit card, PC in your wallet, and DB on a card. These cards provide a great deal of security for the data stored inside them. Some models of smart cards can hold over 100 times the amount of information that is contained in a standard magnetic-strip card. The security and mobility of smart cards have made them increasingly popular, mainly for financial applications. Uses of smart cards include establishing identification when logging on to ISPs or online banks, providing health information that can be used by hospitals or doctors, and making online purchases without the use of traditional credit cards. There are hundreds of smart card operations in use worldwide, with over a billion smart cards in use. Currently, they are most widely used in Europe. Their use is expected to increase as Ovum, a research firm, predicts that 2.7 billion smart cards will be shipped annually by 2003. Some cards can be programmed to support multiple applications as well as application updates. Smart cards can be designed to be inserted into a slot and read by a special reader or to be read at a distance, such as at a tollbooth. The cards can be disposable or reloadable. Smart cards are covered under the International Organization for Standardization (ISO) 7816 standard. The standard entitled "ISO 7816 Identification Cards—Integrated Circuit(s) Cards with Contacts" consists of eight documents that describe all physical aspects of the cards.

Business enterprises looking to incorporate smart cards into their security systems may consider them for many applications, including the following:

- To replace traditional employee ID badges—
  - Provide picture identification,
  - Access to company facilities, including secure areas,
  - Electronic wallet for company cafeteria and vending machines;
- Storage of employee's digital signatures, including certificate authority and private keys;
- Network access identification, including single sign-on;
- Employee medical and health information; and
- Employee business travel profile, including the company's preferred airlines, hotels, and car rental agencies.

CHAPTER 7

Keep Your Data Private

Internet privacy is almost an oxymoron. Privacy issues are taking on increasing importance, as technology is ever more present in daily life. If a company can't assure its customers and employees that sensitive information is secure from the eyes of those who don't need to know, that company won't stay in business without mending its ways.[1]

Privacy is becoming one of the most important areas in which technology and society will have an impact on each other in the coming years. As companies reach out into international markets, they are finding that privacy is a full-time component of their business. Every country can have various laws and cultures that can have an impact on how they do business, including privacy issues. This is a significant challenge. These businesses will have to find ways to utilize increasingly integrated Internet technology without running afoul of a constant changing set of rules.

In this chapter, we will cover ways that your computer information may be captured on the Internet as well as tools that are used to prevent this from happening.

1. Take a look at the Fraud numbers and stats in Chapter 1.

7.1 Who Is Keeping Us Safe?

In the United States, privacy policies are still being formulated and developed. One example of this is HIPAA. The Health Insurance Portability and Accountability Act of 1996 (HIPAA), signed into law on August 21, 1996, includes important new protections for millions of working Americans and their families who have preexisting medical conditions or might suffer discrimination in health coverage based on a factor that relates to an individual's health. The HIPAA provisions amend Title I of the Employee Retirement Income Security Act of 1974 (ERISA) as well as the Internal Revenue Code and the Public Health Service Act and place requirements on employer-sponsored group health plans, insurance companies, and health maintenance organizations (HMOs).

The Federal Trade Commission[2] may get involved if a company's policy is deemed part of its public business, and the FTC is beginning to assume its role as a defender of consumers' privacy. The FTC has a great Web page for Kids and their privacy—http://www.ftc.gov/bcp/conline/edcams/kidzprivacy/index.html

Even the FBI has gotten into the privacy game. The FBI created a tool known as Carnivore. This tool is a combination of hardware and software that enables the FBI to intercept and collect data from traffic on the Internet. More on this later.

7.2 How Are You Being Tracked?

Privacy is not just for companies and employees, it's a concern of the individual computer user as well. Yes, firewalls and routers may help keep the bad dudes out of your computer or network, and that in itself may help protect your personal information. On the other hand, when you use the Internet, you've arrived in a global marketplace stocked with products and services. One important commodity on the Internet is information. You may need to look up information for your next school paper, or to find an old buddy. The Internet is full of information you want and may need. At the same time you provide information as you use the Internet. Every time you visit a site, that site tracks what you have entered. Information is gathered on the Internet both indirectly and directly. When you enter a chat room for a discussion, leave a message on a bulletin board, register with a commercial site, or order a product with your credit card, you directly and

2. http://www.ftc.gov/privacy/protect.htm

knowingly send information onto the Internet. One simple process is to ask for your e-mail address and if you want to receive promotional materials.

Most people realize that a Web site owner can know everything that was viewed on their site, and can even know if this is a return visit by someone using the same machine. This is a lot of information, but it doesn't answer the marketing type of questions that need to be answered for the many sites that depend on advertising for their revenue. Notable are the marketers' need to know who their readers are and what demographic characteristics they possess. In the end the marketers need to know more about the actual people they are in contact with.

Guess what? Web sites resort to the same techniques of data gathering as do magazines and appliance companies. As you visit a Web page you are asked to fill out forms of information about yourself or your family. The reason you do this is for access to data, contents, or even software. Many times this registration process is labled as being "free." In the end it is really a form of payment for access to the services you are after.

Many Internet users are happy to participate in this system of information barter. But once you have an ID (your e-mail address can be an ID) you can be linked to personally identifiable information, and it is even possible that a profile can automatically be built based on this data, whether or not you agree to it.

Another tracking process that can be used is called "cookies." Cookies are pieces of information generated by a Web server and stored in the user's computer, ready for future access. Cookies are embedded in the HTML information flowing back and forth between the user's computer and the servers. Cookies were implemented to allow user-side customization of Web information. Cookies make use of user-specific information transmitted by the Web server onto the user's computer so that the information might be available for later access either by itself or by other servers. In most cases, the storage of personal information into a cookie goes unnoticed. Furthermore, the process of **giving up**, or harvesting the cookies by the Web servers, is not noticed.

Cookies operate by a two-step process. The cookie is first stored in the user's computer. This can happen without their consent or knowledge. During the second step, the cookie is automatically transferred from the user's machine to a Web server. Whenever a user directs their Web browser (1) to display a certain Web page from the server, the browser will, without the user's knowledge, transmit the cookie containing personal information to the Web server (2). Okay, you ask, how can I track which cookies are being put on my computer? One method is to tell your browser to prompt you when a cookie is being put on your computer. Another is to look at the cookie file (or files) that is on your computer. Netscape uses a file called Cookies.txt (3). Just open the file with Notepad and you can look at the cookies.[3] If you don't like your cookies then just delete the file, with the browser shut down. When you restart the browser it will establish your cookie file (see Figure 7.1). In addition, there is software that you can use to manage your cookies.

Take a look at http://www.cookiecentral.com/software.phtml?type=pc for a list. Here are a few examples:

- Cookie Pal—http://www.kburra.com/
- Cookie Crusher v2.6—http://www.thelimitsoft.com/
- NSClean—http://www.nsclean.com/nsclean.html

There are other mechanisms to capture information about who you are. There are features built into Web servers that will capture many variables about your computer and its browser. Additionally, it can capture your computer name or its DNS name and IP address. Here are examples of one method, which uses CGI variables:

- SERVER_SOFTWARE. The name and version of the information server software answering the request (and running the gateway). Format: name/version.
- SERVER_NAME. The server's hostname, DNS alias, or IP address as it would appear in self-referencing URLs.
- GATEWAY_INTERFACE. The revision of the CGI specification to which this server complies. Format: CGI/revision.
- SERVER_PROTOCOL. The name and revision of the information protocol this request came in with. Format: protocol/revision.
- SERVER_PORT. The port number to which the request was sent.
- REQUEST_METHOD. The method used to make the request. For HTTP, this is "GET," "HEAD," "POST," etc.
- PATH_INFO. The extra path information, as given by the client. In other words, scripts can be accessed by their virtual pathname, followed by extra information at the end of this path. The extra information is sent as PATH_INFO. The server should decode this information if it comes from a URL before it is passed to the CGI script.

3. Don't try to edit or save the cookies.txt file because it has a very specific format and you can corrupt the cookie file.

FIGURE 7.1

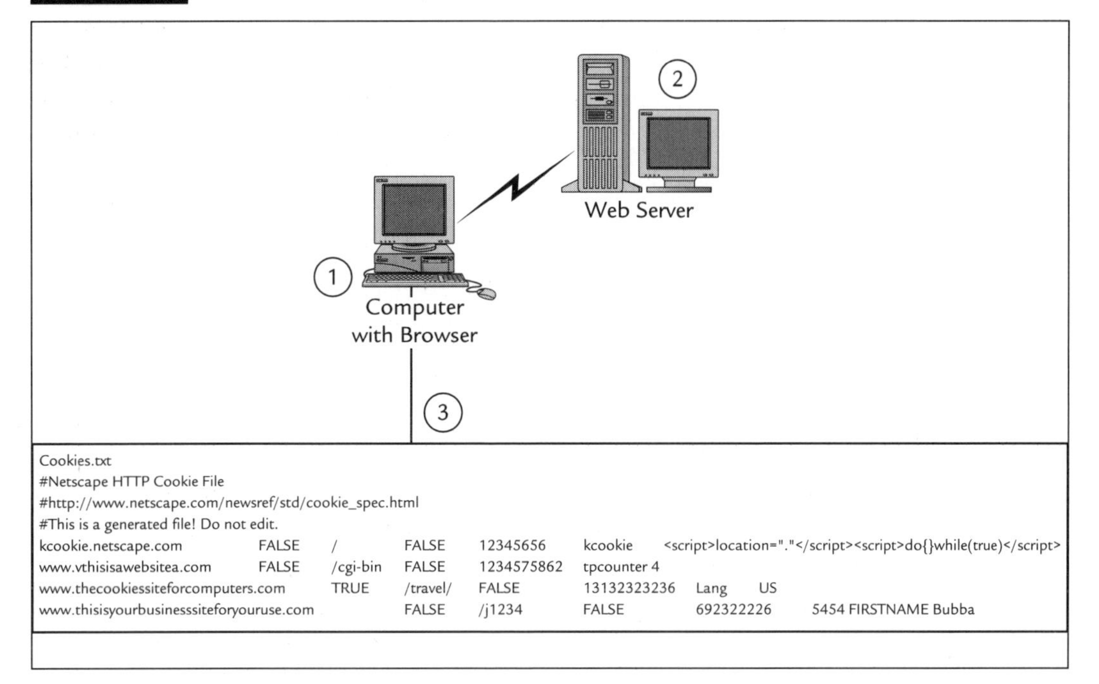

2
Web Server
1
Computer
with Browser
3
Cookies.txt
#Netscape HTTP Cookie File
#http://www.netscape.com/newsref/std/cookie_spec.html
#This is a generated file! Do not edit.
kcookie.netscape.com FALSE / FALSE 12345656 kcookie <script>location="."</script><script>do{}while(true)</script>
www.vthisisawebsitea.com FALSE /cgi-bin FALSE 1234575862 tpcounter 4
www.thecookiessiteforcomputers.com TRUE /travel/ FALSE 13132323236 Lang US
www.thisisyourbusinesssiteforyouruse.com FALSE /j1234 FALSE 692322226 5454 FIRSTNAME Bubba

- PATH_TRANSLATED. The server provides a translated version of PATH_INFO, which takes the path and does any virtual-to-physical mapping to it.
- SCRIPT_NAME. A virtual path to the script being executed, used for self-referencing URLs.
- QUERY_STRING. The information following the ? in the URL that referenced this script. This is the query information. It should not be decoded in any fashion. This variable should always be set when there is query information, regardless of *command line decoding*.
- REMOTE_HOST. The hostname making the request. If the server does not have this information, it should set REMOTE_ADDR and leave this unset.
- REMOTE_ADDR. The IP address of the remote host making the request.
- AUTH_TYPE. If the server supports user authentication and the script it protects, this is the protocol-specific authentication method used to validate the user.
- REMOTE_USER. If the server supports user authentication, and the script is protected, this is the username they have authenticated.

- REMOTE_IDENT. If the HTTP server supports RFC 931 identification, then this variable will be set to the remote user name retrieved from the server. Usage of this variable should be limited to logging only.
- CONTENT_TYPE. For queries that have attached information, such as HTTP POST and PUT, this is the content type of data.
- CONTENT_LENGTH. The length of the said content as given by the client.
- HTTP_ACCEPT. The MIME types that the client will accept, as given by HTTP headers. Other protocols may need to get this information from elsewhere. Commas as per the HTTP spec should separate each item in this list.
- HTTP_USER_AGENT. The browser the client is using to send the request. General format: software/version library/version.

This kind of information is valuable to marketers because it helps them target their sales efforts. The more "they" know about you the better they can market their products to the general consumer.

Starting April 21, 2000, a new law[4] puts parents in charge of their kids' personal identifying information (for children under 13). Web sites that ask for certain information about kids under 13 have to obtain parental permission to get this information. This puts the parents in control of data leaving their house. This also means that parents need to work with their children on how to read and interpret questions on various Web pages. This law is important because it can stop Web site operators who might misuse information they collect from kids. This law protects children by asking their parents to give Web sites their permission to collect information. Some of the important things to know about surfing, privacy, and your personal information include:

- Kids. Don't tell other kids your screen name, user ID, or password.
- Kids. Surf the Internet with your parents. If they aren't available, talk to them about the sites you're visiting.
- Never give out your last or family name, your home address, or your phone number in chat rooms, on bulletin boards, or to online pen pals.
- Look at a Web site's Privacy Policy to see how the site uses the information you give them. (This is a good step before you let your kids visit a site.)

4. http://www.ftc.gov/bcp/conline/edcams/kidzprivacy/biz.htm

7.3 The FBI and Carnivore

As promised we will talk a bit more about Carnivore. This product provides the FBI[5] with the ability to intercept and collect data on the Internet. A special device, now known as "The Collector," is installed at an Internet Service Provider (ISP). The collector can be configured to capture and save data from specific users or sites. The collector has a central specific feature, the ability to sniff the network. This process can capture IP packets. If you have forgotten what an IP packet is, then review Chapter 3. The IP data can carry different types of TCP services, such as FTP, e-mail,[6] and http traffic. Carnivore can listen and capture any of this data. Use of Carnivore is controlled by the Department of Justice and/or by court orders. Illegal use of the tool is punishable by imprisonment of up to five years, a fine, or both. Mario Figueroa wrote a great study on the Carnivore tool that you might want to check out: http://www.sans.org/infosecFAQ/legal/carnivore.htm

7.4 Privacy Tools

- Security: Encryption: Pretty Good Privacy. http://www.stack.nl/~galactus/remailers/index-pgp.html
- PGP is a file encryption program that is generally considered unbreakable. It can also create digital signatures.
- Digicash—electronic anonymous payments—http://www.digicash.com/ Buying on the Internet can be done with a credit card, but this is not very secure. It is also not very anonymous. Your credit card company knows what you are buying, as well as where and when. The person you are buying from also knows your name. Digital cash is just like its real-life counterpart.
- Security: Encryption: Disk encryption. http://www.stack.nl/~galactus/remailers/index-diskcrypt.html (more on this in a later chapter).
- Security: File wiping. http://www.stack.nl/~galactus/remailers/index-wipe.html (a normal "delete" does not actually erase files). The data itself remain on the disk but it's just not part of a file anymore. By using a wiper, the data are replaced with random junk first. This prevents bad dudes with undelete capability from recapturing your erased files.

5. http://www.fbi.gov/programs/carnivore/carnivore2.htm
6. Example: SMTP messages.

7.5 Privacy References

- American Civil Liberties Union (ACLU). A national civil liberties organization originally founded in 1920, the ACLU conducts extensive litigation on Constitutional issues including privacy and free speech. The ACLU Washington office lobbies Congress for civil liberties and civil rights issues. E-mail: info@aclu.org 125 Broad Street, NY, NY, 10004-2400. Executive Director: Ira Glasser.
- Consumer Project on Technology. The CPT was created by Ralph Nader in the Spring of 1995 to focus on a variety of issues, including telecommunications regulation, pricing of ISDN services, fair use under the copyright law, issues relating to the pricing, ownership, and development of pharmaceutical drugs, impact of technology on personal privacy, and several other issues. Box 19367, Washington, DC 20036, (202) 387-8030 (tel), (202) 234-5176 (fax). Director: James Love.
- Center for Media Education. A national nonprofit organization dedicated to improving the quality of electronic media, especially on the behalf of children and families. Guides, reports, and other information on children's and consumer privacy. E-mail: cme@cme.org 1511 K Street NW, Suite 518, Washington, DC 20005. (202) 628-2620 (tel), (202) 628-2554 (fax).
- Privacy International (PI). An international human rights group based in London, England with offices in Washington, DC and Sydney, Australia. Privacy International has members in over 40 countries and has led campaigns against national ID cards, video surveillance, and other privacy violations in numerous countries including Australia, New Zealand, the United Kingdom, and the Philippines. The PI group also publishes the International Privacy Bulletin and sponsors yearly international conferences on privacy issues. E-mail: pi@privacy.org Privacy International, 1718 connecticut Avenue, NW, Suite 200, Washington, DC 20009.
- Privacy Rights Clearinghouse. A California-based organization formed in 1992. The Clearinghouse has produced many fact sheets and an annual report, and maintains a toll free hotline to provide advice to consumers about their rights. E-mail: prc@privacyrights.org 5384 Linda Vista Road, #308, San Diego, CA 92110-2492 (619) 298-3396 (tel), (619) 298-5681 (fax). Director: Beth Givens.

CHAPTER 8

Encryption for Your PC

Cryptography is one of the oldest systems of protecting data. Historians have found evidence of this dating back at least 4000 years. Cryptography is believed by many to have been created around 2000 B.C. in Egypt. The ancient Chinese also used codes to hide the meaning of their words. Over the years, various systems have been used, ranging from a simple substitution of letters or numbers to complex mathematical theorems.

Understanding encryption is a key component to securing information as it goes from your computer to the next computer and vice versa. In this chapter we cover Public/Private Key, RSA, Digital Certificates, SSL, and other methods you can use to help ensure your information is not being accessed without your knowledge.

8.1 A History of Cryptography

One of the simplest forms of cryptography is a substitution of letters for numbers. The example shown here was a popular prize in cereal boxes many years ago:

A	B	C	D	E	F	G	H	I	J	K	L	M	N	O	P	Q	R	S	T	U	V	W	X	Y	Z
1	2	3	4	5	6	7	8	9	1	1	1	1	1	1	1	1	1	1	2	2	2	2	2	2	2
									0	1	2	3	4	5	6	7	8	9	0	1	2	3	4	5	6

Granted, the bad dudes may have been able to figure this one out, but most codes are not this simple. Cryptology is the process of changing text into some type of code or text (called ciphertext) that is not readable by the general reader. Ciphertext is the result of using a key (sometimes secret) and creating a body of text that needs to be deciphered. A key is typically some quantity or mechanism to encrypt or decrypt text or ciphertext.

Now that we know what a key is, and what ciphertext is, we can begin to encrypt and decrypt data. Here is a very simple example that uses the letter/number format.

Start out with the text "HELLO." If we encrypt it with our encryption system, we have 8 5 12 12 15 and the formula is:

Text → Encryption System → Ciphertext
HELLO → Table Look up → 8 5 12 12 15

Now using the same Key we will decrypt the ciphertext

Ciphertext → Encryption System → Text
8 5 12 12 15 → Table Look Up → HELLO

Throughout history, all governments have used some type of encryption. During the Middle Ages there was considerable use of encryption. Many of the early European governments used cryptography, encrypting communiques for their government ambassadors.

Over time encryption was enhanced by various tools. One of these, a Cipher Wheel, was invented by Thomas Jefferson. This tool consisted of a set of wheels, each with a random order of the letters of the alphabet. The key to the system was the order of the wheels. Each wheel was placed on an axle, and the message was encoded by aligning the letters along the axis of the axle such that the message was created.

Any other row of aligned letters could then be used as the ciphertext. The decryption required that the person receiving the message configure the letters of the ciphertext along the axis and find a set of readable letters. The recipient then had a readable message.

Go to your favorite search engine and do a search for "Cryptography and Shakespeare." There are many listings for URLs and books on the use of code in Shakespearean works. Many arguments have been made that Christopher Marlowe or Thomas Kyd actually wrote the various plays and sonnets and that the clues are encoded in the writings. Allowing for a brief moment of facetiousness, it may be that if you somehow decoded the plays, you could perhaps find that Romeo actually loved a girl named Ethel!

As you can see, encryption and cryptography are not new, and they are not a technology created for the Internet. They are as old as language itself and have been used for many different purposes, mostly to keep secrets from an adversary. If you study any war throughout history, you will find the use of some type of encryption. During the American Civil War, both the Union and Confederate armies used ciphers. During World War II, the Americans were able to break the Japanese codes, known as Purple codes. The ability to decrypt the information contained in the code assisted the Americans in battles with Japan. The Purple team was led by William F. Friedman, who during his spare time at Cornell University worked with cryptologists in trying to prove that Sir Francis Bacon through his encrypted signature in plays actually wrote works credited to Shakespeare! In World War II, American military forces used the Navajo Native American language to transmit messages by telephone and radio—a code that the Japanese never broke. Its syntax and tonal qualities, not to mention dialects, make it unintelligible to anyone without extensive exposure and training. It has no alphabet or symbols, and is spoken only on the Navajo lands of the American Southwest. One estimate indicates that fewer than 30 non-Navajos, none of them Japanese, could understand the language at the outbreak of World War II.

At the same time during World War II, German codes were predominantly based on the "Enigma" machine. On an old farm outside of London known as Bletchley Park, Alan Turing, a leading mathematician, developed an electromechanical machine that would enable code cracking of the Enigma keys. With this system and the capture of Enigma machines from U-boats, the Allies were able to learn the planned activities of U-boat, Panzer tank, and bombing raids.

A great Enigma emulator in the form of an Applet can be found at http://www.ugrad.cs.jhu.edu/~russell/classes/enigma/

Here is some code to make with this applet; see if you can crack an Enigma code from World War II: NMQXIOWFPB. E-mail the results to timspeed@home.com (sorry, no prizes for this!)

8.2 Key Types

What is the impact then of all this wonderful history? The answer can be found in the following paragraphs. First, let us take one more look at the keys and how they are used in encryption. There are basically two types of key-based algorithms: symmetric (secret-key) and asymmetric (public-key). The difference between these is that the symmetric keys use the same algorithms for encryption and decryption. The asymmetric algorithm uses a different key for encoding, one for creating the ciphertext, and another for decoding, or translating the ciphertext into readable text. You may have heard of the term, **Public-Private Key**; this is the technique that current encryption systems use within today's Internet environment.

8.3 How a Public-Private Encryption System Works

The system will generate a key pair for an assigned user. One public key and one private key are generated. These keys are mathematically related so that the private key can decrypt any messages that are encrypted by the public key. The following is an example of how a message is encrypted:

1. The public/private key pair is created.
2. The public key is placed in a public directory. A directory is a storage facility that can house usernames and information about the users (i.e., e-mail addresses, phone numbers, and the public key).
3. The private key is stored in an area that only the designated user can access, such as their local PC or laptop. Note: This example does not address roaming users and the management of keys. (See Figure 8.1.)
4. You can now send an encrypted message. From the directory you select the intended recipient's user name (This is managed via a software program).
5. The message is encrypted using the targeted user's public key. (See Figure 8.2.)
6. The data are now transferred between systems, applications, or e-mail, as ciphertext. You now have an encrypted message that is difficult to read by a third party. (See Figure 8.3.)

Okay, but how can we read the message? This is where the private key is used.

7. The user then retrieves the message and decrypts it with his or her private key. The private key may be locked with a password that only the user knows. The message is now readable by the targeted user. (See Figure 8.4.)

8.3.1 RSA: Public and Private Keys

We now have a better idea of how the public/private system works. It is based on a technique patented by Diffie-Helman in 1974 and formatted into architecture by Rivest, Shamir, and Adelman (RSA). Take a look at http://www.rsa.com and http://www.verisign.com for more information.

FIGURE 8.1

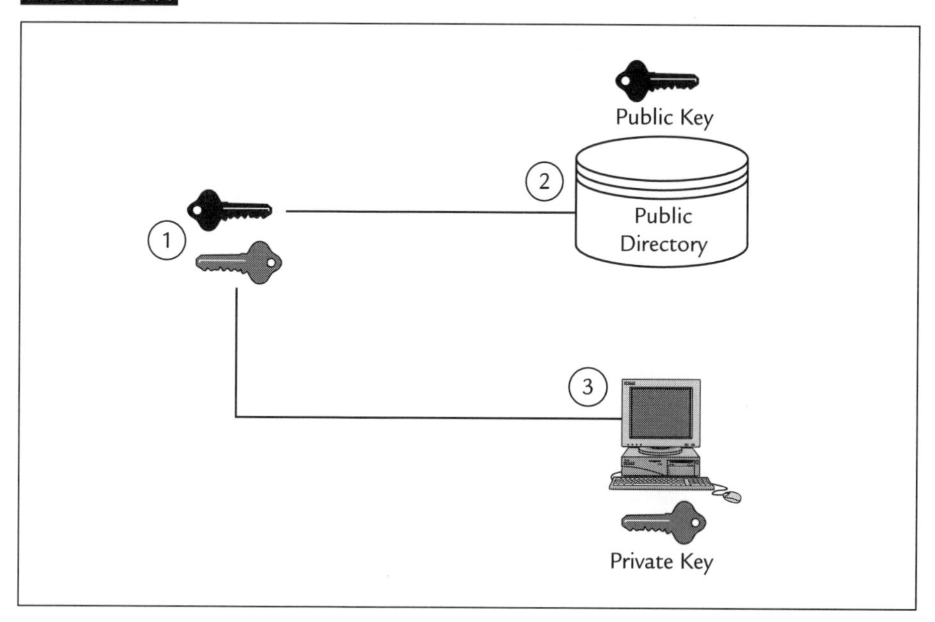

FIGURE 8.2

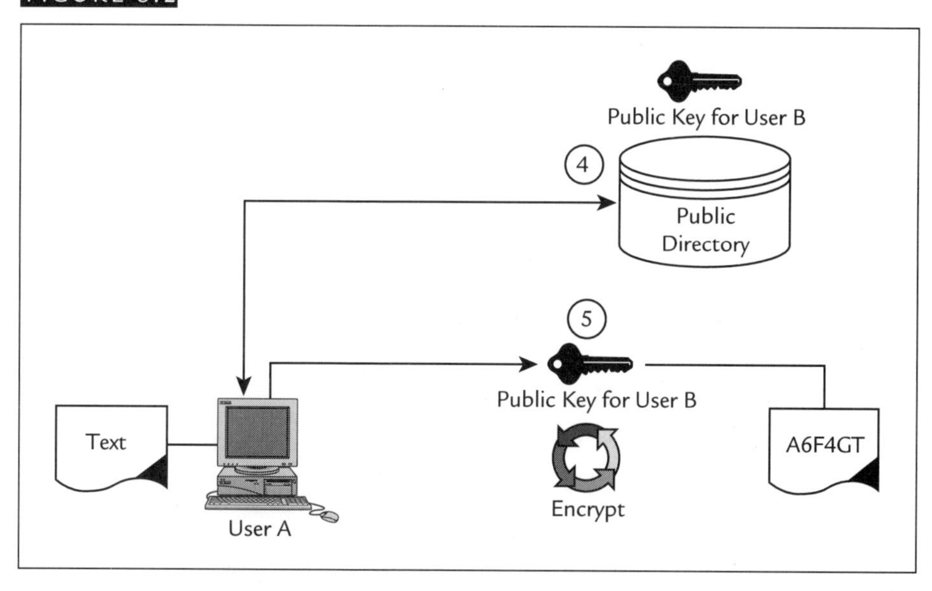

One example of the RSA implementation is PGP, or Pretty Good Privacy. Philip Zimmermann, who originally created PGP, was the first to make military-grade cryptography available to the general public. His PGP can be used to send encrypted messages via almost any e-mail system. All that is

FIGURE 8.3

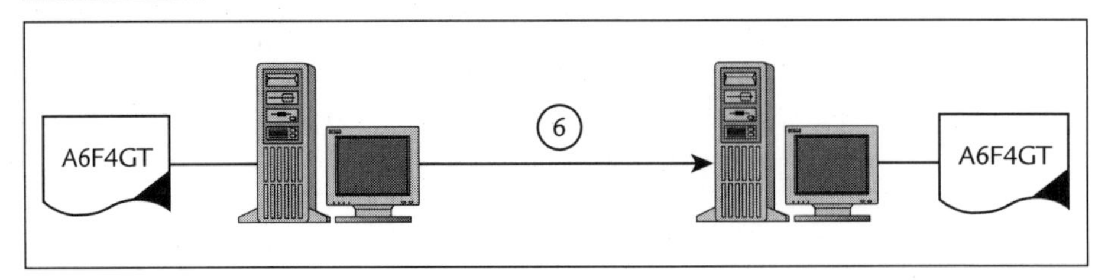

FIGURE 8.4

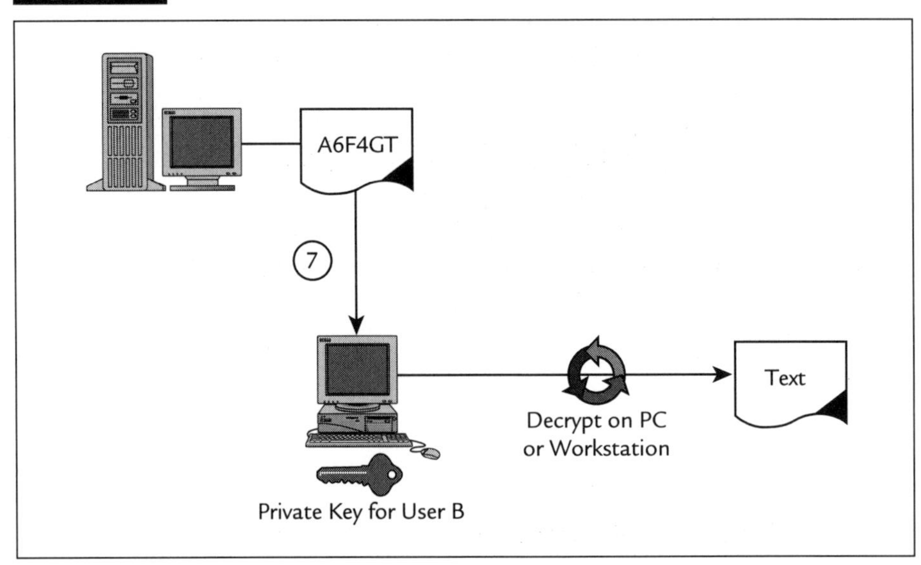

needed is software available from http://www.pgp.com and the public-key of the party to whom you want to send an encrypted message.

8.3.2 PGP

One of the many available systems today to send encrypted messages is the PGP. See also the following references for software and information:

http://www.ibm.com
http://www.lotus.com
http://www.verisign.com
http://www.entrust.com

There are several methods to encrypt messages. One standard is S/MIME. There are also secret key systems and other systems to encrypt data as it travels from one location to another.

8.3.3 Digital Signatures

A process that can be used from a byproduct of public/private keys is known as "digital signatures." Digital signatures can be used to authenticate messages and prevent forgeries and/or tampering. Two other methods, known as block ciphers and stream ciphers, are very intriguing but will not be covered in this book.

8.3.4 S/MIME

The S/MIME method is used to send encrypted mail from one person to another and it has nothing to do with Marcel Marceau! The problem we have is that important messages often have to be sent via the Internet, but it is a potentially dangerous place where someone unscrupulous can easily intercept our messages (the "bad dudes"). Once the "bad dudes" have it, they can then read it unless you encrypt the message via a method such as S/MIME.

As we have said before, S/MIME provides a method to send and receive secure MIME messages. Thus what exactly is a MIME message? The MIME method is described in the IETF standard RFC 1521 and explains how an electronic message is formatted. Multipurpose Internet mail extensions (MIME) are a set of specifications that describes a method to offer text via various character sets, and with multimedia.

8.3.5 Digital Certificates

Certificates are digital identities that are linked to a specific user or person. In our example, a certificate will be placed into each user's e-mail system, one certificate is placed into the public directory (the public key), and the other part is placed into the e-mail client system (the private key).

8.3.6 How It All Works

In the example shown in Figure 8.5, Bob sends a message to Bubba. Bob finds Bubba's public key in the directory and sends him a message. Bob's workstation software encrypts the message and it is then sent via the Internet (SMTP) to Bubba's workstation (via a Service Provider and a POP Account). When Bubba opens the message it is automatically decrypted. Now Bubba can reverse the process. If he has Bob's public key, or access to the directory where Bob's key is stored, then Bubba can send an encrypted message back to Bob. This process is accomplished by the S/MIME protocol.

The solution for our first problem is to implement a mechanism to send S/MIME messages between the home office and the person in the field.

FIGURE 8.5

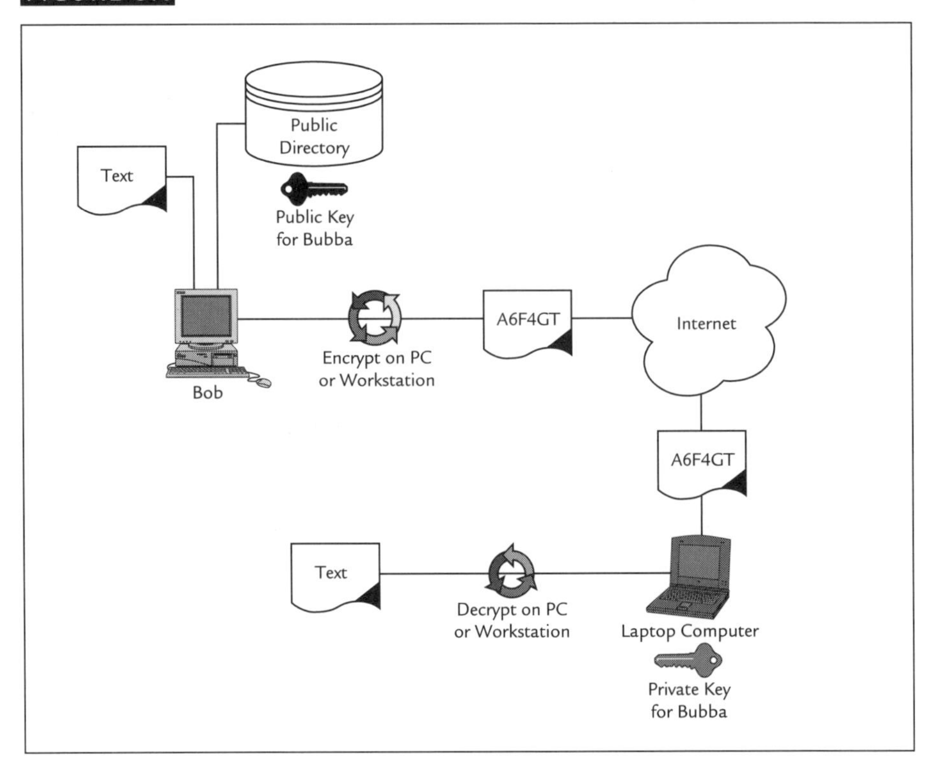

The same digital certificate that is used for reading encrypted mail can also be used to digitally sign documents. When the document is signed, you can then tell who actually sent the document. With messages sent on the Internet, it is easy to modify the From field and spoof the identity of the sender. Okay, no problem. We will require that the sender digitally sign all orders so we can prove that the messages really originated from the vendor. There are many issues involved in this problem and we will stick with our case in point, that is, digital signatures. (The assumption is made that the order did arrive and our order-processing department did not make an error.) This process of proving who actually sent the message is called Nonrepudiation. This service provides virtually unforgeable evidence that a specific action occurred, or in our case, that a transaction was fulfilled. This is all possible via a certificate. (Another assumption made is that the vendor has not lost control of the certificate—stay with us on that.) Nonrepudiation can be used by both the sender of the order and recipient, that is, the business receiving the order, to prove to a third party (such as a judge) that the sender did indeed send the transaction and, as part of this, that the

FIGURE 8.6

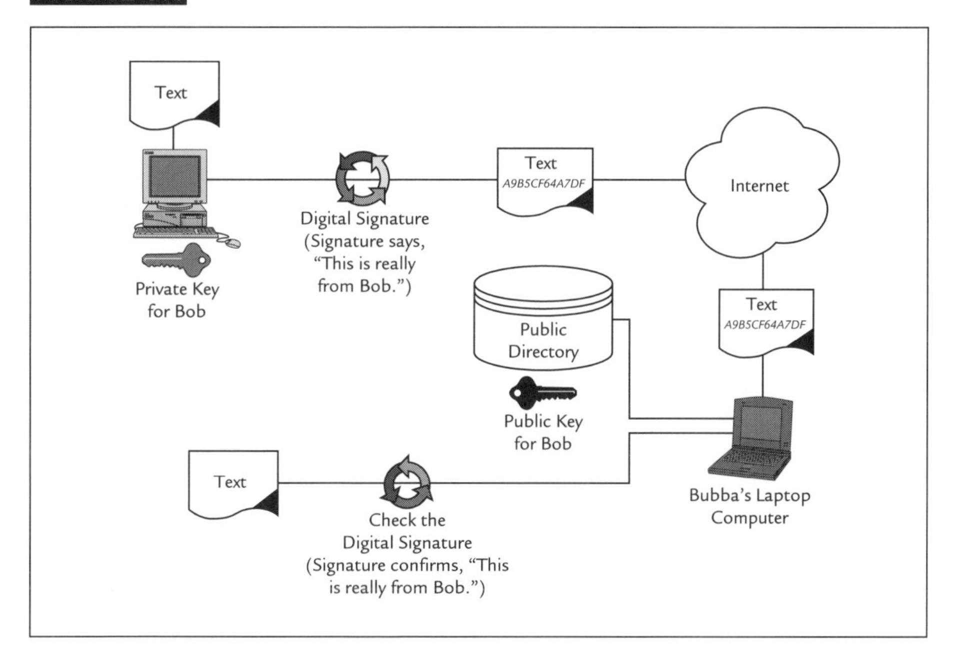

recipient received exactly the same transaction that was sent. Remember the MD2 and MD5 message digests? If any one character of a message was changed, then up to half of the message digest would change. It is very difficult to modify a message and keep the message digest the same (for most of the world's population it is impossible).

In our example as shown in Figure 8.6, Bob digitally signs a message and sends it to Bubba. The software that Bubba has will automatically attempt to verify that the signature is from Bob via the public directory. Now Bubba knows the message is really from Bob.

8.4 Now the Packet Sniffer

Data are transmitted between your browser and the Web server via some type of network and protocol. The network could be your network at the office or a dial-in system from your house. There are also networks that connect to the cable in your house. The protocol that is used in most cases by the Internet is TCP/IP. Using a packet sniffer, the "bad dudes" can hook on to your network, or at your ISP, and capture your network packets. There are many places on the Internet where someone can "steal" your packets. A network packet, for this discussion, is an envelope of data. Much like you would send a letter in an envelope to a friend via the Post Office, you would send e-mail via packets of data via a network. This is all done for you via software and protocols. The TCP/IP is the underlying protocol of the Internet.

With a packet sniffer, these packets can be captured and read. It is possible to extract all types of information, including:

- Where is the packet going?
- Where is the packet from?
- Are the data in the packet encrypted?
- Is there a username in the packet?
- Is there a password in the packet?
- The data contained in the packet, such as a message or a part of a message, for example, your credit card number!
- And much more.

8.5 Securing the Link with Secure Sockets Layer (SSL)

Most browsers today use some type of "Root Certificate." This root certificate is a mechanism that identifies the company issuing the certificate. There are companies known as (actually that act as) certificate authorities (CA). These CAs will act as an authority that certifies that the server you are accessing is really the server you want. Say, for example, you go to www.amazon.com and purchase something. You naturally want to be sure that you are actually providing your credit card information to *Amazon.com* and not to www.fakeyououtwithafalseaddress.com; the CA will certify that you are talking with the server to which you want to be connected. As there are mechanisms that can route you to the wrong server, using a CA, such as Verisign, allows you to be sure that you have connected to the correct server. This process, known as secure sockets layer (SSL), will encrypt the data at the network layer so that your transaction is safe.

Now your question is, "How can I turn on SSL ?" The answer for the most part is simple:

- At the URL enter https (note the "s"). Example: https://www.thisismywebpageanditissecure.com

Stay with us here, we are trying to make the point that SSL will keep the transaction safe. You may point out that your credit card information still may not be safe. Agreed, there have been some break-ins in which credit card data were stolen. Yes, that is correct, stolen. Now in this case, SSL could have been used and the data still would have been ripped off. How is this possible? Easy. The transaction was safe but someone broke into another part of the system and ran off with the credit card data. Security needs to cover many facets: not much good if you lock the front door but don't have a lock on the back door.

At some point you have likely received one of the types of pop-up windows from your browser as shown in Figure 8.7.

This is what is known as a Basic Authentication dialog box. Typically the username is some name that a program has assigned to you or you have assigned yourself. The Web is full of places that require a username. The username is a mechanism that identifies who you are in relation to the program or data you are trying to access. The password is the key that allows you in under that username. This is a simple and effective mechanism to access "controlled" data, but it is not very secure. In basic HTTP authentication, the password passed over the network is not encrypted, and it is not plain text either—it is "unencoded." Anyone watching packet traffic on the network will not see the password in the clear, but the password will be easily decoded by anyone who happens to catch the right network packet. With a packet sniffer you could monitor the traffic on a network and extract the password, then use a simple decoder to extract the password. If you want to send the username and password then use SSL. This method

FIGURE 8.7

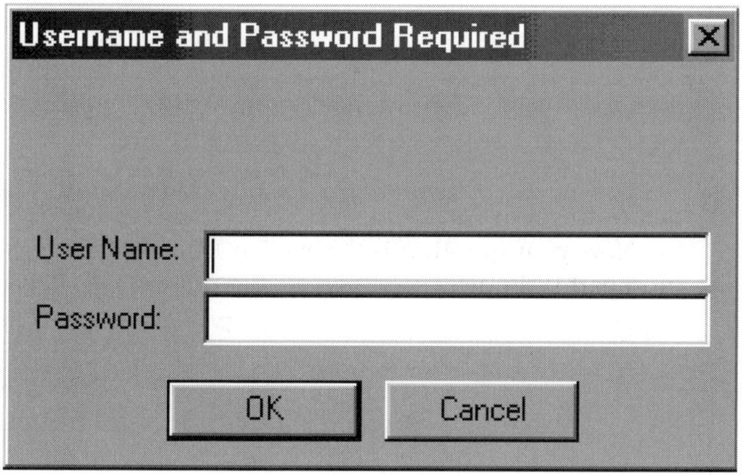

will encrypt the data at the network level so that someone with a sniffer cannot easily decode (decrypt) the data or your passwords.

So far in the process we have talked about the SSL handshake and the encryption keys and certificates. One item left to talk about is certificates and how to use and manage them.

8.6 Using and Managing Certificates

Certificates are, in effect, signed documents. In an SSL transaction, each device will have one of these "signed documents." We use different forms of signed documents in our everyday lives. In most countries, including the US, there are agencies (e.g., State Departments of Motor Vehicles) that certify people to legally drive a car.

The steps for obtaining a driver's license are very similar between all agencies:

- The user requests a license (a certificate).
- The user makes a payment (always money involved!).
- The user may have their picture taken and will sign the document.
- The agency will "certify" that the license is good and will provide some type of unique number that only that particular license will have.
- The license will expire at some point.
- At some point you may need to recertify your license.
- The license gives the user the right to drive a car and is used for identification purposes.

In the preceding example, the Department of Motor Vehicles is the Certificate Authority, or CA. The CA in this case will certify that the holder of the license can drive a car and that they are really who they say they are. As far as identification goes we trust the holder of the license for the following items:

- The picture matches the face of the holder.
- The signature on the license matches the signature of the holder.

Why do we trust the license? We trust the agency that "certified" the license and so we trust this third party because the third party has implemented some type of due diligence in determining the true identify of the user. If we trust the third party, then we trust the identity of the holder of the card. Get it? If not, you may want to review this section again; this is critical in order to understand the rest of the certificate process.

How about the scenario depicted in Figure 8.8?

With Internet certificates, the process is much the same. Certificates are signed by certificate authorities (CAs). The CA will issue certificates based on a request from the user or server. A certificate authority is a commonly trusted third party (like the government agency shown here), that is relied upon to verify the matching of public keys to the user's identity. This process can also verify items like:

- E-mail name;
- A digital signature; and
- Access privileges.

To make this process work, all parties must trust the CA. We use digital certificates instead of a card or license. With a CA and these certificates, we can verify a user's or server's identity over the Internet. Therefore, a certificate authority, or CA, refers to either the software or the service that issues digital certificates. A certificate authority acts as the third party in a digital transaction: When a user is trying to prove his or her identity to a vendor so he or

FIGURE 8.8

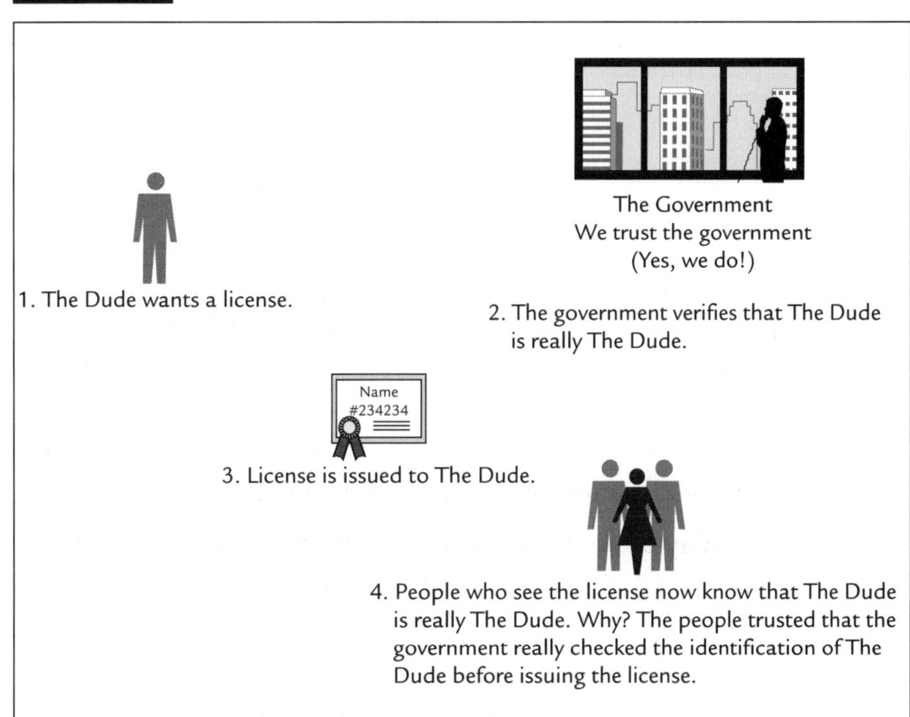
The Government
We trust the government
(Yes, we do!)
1. The Dude wants a license.
2. The government verifies that The Dude is really The Dude.
Name
#234234
3. License is issued to The Dude.
4. People who see the license now know that The Dude is really The Dude. Why? The people trusted that the government really checked the identification of The Dude before issuing the license.

she may access his or her account, the vendor can verify the user's identity via the certificate authority. Digital certificates work via a technology known as public key encryption. The owner of a certificate holds two keys, namely, a public key and a private key:

The Public Key: This key allows anyone to encrypt data to send to a specific user.

The Private Key: This key is accessible only to the user or owner. The owner of the key, using the private key, can send signed messages and decrypt information.

The CA will issue a certificate to a user or server. The certificate will have information much like that shown in Figure 8.9, and should include the following items:

- Certificate Owner. The certificate owner is the person who has access to use the certificate. This could be protected by a password or be placed onto a smart card or other device.
- Name. This is the name assigned to the owner of the certificate.
- Key Serial Number. Each certificate should have some type of number that identifies it and is unique.
- Expiration Date. All certificates should have an expiration date.
- Private Key. The private key is not shared outside of the certificate.

FIGURE 8.9

A Digital Certificate

Certificate Owner:

Name:	Bubba Smith
Key Serial Number:	#8629728212
Expires:	5/10/2002
Private Key: (Hidden)	MIIEfTCCA+agAwIBAgIQed4BZxYqgUuPCMTE5
Public Key: (Hidden)	MDAwMDAwWhcNMDAwMjE4MjM1OTU5WjC5

Certificate Issued By:

Name:	Billy Jo Bob CA Inc.
State:	Texas
Digital Fingerprint:	A3:F3:68:38:AC:95

- Public Key. The public key is sent to other users or a shared directory service.
- Certificate Issued By. This section has information about the CA.
- Name. This is the name of the CA.
- Digital Fingerprint. This is a number that is unique to the certificate. This can be used to verify whether a signature is valid.

As we have shown, certificates have a limited life. They are requested and created, and then they are either revoked or expire. Revocation is important if private keys are compromised or there has been a change in status or policy. Revocation of a certificate is accomplished through use of a certificate revocation list (CRL). Someone who is going to use a certificate might want to check against a CRL to ensure the validity of the certificate. A certificate authority will sign all certificates (see Figure 8.10) that it issues with its private key. The corresponding certificate authority public key is itself contained within a certificate, called a CA certificate. A browser must contain this CA certificate in its "Trusted Root Database" in order to "trust" certificates signed by the CA's private key. Therefore, the browser will have a trusted root as shown in Figure 8.11 and the server will have a certificate that is signed by the CA.

Presented in Figure 8.12 are some examples of the Root certificates that ship with a Netscape browser. There are more than 50 in the Netscape browser.

Your company may choose to create their own closed, "private" certificate infrastructure for internal use. This can be accomplished with software

FIGURE 8.10

FIGURE 8.11

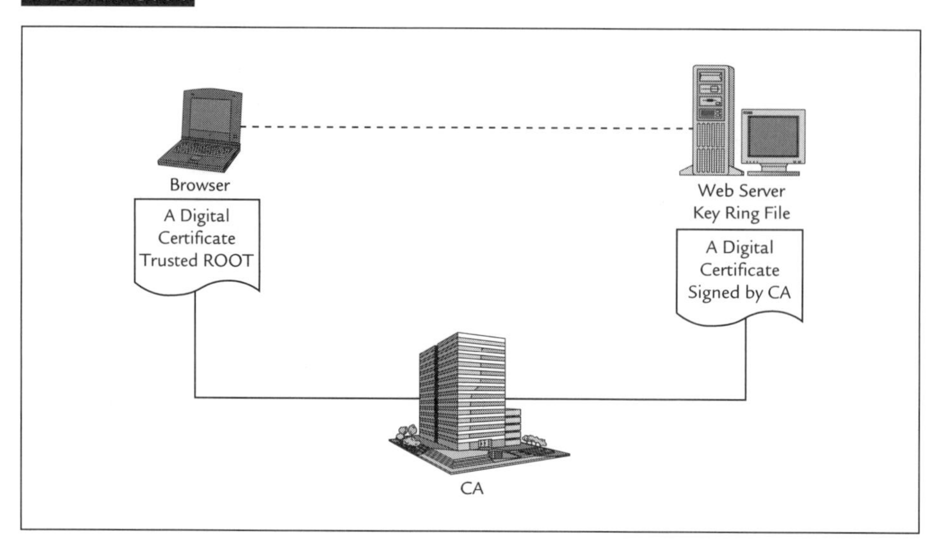

FIGURE 8.12

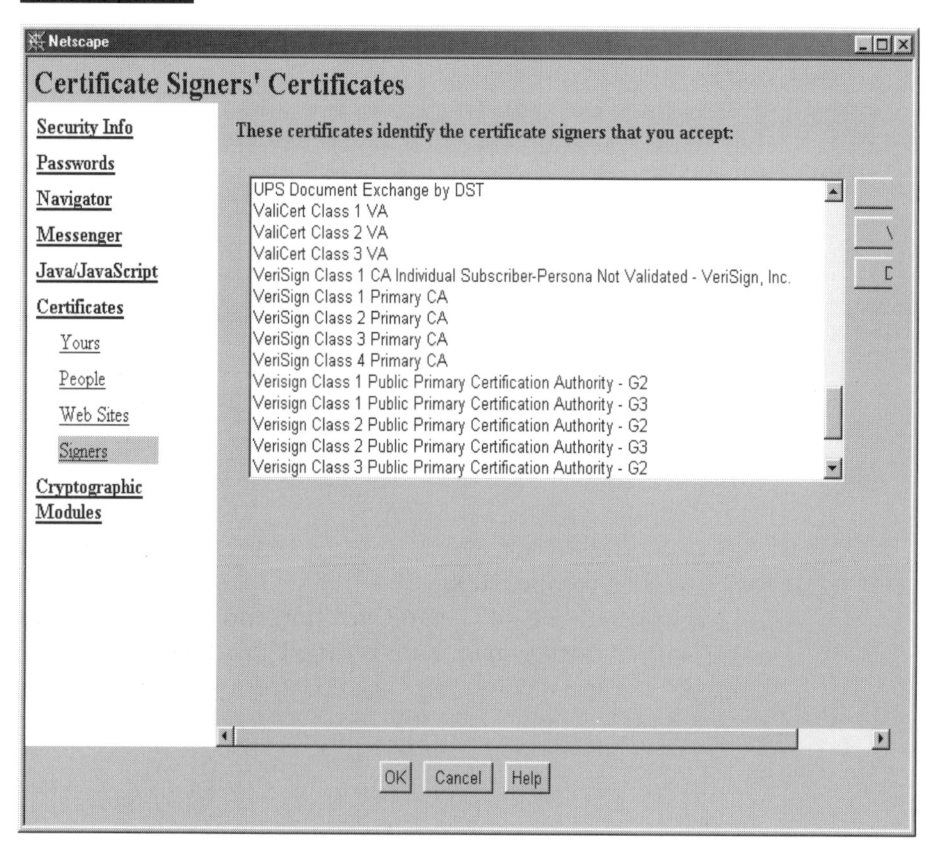

that is provided with many Web servers or you can purchase your own software, or have a service provider as your CA. You can also use Public CAs.

Thus how can we send encrypted mail from me to you? Here is one example. Request a signed message from the person to whom you want to send a message. Once you get this message add a new user (this person) to the personal address book in your mailer program. Many programs will allow you to add new users. Here are the steps (in this example a vendor is a single user with a single certificate and not an organization):

- The user will tell Person A to send a digitally signed message.
- The user will receive the message and then add the person's name to the address using an action dialog box, button, and/or script.
- This script will add Person A's name, e-mail address, and public key to the user's personal mail directory.
- The user can now end an encrypted message to that particular user.
- Repeat the process for each additional person.

The user sends a digitally signed message to Person A and Person A follows the same steps.

8.7 Reference Books about Encryption

Bamford, James. *The Puzzle Palace: A Report on America's Most Secret Agency.* New York: Viking. 1983.

Diffie, Whitfield and Susan Eva Landau. *Privacy on the Line: The Politics of Wiretapping and Encryption.* Cambridge: MIT Press. 1998.

Herkommer, Mark. *Number Theory: A Programmer's Guide.* New York: McGraw-Hill. 1999.

Kahn, David. *The Codebreakers: The Comprehensive History of Secret Communication from Ancient Times to the Internet.* New York: Scribner. 1996.

Kaufman, Charlie, Radia Perlman, and Mike Speciner. *Network Security: Private Communication in a Public World.* Upper Saddle River: Prentice Hall. 1995.

Marks, Leo. *Between Silk and Cyanide: A Codemaker's War 1941-1945.* New York: Touchstone. 2000.

Menezes, Alfred J., Paul C. van Oorschot, and Scott A. Vanstone. *Handbook of Applied Cryptography.* Kansas City: CRC. 1996.

Schneier, Bruce and David Banisar. *The Electronic Privacy Papers: Documents on the Battle for Privacy in the Age of Surveillance.* New York: Wiley. 1997.

Schroeder, Manfred. *Number Theory in Science and Communication: With Applications in Cryptography, Physics, Digital Information, Computing, and Self-Similarity.* Heidelberg: Springer-Verlag. 1997.

Stallings, William. *Cryptography and Network Security: Principles and Practice.* Upper Saddle River: Prentice Hall. 1998.

Stinson, Douglas. *Cryptography: Theory and Practice.* Kansas City: CRC. 1995.

Tung, Brian. *Kerberos: A Network Authentication System.* Reading: Addison Wesley. 1999.

Wayner, Peter. *Disappearing Cryptography: Being and Nothingness on the Net.* San Francisco: Morgan Kaufmann. 1996.

APPENDIX 1

Security Hardware and Software Reference Section

This reference section includes a listing of hardware and software tools that may be used in securing your work or home PC and laptop. The major categories included are as follows:

A1.1 Encryption

A1.2 Filters

A1.3 General Protection

A1.4 Personal Firewall

A1.5 Physical Security

A1.6 User Authentication

A1.7 Virus Protection

A1.1 Encryption

Company name: Armadillo Limited
Address: P.O. Box 667694; Charlotte, NC 28266
Phone number: (704) 987-5003
E-mail address: (704) 896-7818
URLs: http://www.armadillousa.com/gatekeeper.htm

Category: Encryption
Product name: GateKeeper™
Product Description: Smart-card based 1024-bit RSA, RC4, 3DES file and email encryption system. GateKeeper is a personalized encryption system designed for data security of individual users in a corporate and/or personal environment. By using 1024-bit RSA, RC4, Triple-DES (3DES) encryption methods and the proven security of the smart card, the GateKeeper™ protects the integrity and confidentiality of the user's files (documents, texts, spreadsheets, graphics, etc.), program files (stored in data disk, hard drive, etc.), and/or messages transmitted through the Internet. GateKeeper utilizes encryption methods that have been tried, tested, and developed in the US; 1024-bit RSA, RC4, and 3DES are widely used by telecommunication corporations, financial institutions, and government agencies in the US. GateKeeper is a hardware/software-combined system that supports Windows™ 95, 98, and 2000 operating systems. GateKeeper is ideal for individuals or small- to medium-sized businesses seeking to protect the vital contents on a computer and private information transferred through the Internet. GateKeeper is convenient, easy-to-use, virtually tamperproof and is available for immediate purchase directly from the publisher's Web site at www.armadillo.com.hk/gatekeeper.htm. The product comes complete with a smart card, smart card reader, power adapter, and software on CD-ROM.

Company name: CyPost Corporation
Address: 900–1281 West Georgia; Vancouver, BC V6E 3J7
Phone number: (604) 904-4422
E-mail address: info@cypost.com
URL: http://www.cypost.com
Category: Encryption
Product name: Navaho Lock with Voice
Product description: Encrypted voice e-mail. Navaho Lock with Voice allows users to record, compress and encrypt private voice email for transmission across any digital network without sacrificing the tone, feeling, or integrity of the message. Navaho Lock with Voice also reduces the time spent typing traditional text-based email messages. A summary of new major features follows.

- Electronic Shredder. Navaho Shredder offers a high level of disk sanitization allowing users to securely delete files and documents from any computer. Navaho Shredder has been designed to meet and exceed the US Department of Defense standard (DOD 5220.22-M) for data removal. The program is currently capable of overwriting data stored on disk a total of nine times, exceeding the DOD standard for data removal.

- Built-in Compression. Navaho Lock with Voice automatically compresses all documents and files by as much as 70%, thereby maximizing disk space and dramatically reducing transmission times.
- Choice of Encryption Strength. Navaho Lock with Voice offers the widest selection of encryption standards including 40-, 56-, 112-, 128-, and 168-bit key-lengths and algorithms to meet the individual security needs of your business. Users are able to customize security settings and select unique pass phrases by contact or group.
- New Drag-and-Drop User Interface. Further improving ease of use and increasing user productivity, the new drag-and-drop user interface allows users to encrypt, compress, or shred files by simply dragging and dropping them into the Drop area.

Company name: DSEnet
Address: 5201 South Westshore Blvd.; Tampa, FL 33611
Phone number: (813) 902-9597
E-mail address: questions@dsenet.com
URL: www.dsenet.com
Category: Encryption
Product name: DSEnet Encryption
Product description: DSEnet Encryption provides users with the ability to securely encrypt and store their information. There is no better way to keep intruding hackers, nosy coworkers, pesky younger siblings, and cunning competitors from your critical information. Encrypt documents, spreadsheets, presentations, e-mail attachments, graphs, charts, images, music, and most files residing on your computer with DSEnet Encryption. DSEnet Encryption is an easy-to-install, quick-to-learn and simple-to-use software utility that secures data stored on a computer's hard drive.

Keys:

- encryption prevents unwanted access
- easy to learn and operate, little training required
- easy to use explorer style interface
- encrypts individual files, groups of files and folders
- DSEnet Encryption occupies only 4 MB of disk space.
- user key and password combination protects data
- strong 256-bit encryption algorithm

Operating requirements: Microsoft Windows 95, 98, Me, NT 4.0, 2000 Professional / Advanced Server, 32MB-RAM.

A1.2 Filters

Company name: Armadillo Limited
Address: P.O. Box 667694; Charlotte, NC 28266
Phone number: (704) 987-5003
E-mail address: (704) 896-7818
URL: http:/ /www.armadillousa.comlmaincatalog.html
Category: Filters
Product name: R.A.T. Control™
Product description: Smart-card based Internet filtering/blocking system—the only parental control software that is 100% effective against accessing nonapproved Internet sites. **R.A.T.™ Control is the first 100% effective Internet blocking/filtering product to combine hardware and software security.**

Using R.A.T.™ Control, parents select appropriate Web sites according to their own values, taste and their children's maturity level. When supervision is not available, the system shelters children in a library of parent-approved sites and prevents their intentional or accidental access to objectionable sites.

R.A.T.™ Control combines the use of a high-security smart card key with personalized password security to create a seamless lockout system to provide the most effective protection against access to unapproved sites. Parents actively choose which Web sites are good for their children instead of relying on filtering software to block out known objectionable sites and sites that use objectionable keywords.

This product is convenient, easy-to-use, and virtually tamperproof. User friendly, R.A.T.™ Control employs clear graphics and icons that users of all ages can navigate with ease. Parents can also give each site a name and description for the convenience of their children.

R.A.T.™ Control is available for immediate purchase direct from the publisher's Web site, http://www.armadillo.com.hk/maincatalog.html. The product comes complete with a smart card, reader, and software (CD-ROM).

Company name: Charles River Media
Address: 20 Downer Avenue, Suite 3; Hingham, MA 02043
Phone number: (800) 382-3505
E-mail address: info@charlesriver.com
URL: www.charlesriver.com
Category: Filters
Product name: Internet Watchdog

Product description: Allows the user to record and monitor computer activity.

Company name: surfControl a Division of JSB
Address: 100 Enterprise Way, Mod A-1; Scotts Valley, CA 95066
Phone number: (831) 431-1400
E-mail address: surfsales@CONTROL.com
URL: www.surfcontrol.com
Category: Filters
Product name: surfCONTROL Family of Products
Product description: Controls the use of your Internet.

Company name: Blue Ocean Software, Inc.
Address: 15310 Amberly Drive, Suite 370; Tampa, Florida 33647
Phone number: (813) 977-4553
E-mail address: info@bluocean.com
URL: www.blueocean.com
Category: Filters
Product name: Track-It
Product description: Record keeping system.

Company name: SonicWall, Inc.
Address: 1160 Bordeaux Drive; Sunnyvale, CA 94089-1209
Phone number: (408) 745-9600
E-mail address: sales@sonicwall.com
URL: www.sonicwall.com
Category: Filters
Product name: SonicWALL DMZ
Product description: Provides protection from hackers and content filters.

A1.3 General Protection

Company name: CyPost Corporation
Address: 900–1281 West Georgia; Vancouver, BC V6E 3J7
Phone number: (604) 904-4422
E-mail address: info@cypost.com
URL: http://www.cypost.com
Category: General protection
Product name: Navaho ZipSafe

Product description: Navaho ZipSafe is the easiest and fastest way to ensure that no one reads confidential data on hard disks, network drives, or floppies. Navaho ZipSafe compresses (by up to 70%) and protects data in one step, enabling you to organize documents files and folders instantly for secure storage or transport.

- Built-in compression. Reduces file size on hard drives and floppy disks by as much as 70%.
- Drag-and-drop feature. Application works behind the scenes to allow users to encrypt and compress files by simply dragging and dropping them into the Drop area.
- Shredder. This feature makes files unrecoverable to programs that rebuild files after deletion.
- Choice of encryption. Navaho ZipSafe supports a variety of algorithms including 40-, 56-, 112-, 128-, and 168-bit.
- Works with all file formats. Navaho ZipSafe quickly and easily encrypts and compresses digital images, spreadsheets, Word documents, files, folders, and even entire directories.

Company name: Delta Design UK.com
Address: 10 Wratting Road; Haverhill, Suffolk, CB9 0DD, United Kingdom
Phone number: n/a
E-mail address: marketing mail@deltadesignuk.com / for publication: mail@deltadesignuk.com
URL: http://www.deltadesignuk.com/
Category: General protection
Product name: Net-Commando 2000
Product description: Hacker protection/prevention/detection, Trojan horse virus protection/prevention/detection/removal, system analysis and Internet tracing. This package uses various methods of detection, prevention and monitoring to deny remote access to your computer. It does this by monitoring areas of your computer where Internet viruses aim their auto-start procedures. It warns of hackers attempting to access your computer, and provides an address for you to backtrack them—as well as tools to assist you in reporting the hacker to the ISP. The program also includes many system analysis tools, including NetStat (protocol statistics), which lists all open ports and allows one to terminate an established TCP port.

Company name: Finjan Software
Address: 2860 Zanker Road, Suite 201; San Jose, CA 95134

Phone number: (408) 324-0228
E-mail address: info@finjan.com
URL: www.finjan.com
Category: General protection
Product name: SurfinShield Corporate
Product description: SurfinShield Corporate is a centrally managed PC security solution that proactively monitors the actual behavior of downloaded active content including executables, scripts, ActiveX, and Java. By monitoring code behavior in its protected "SafeZone," SurfinShield enforces its security policy and automatically blocks malicious activity before damage can be inflicted. Unlike traditional anti-virus technology, SurfinShield represents a new way to combat Trojans, Internet worms, and hostile Web pages based on code behavior, not by static signature recognition. Because SurfinShield does not rely on database updates, it defends against new variants, unknown, and "yet-to-be-created" attacks on the "first strike."

Features and Benefits:

- Behavior Monitoring. Checks active content in realtime in SurfinShield's sandbox including Executables, ActiveX controls, Java applets, Scrap files (.shs), and all Windows scripting host files (e.g., .VBS, .JS, .WSH, etc.). Companies can have protection from all "ILOVEYOU" type worm attacks without having to wait for anti-virus updates.
- Palm-to-PC Sync Protection. Palm Pilots can be used to deliver malicious programs or Trojans to PCs using the synchronization process. SurfinShield monitors all Palm OS-based PDA sync processes for executable programs and protects PCs from sync attacks.
- Multimedia Surveillance Protection. SurfinShield now protects against audio/video recording from Trojans by preventing the PC microphone or camera from automatically being turned on and by monitoring network connections.
- White Listing. Applications from trusted partners enables secure e-business. Companies can allow trusted applications to enter the network with full permissions while unknown code is still subject to monitoring.
- Application Auto-Launch Blocking. Prevents Microsoft Office Suite applications from being automatically launched by Web browsers, Microsoft Outlook and Qualcomm's Eudora e-mail client.
- SurfinConsole™. Centralized management console enables security managers to easily implement and enforce group and individual security policies for all computer users throughout an organization.

- Smart Kill. SurfinShield can identify and surgically kill specific malicious codes. Applications and Web browsers are left undisturbed and user productivity is not hindered.
- Mobile PC Protection. SurfinShield Corporate's monitoring "engine" resides on the PC and will continue to operate when taken on the road. This results in ongoing protection for PC users who are connecting to the Internet from outside the corporate network.

SurfinShield Corporate consists of a console, a server, and a client module. The central console is designed for ease of use, allowing administrators to set both granular and corporate-wide security policies. The central server holds security policies and logs the security events of each desktop. Should one client face an attack, it will update all other SurfinShield Corporate clients, automatically blocking the hostile element upon contact. The client module of SurfinShield Corporate houses the behavior monitoring "engine." The client is not dependent on the server for protection and will continue to defend against attacks when removed from the corporate network.

A "first strike" is the first time a new malicious code attack is launched. First-strike security uses content inspection and behavior-monitoring technology to detect and prevent malicious attacks before damage is caused. Because Finjan products do not rely on database updates, they defend against new variants, unknown, and even "yet-to-be-created" attacks on the "first strike."

SurfinShield Client System Requirements:

- Pentium 133 processor and above
- Windows 9x/ME/NT 4.0/2000
- 16-MB RAM (32-MB RAM recommended)
- 15-MB of free disk space

SurfinShield Server System Requirements:

- Pentium 266 processor and above
- Windows NT 4.0/2000/Solaris 2.6
- 64-MB RAM (128 MB recommended)
- 24 MB of free disk space

SurfinConsole System Requirements:

- Pentium 200 processor and above
- Windows 9x /NT 4.0/2000
- 64-MB RAM (128 MB recommended)
- 15 MB of free disk space

Company name: Intego, Inc.
Address: 6301 Collins Avenue Suite #1806; Miami, Florida 33141

Phone number: (305) 868-7920
Contact name: Olivier Depoorter
E-mail address: odepoorter@intego.com
URL: www.intego.com
Category: General protection
Product name: ContentBarrier
Product description: Blocks all offensive material from the Internet. Intego, a leading provider of Macintosh Internet security utilities announced ContentBarrier thorough and efficient Internet filtering software for Macintosh. ContentBarrier 1.0 helps parents protect their children by monitoring Internet usage to avoid contact with dangerous Web sites, chat rooms, email, newsgroups, and downloads.

ContentBarrier allows parents to select or customize specific categories of potential danger, log Internet usage, control access days and times, and receive email alerts when certain activity occurs. ContentBarrier works with multiple users, so if there are several children in a household, different criteria can be set according to their age. ContentBarrier has a high-content filter engine for sophisticated filtering. Its pre- defined categories let you choose what you don't want your children to see. Inappropriate Web sites are blocked, thus shielding your children from things they are too young to see. ContentBarrier also supports the new version of Intego's NetUpdate, the automatic software update engine. Users can program updates for specific days and times, and NetUpdate will check the Intego server to find out if updates are available for all of Intego's Barrier products installed on your computer.

Intego's programs have received many awards in the US, Europe, and Asia. These include awards from Macworld, MacHome, MacNN, and MacAddict. In France, UniversMacWorld recently gave NetBarrier their 2000 trophy for the best Internet program.

Laurent Marteau, CEO, Intego, reported that "When children surf the Internet, they can see whatever they want, unless a parent is there to watch over their shoulders." He went on to say that "ContentBarrier sets up a protective wall around your computer making the Internet a safer place for children."

ContentBarrier features:

- Blocks and filters all offensive material from the Internet
- Multiple users—if you have several children, you can adjust the settings for their age and maturity
- Multiple levels of protection
- Predetermined categories for safe and easy content filtering (sexually explicit sites, violence, hate/racism, online chat, etc.)

- Limits Internet access by day and time
- Allows you to inspect your child's computer and make a full inventory of all pictures, movies, music files or Web pages
- Anti-predator function to block predatory language in chat sessions
- Trusted site selection—you can set the program to block all sites except those you select
- Keeps a detailed log of each user's Internet sessions. Records traffic data for an overview of Internet use
- Automatic updates with Intego's NetUpdate function
- Password protection to prevent unauthorized users from changing program settings
- Automatic e-mail notification of certain events

ContentBarrier is also used by companies to restrict inappropriate employee Web site usage. Many employees do their shopping on the Internet, play network games, send and receive personal e-mail or download MP3 files while at work, thereby reducing productivity and using valuable network bandwidth. ContentBarrier can solve this problem by blocking access to many different types of sites, and contains specific categories of Web sites designed for business use.

If your employees spend their working time surfing sexually explicit sites, this not only reduces productivity, but it may even expose you to liability for sexual harassment. Sending private e- mail over your mail server can also expose you to liability , and even prosecution, as your business is responsible for what circulates on its network.

ContentBarrier business features:

- Helps increase productivity and optimizes bandwidth; and
- protects your company from liability.

System requirements are a Mac OS compatible computer with a Power PC processor, OpenTransport, Mac OS 8.1 or higher, and 32-MB RAM. It is also compatible with Mac OS 9.1. A Mac OS X version will be available Q1 2001. Also available in French and Japanese versions.

ContentBarrier is available immediately from retailers including buy.com, CompUSA, MacZone, Outpost.com, Computertown, Club Mac, MacWarehouse, MacMall, ComputerWare, Computer Store Northwest, J&R, Microcenter, CDW, Developer Depot, and from 200 Apple Specialists (see list on the Intego Web site), and online at httQ://www.intego.com.

Company name: Intego, Inc.
Address: 6301 Collins Avenue Suite #1806; Miami , Florida 33141
Phone number: (305) 868-7920

Contact Name: Olivier Depoorter
E-mail address: odepoorter@intego.com
URL: www.intego.com
Category: General protection
Product name: Internet Security Barrier
Product description: The Internet Security Suite for the Mac. Intego, a leading provider of Macintosh Internet security utilities announced Internet Security Barrier, a total Internet security suite for the Macintosh. Internet Security Barrier includes NetBarrier and its three powerful modules: Firewall, Antivandal, and Internet Filter; VirusBarrier, the acclaimed antivirus program for Macintosh; and ContentBarrier, the thorough and efficient Internet filtering program for a full security suite to protect Macs from all Internet dangers. This suite is the perfect solution to Internet security problems.

Intego's programs have received many awards in the US, Europe, and Asia, for example, awards from *Macworld, MacHome, MacNN,* and *MacAddict.* In France, *UniversMacWorld* recently gave NetBarrier their 2000 trophy for the best Internet program.

Internet Security Barrier 1.0 also supports the new version of Intego's NetUpdate, the automatic software update engine. Users can program updates for specific days and times, and NetUpdate will check the Intego server to find out if updates are available for all of Intego's Barrier products installed on your computer.

As noted by Laurent Marteau, CEO, Intego, "Security issues are the biggest computer problem in recent years." And, continuing, he noted, "Hackers, viruses, and inappropriate content are a plague. Our goal was to develop a full suite of security software for the Macintosh, so Mac users can be protected from every security risk. We're proud to be able to offer such a comprehensive package."

Internet Security Barrier Features include:

- NetBarrier's fully customizable Firewall
    - Anti-vandal to protect your computer from hacker attacks
    - Internet Filter
    - Spam Filtering
    - Ad banner blocking
- VirusBarrier's protection against all known viruses
    - Protection against Word and Excel macroviruses
    - Scans compressed files—checks all types of archives recognized by Stuffit Expander (Zip, CompactPro, DiskDoubler, tar, BZip, arc, etc.)
    - Turbo Mode makes scanning from 5 to 40 times faster
    - Contextual Menu module for quick virus scanning

- ContentBarrier's predetermined categories for safe and easy content filtering (sexually explicit sites, violence, hate/racism, online chat, etc.)
  - Blocks and filters all offensive material from the Internet
  - Multiple users—if you have several children, you can adjust the settings for their age and maturity
  - Multiple levels of protection

System requirements are a Mac OS compatible computer with a Power PC processor, OpenTransport, Mac OS 8.1 or higher, and 32-MB RAM. It is also compatible with Mac OS 9.1. A Mac OS X version will be available Q1 2001. Also available in French and Japanese versions.

Internet Security Barrier is available immediately from retailers including buy.com, CompUSA, MacZone, Outpost.com, Computertown, Club Mac, MacWarehouse, MacMall, ComputerWare, Computer Store Northwest, J&R, Microcenter, CDW, Developer Depot, and from 200 Apple Specialists (see list on the Intego Web site) and online at htm://www.intego.com.

Intego, the i-security software company, publishes security software for the Macintosh, and its products are currently sold in 65 countries. With three essential products, Intego focuses on all aspects of the computer security market—antivirus protection, intrusion prevention, and content control.

In less than two years, NetBarrier has become the world leader in personal firewalls for the Macintosh. VirusBarrier, Intego's acclaimed antivirus solution, has been a resounding success since its launch in July 2000. And ContentBarrier, Intego's new parental control program, was to be available to reinforce its product line in January 2001.

Intego was founded in May 1999 by a group of highly motivated engineers and high-profile marketing, finance, and sales managers to leverage their extensive knowledge of network security and the Mac environment to corporate, individual, and educational users worldwide. Intego has grown 500% in the year 2000, and 2001 will help maintain this exceptional growth through the release of other new and innovative computer security products. The privately held company has headquarters in Miami, Florida, and Paris, France.

Company name: MFX Research
Address: 19–23 Bridge Street; Pymble New South Wales 2073 Australia
Phone number: +61 2 9440 0200
E-mail address: info@mfxr.com
URL: www.mfxr.com
Category: General protection
Product name: MFX Verify

Product description: MFX Verify is a toolset designed to monitor and protect the condition of your applications and operating systems files from ANY form of corruption, decay, or degradation.

MFX Verify continuously checks critical system and application files. As soon as any corruption is detected, regardless of the cause, the files are immediately restored to their original state.

Examples of some of the day-to-day problems solved by MFX Verify:

- Your PC "hangs."
- Your system has not closed properly.
- Your .exe or .dll files have become corrupted.
- You inadvertently delete a monitored file.
- A virus attaches to an .exe file.

In all of the forementioned examples, MFX Verify immediately detects what has happened, and undoes any damage done to the file. MFX Verify is unique—and because it is complementary to other utility software, it "plugs the holes" in the control of systems and applications. Unlike other "so-called" restoration systems, MFX Verify operates by making a byte-by-byte comparison, not simply a checksum, file size, or date stamp comparison. It offers users the ability to define which files they wish to protect. The major cause of errors in PCs is the corruption of application and system executable and library files. By keeping these files in their original condition, "up time" is dramatically improved. Rather than permitting a problem to occur, and then trying to fix it, MFX Verify prevents the problem from happening in the first place. MFX Verify also permits the frequency of scan to be run continuously or set at intervals. MFX Verify operates in a fully automated or user-selected format, on compiled file types, such as .exe, .com, .dll, and .sys. MFX Verify is very fast—the throughput is up to 20Mb/s. With full log and reporting facilities, MFX Verify maintains the integrity of the files from the time of installation. MFX Verify SDK provides the same protection on Windows NT and 2000 systems.

Company name: MFX Research
Address: 19–23 Bridge Street; Pymble New South Wales 2073 Australia
Phone number: +61 294400200
E-mail address: info@mfxr.com
URL: www.mfxr.com
Category: General protection
Product name: MFX ValidSite
Product description: This product allows the user to control the information that is published on their Web site. ValidSite from MFX Research

ensures that ONLY the information YOU want to display is publicized on your Web site. ValidSite's unique "file trap procedure" provides for:

- Total and automatic revalidation of a Web site's contents.
- Regular updates to the sites contents, ensuring that only the correct information is being seen by visitors to the site.
- Permits approved updates of information on the site; and
- Eliminates any site rebuild costs should an attack take place.

Should a hacker enter the site, ValidSite will automatically remove all traces of the attack. ValidSite dramatically reduces Web site maintenance and updates costs. ValidSite is simple to use, does not require any extra hardware, requires little or no systems knowledge, and can be installed in seconds. ValidSite ensures that only the "authorized version" of your site can be viewed by your customers, staff, investors, or any visitor to the site. As more companies are relying upon their Web sites to act as both a shopfront for their products and services, and as a window to their company, the need to protect the contents of their Web site is critical. The protection of this investment is paramount to companies and organizations. Full details of ValidSite can be obtained from the MFXR Web site.

Company name: MFX Research
Address: 19–23 Bridge Street; Pymble New South Wales 2073 Australia
Phone number: +61 294400200
E-mail address: info@mfxr.com
URL: www.mfxr.com
Category: General protection
Product name: MFX WebSiteLock
Product description: Protect your Web site from attack and alteration. WebSiteLock is the world's first software toolset to "lock" and protect the contents of an organization's Web site.

- Automatically monitors and secures your Web site.
- Can constantly monitor all files on a Web site.
- Monitors each byte, and at the first change, reverts to the original and correct byte.
- Permits an immediate and automatic rebuild of any "tampered" files with the original files.
- Immediate reporting of any attack to the System Administrator.
- Not just an Intrusion Detection System, WebSiteLock actually maintains the integrity of your Web site.
- Prevents the Web site files from being corrupted, which is essential for the protection of full e- Commerce sites.
- Can protect both dynamic and static files.

- Allows authorized users to make changes to the Web site, but blocks everyone else.
- Protects your critical firewall files.

As more and more companies rely upon their Web sites to act as both a shopfront for their products and services, and as a window to their company, the need to protect the contents of their Web site has become critical. The protection of this investment is paramount to companies and organizations.

Significant amounts of interest, time, and money are invested in firewalls and other software and hardware solutions to prevent intrusion. In spite of this, we all know that even the most secretive and security-conscious organizations have been "hacked"—from our own Prime Minister's site to the CIA site in Washington. Commercial sites such as Nike and MGM have been entered and details altered, deleted, or added. Many smaller companies and organizations have been targeted and the costs suffered by the disruption have been experienced by all sectors of business, the utilities, and the government. Hackers often attack a site out of curiosity, mischief, and "fun" to prove how clever they are—not necessarily to prove how negligent you are. Regardless of the motive, the impact is the same—You pay *for* the consequences! ! ! Because your firewall alone, is never enough.

Further, the damage being caused by someone from within, or someone with inside knowledge who has recently left the company, can be of greater impact. This person can be far more "focused" and specific in the damage he or she may cause. WebSiteLock is aimed at organizations that have their own server(s) to manage their site.

Company name: Palisade Systems Inc.
Address: 2625 North Loop Drive, Suite 2120; Ames, IA 50010
Phone number: (515) 296-6500 or (888) 824-0720
E-mail address: info@palisadesys.com
URL: http:llwww.palisadesys.com
Category: General protection
Product name: PacketPup
Product description: PacketPup is free-to-download software available from www.packetpup.com that quickly and easily shows you whether you should be concerned about bandwidth allocation on your network. PacketPup tracks the use of file-sharing and streaming applications such as Napster, Gnutella, iMesh, RealAudio/RealVideo, Scour Exchange, Shoutcast, and Windows Media, displaying its data in graphical form. It then provides a Return on Investment (ROI) interface that helps you determine both usage and how much that usage costs your organization. If PacketPup

shows you that you have a bandwidth problem, PacketHound, a hardware-based blocking appliance, is a great solution.

PacketPup protects PC networks by alerting administrators to possible bandwidth and security issues associated with the use of file-sharing and streaming applications. Used unchecked, these applications (including Napster, Gnutella, RealAudio/RealVideo, etc.) can make PCs vulnerable to problems, clogging network bandwidth and exposing the network to security holes by opening backdoors and creating virus vulnerabilities.

Company name: Palisade Systems Inc.
Address: 2625 North Loop Drive, Suite 2120; Ames, IA 50010
Phone number: (515) 296-6500 or (888) 824-0720
E-mail address: info@palisadesys.com
URL: http://www.palisadesys.com
Category: General protection
Product name: PacketHound
Product description: PacketHound is a network appliance that allows system administrators to manage or block access to bandwidth- and productivity-eating Internet technologies such as Napster, Gnutella, iMesh, RealAudio/RealVideo, Scour Exchange, and Windows Media. PacketHound protects your organization by allowing you to impose a flexible, organization-specific rule set. You can, for example, block an entire network, or block all access except in one computer lab, or block on a machine-by-machine basis. You can also use time-based rules to shut down access during critical hours but allow it at other times.

PacketHound protects PCs from the bandwidth and security issues associated with the use of file-sharing and streaming applications. Networked PCs are vulnerable to the actions of others on the network; if others are running Napster or Gnutella, all computers have less bandwidth and are potentially vulnerable to security issues—network use of peer-to-peer clients can open security holes and expose an organization to viruses and Trojan horses.

Company name: Pedestal Software
Address: 11 Medway Branch Road; Norfolk, MA 02056
Phone number: (888) 664-7174
E-mail address: info@pedestalsoftware.com
URL: http:/ /www.pedestalsoftware.com
Category: General protection
Product name: SecurityExpressions

Product Description: Enterprise security management, administration, reporting, and lockdown. SecurityExpressions automates the process of deploying, assessing, and maintaining consistent security policies on networks of Windows NT and 2000 systems. It helps organizations with security management and large-scale systems lockdown. SecurityExpressions helps protect Internet PCs by locking them down according to industry-standard guidelines. Security "expressions," similar to mathematical ones, are at the core of this host and application policy management system. SecurityExpressions first assesses the vulnerability state by seeing how well the PC complies with the lockdown policy. Changes are recommended for non-compliant settings and SecurityExpressions automatically fixes them either interactively or in unattended mode. History logging provides an audit trail of changes and modifications may be rolled back to their previous state if problems arise.

Company name: Secure Computing Corporation
Address: One Almaden Boulevard, Suite 400; San Jose, CA 95113
Phone number: (800) 379-4944
E-mail address: NA
URL: www.securecomputing.com
Category: General protection
Product name: SafeWord Plus
Product description: Supports smart cards, Secure Computing's Server for Virtual Smart Card, and general smart cards.

Company name: Secure Computing Corporation
Address: One Almaden Boulevard, Suite 400; San Jose, CA 95113
Phone number: (800) 379-4944
URL: www.securecomputing.com
Category: General protection
Product name: Sidewinder 5
Product description: Provides internal and perimeter security.

Company name: Texar Software Corp.
Address: 1101 Prince of Wales Drive; Ottawa K2H 9N6, Canada
Phone number: (613) 274-2200
E-mail address: info@texar.com
URL: www.texar.com
Category: General protection
Product name: Secure Realms

Product description: An access control solution that controls access to both legacy-based applications and to the Web.

Company name: WatchGuard Technologies
Address: 316 Occidental Ave. S., Suite 2000; Seattle, WA 98104
Phone number: (206) 521-8340
E-mail address: information@watchguard.com
URL: www.watchguard.com
Category: General protection
Product name: WatchGuard LiveSecurity System w/FBII Plus and w/FBI-Fast VPN
Product description: Provides VPN and security for the Internet.

Company name: Webroot Software, Inc.
Address: P.O. Box 3531; Boulder, CO 80307
phone number: (800) 772-9383
Category: General protection
E-mail address: Infocom@webroot:com
URL: www.webroot.com
Product name: Window Washer™
Product description: Window Washer is a utility, not unlike ScanDisk, Disk Defragmenter, etc., that every computer should have, whether it is used in the home or office. Window Washer automates the cleaning of all unnecessary system and Internet files. In the case of system files, Window Washer cleans the following:

- Recycle Bin. This area continues to hold deleted information long after it is useful. Deleting its contents is important for home users as many do not know the Recycle Bin does not empty itself. In the case of businesses, this serves the important function of completely removing sensitive material.
- Registry Streams. This area tracks programs that are used most often. Clearing the Registry Streams is important for home users since it contains useless data that continually takes up space. In the case of businesses, eliminating this information prevents others from finding information regarding the computer's recent activity.
- Windows Run & Find History. These memory blocks were created for convenience, but only take up space in the average consumer's computer. On business computers, they can also act as an open window into the user's activity.
- CHK Scan Disk Files. These files can be used to reconstruct old, deleted files. Eliminating these files removes useless fragments and, in the case of businesses, prevents other users from reconstructing old files.

- Recently Viewed Pictures. Deleting these items can protect children from inappropriate material parents do not wish them to view. For businesses this can prevent the theft of online schematics and PowerPoint presentations.
- Recently Opened Documents. Removing the information stored in this area keeps others from discovering which documents have been opened recently.
- MS Office 97 and 2000 Tracks. These files are similar to Recently Opened Documents. By deleting the MS Office tracks, a user keeps secret the documents that have recently been modified, whether it is changes to a home checking account or changes to the company's new formula for household cleaners.
- Windows Temporary Files Folder. By eliminating these files users prevent anyone from determining which programs have recently been installed and what items have been downloaded.

This list is considerably expandable through the use of Window Washer's free plugins (now over 130) and the custom cleaning feature. The plugins enable the user to clean programs sucn as Adobe Acrobat Reader, MSN Instant Messenger, Real Player, etc. For browsers such as Internet Explorer, Netscape, Opera, Neoplanet, etc., Window Washer cleans:

- Cache. This area stores accessed Internet pages. By deleting this, users do not have to worry about anyone seeing which sites have recently been viewed.
- Cookies. By deleting the cookies from a user's browser, it prevents third-party services from tracking the sites to which the user has gone.
- History. By deleting this, the user prevents others with access to the computer from being able to find out which sites have been visited. This can help keep research and financial information secret.
- Mail Trash. This function of Window Washer completely eliminates emails once they have been removed from the deleted folder in mail managers. Many users believe that when the deleted items folder is emptied the emails are gone forever. Window Washer completely secures old correspondence by deleting them from the system entirely.
- Drop Down Address Bar. As this area tracks all URLs that have been input into the browser, deleting this information helps secure a user's browsing history.
- Auto Complete Data Forms. By removing this information, home users can protect their credit card information and business users can keep login and password information secure.
- Downloaded Program Files. Deleting this information gives both home and business users the comfort of knowing that no one can discover which Internet programs have been downloaded onto the computer.

The functionality of Window Washer offers the user two major benefits— privacy and performance. Whether it is the home user who doesn't want friends, spouses or children to view his or her latest letter to the IRS or whether it is a business person writing a letter to the human resources department, Window Washer protects their privacy according to DOD standards.

In the process of protecting the user's privacy Window Washer also recovers valuable hard drive space, restoring overall performance to the machine's original speed. As I'm sure you know, unless these areas are routinely cleaned, they accumulate rapidly, using more and more hard drive space. Most computer users are not aware of how to clean these areas and those who do know tend to avoid doing so because of the tedious and boring nature of the task.

The Windows™ operating system was designed for convenience and ease of use, not security. Hackers can enter computer systems through a variety of surreptitious means. This enables them to access private information, thereby compromising an individual's safety and right to privacy. Window Washer, when used routinely, plugs many of the security holes left open by the operating system's original design.

Window Washer is currently available on the Webroot Web site, http://www.webroot.com, and through a variety of Internet resellers. In the retail channel, Window Washer is carried by AOL, CompUSA, Fry's Electronics, Hastings, and others.

Company name: Webroot Software, Inc.
Address: P.O. Box 3531; Boulder, CO 80307
Phone number: (800) 772-9383
Category: General protection
E-mail address: Infocom@webroot:com
URL: www.webroot.com
Product name: WinGuardian
Product description: As children begin to use computers at younger and younger ages, they often become sophisticated enough to disable filtering and blocking software. WinGuardian is a Windows TM monitoring utility that is an alternative to filtering and blocking for parents, schools, and other organizations. This helpful tool runs completely hidden and is able to monitor everything a user does on a system. WinGuardian can keep track of which programs a user runs, log any text that is typed into a program, log all Web sites that are visited, and even capture screenshots at specified intervals. The logs can be reviewed to determine if a user is run-

ning inappropriate programs such as games or visiting Web sites that the system owner considers offensive. Alternatively, WinGuardian can display an acceptable use policy (AUP) on the computer screen. A user must read the AUP and then click on the AGREE button before he or she is allowed to access the system. Knowing that the system is being monitored is a strong deterrent from using inappropriate programs or viewing inappropriate Web pages. WinGuardian also gives you the option to "lock down" the Windows 95/98/Me environment so that users can only run authorized programs.

Company name: World Wide Digital Security, Inc. (WVVDSI)
Address: 4720 Montgomery Lane, Suite 800; Bethesda, MD 20814
Phone number: (301) 656-0521, ext. 0085
E-mail address: isolav@wwdsi.com
URL: http:llwww.wwdsi.com
Category: General protection
Product name: SAINT™ (System Administrator's Integrated Network Tool)
Product description: The most current version is bundled with SAINTwriter and/or SAINTexpress™. Older versions can be downloaded separately. SAINT is a vulnerability assessment tool used to scan networks for vulnerabilities that hackers might exploit to gain access. SAINT also supports extensive documentation on how to use the product, about the vulnerability, and how to fix the vulnerability. SAINT provides links to more information on the vulnerabilities found, and when possible, links to sites where patches can be downloaded to fix vulnerabilities. SAINT provides a variety of scanning intensity options ranging from *light* to *heavy plus*. Additional options include the SANS Top 10 and user-customized scans.

Company name: World Wide Digital Security, Inc. (WVVDSI)
Address: 4720 Montgomery Lane, Suite 800; Bethesda, MD 20814
Phone number: (301) 656-0521, ext. 0085
E-mail address: isolav@wwdsi.com
URL: http:llwww.wwdsi.com
Category: General protection
Product name: SAINTwriter™
Product description: SAINTwriter is a report writing module that attaches seamlessly to SAINT. SAINTwriter allows the user to generate easily various types of reports, ranging from executive summaries to technical detail reports. Users can quickly and easily create customized reports and save the report formats for future use.

Company name: World Wide Digital Security, Inc. (WVVDSI)
Address: 4720 Montgomery Lane, Suite 800; Bethesda, MD 20814
Phone number: (301) 656-0521, ext. 0085
E-mail address: isolav@wwdsi.com
URL: http:llwww.wwdsi.com
Category: General protection
Product name: SAINTexpress™
Product description: SAINTexpress is an automatic service that updates SAINT every time it is used. When a SAINT scan is initiated, SAINTexpress checks the WWDSI Web site to see if a newer version of SAINT is available. If available, SAINTexpress downloads the newer version of SAINT and runs the scan using this newer version. This guarantees that the scan is testing for the most recently discovered vulnerabilities and using the most advanced version of SAINT. This service is important because SAINT is updated at least once every two weeks or whenever a new critical vulnerability is discovered.

Company name: World Wide Digital Security, Inc. (WVVDSI)
Address: 4720 Montgomery Lane, Suite 800; Bethesda, MD 20814
Phone number: (301) 656-0521, ext. 0085
E-mail address: isolav@wwdsi.com
URL: http:llwww.wwdsi.com
Category: General protection
Product name: WebSAINT™
Product description: WebSAINT is WWDSI's Web-based vulnerability assessment scanner. The network scan is run from the WWDSI Web site and the report of the findings is sent to the user via secure http. WebSAINT is designed for people who are responsible for the security of their networks but do not have the time or expertise to download and configure the software, perform the scan, and create the reports.

A1.4 Personal Firewall

Company name: Computer Peripheral Systems, Inc. (CPS)
Address: 5096 Bristol Industrial Way, Suite B; Buford, GA 30518
Phone number: (770) 945-0643
E-mail address: cpsinc@randomc.com
URL: http://www.cpscom.com
Category: Personal firewall
Product name: Mini Firewall

Product description: Hardware security product for LANs with modem connections. Used to prevent modem connections to the Internet from gaining backdoor access to the corporate LAN. It connects between the modem and the LAN and physically breaks the LAN connection when the modem is in use. The LAN connection is re-established when the modem goes back on-hook or after user-specified software is executed.

Company name: DSEnet
Address: 5201 South Westshore Boulevard; Tampa, FL 33611
Phone number: (813) 902-9597
E-mail address: questions@dsenet.com
URL: www.dsenet.com
Category: Personal firewall
Product name: DSEnet Firewall
Product description: DSEnet Firewall is a personal firewall that protects networked PCs from remote attacks. Install DSEnet Firewall on a PC using the friendly interface, and apply the necessary access rights for the Internet. DSEnet Firewall is an ideal low-cost solution for small- to medium-sized businesses, home offices and home users. Now, connecting to the Internet does not require the resources or support of a large corporate security infrastructure. Put DSEnet Firewall on a PC and browse the Internet safely and securely.

Use DSEnet Firewall to restrict access to specific services for example, web browsing, or email. Even advanced rules can be created on a per user basis. Allow and block various users from Web addresses, ports, and protocols. Parents can blacklist Web sites that are off limits to children, or whitelist only the acceptable Web sites children are allowed to browse. Businesses can limit employees to work-related Web sites, prevent downloads and restrict Internet e-mail.

DSEnet Firewall can be accessed with the icon located in the lower right corner of the taskbar. Logging in provides users with their profiles. The Configuration Panel is accessible only with an administrator password. All user profiles, settings and rights can be configured in this panel.

DSEnet Firewall:

- Prevents unauthorized access from the internet
- Stealth mode hides your PC from the Internet world
- Runs seamlessly while surfing the Internet
- Great help files and instructions
- Basic users can use the firewall with minimal effort
- Computer wizards can, in detail, control every TCP and UDP port
- Runs on Windows 95, 98, and NT 4.0

- Control access to unacceptable Web sites
- Low-cost solution with no additional hardware required
- Supports multiple user profiles
- Simultaneously notifies the user and blocks intrusion attempts
- Flexible control of Web browsing
- Restricts access by IP address, URL, port and protocol
- Easy to install and easy to use explorer style interface
  System Requirements: Win 95,98, NT, Me, 2000; 32-MB RAM & TCP/IP

Company name: Intego, Inc.
Address: 6301 Collins Avenue, Suite # 1806; Miami, Florida 33141
Phone number: (305) 868-7920
Contact name: Olivier Depoorter
E-mail address: odepoorter@intego.com
URL: www.intego.com
Category: Personal Firewall
Product name: NetBarrier
Product description: First personal firewall for the Mac. Intego, a leading provider of Macintosh Internet security utilities, announced that it has won the prestigious International award, the UniversMacworld Award for the Best Internet Software of 2000 for NetBarrier. NetBarrier is the first personal Firewall for Macintosh with Firewall, Antivandal, and Internet Filter components that make NetBarrier the all-in-one solution for complete personal Internet security .

Intego has won over 20 awards in the US, Europe, and Asia, among which are awards from *Macworld; MacHome, MacNN, and MacAddict.* In just two years, NetBarrier has become the worldwide leader in personal firewall software for the Mac. In the words of Laurent Marteau, CEO, Intego, "We are extremely excited about winning this international award for our Internet security software. To be chosen the Best Internet Software among this fast-paced Internet community is truly an honor."

NetBarrier provides three powerful modules: Firewall, Antivandal, and Internet Filter to make NetBarrier the all-in-one solution for complete personal Internet security. Designed with maximum ease of setup and use, NetBarrier is the "must have" in Internet security software. New security features in NetBarrier 2.0 include control of unwanted Internet cookies, banner ads, and spam, the ability to filter personal information sent when connected to a Web site, updates to the program's Firewall settings, gauges to monitor data traffic by protocol or application, and log exporting. NetBarrier 2.0 also supports the new version of Intego's NetUpdate, the automatic software update engine. Users can program updates for specific days and times, and NetUpdate will check the Intego server to find out if updates are available for all of Intego's Barrier products installed on your computer.

Among the many awards Intego's programs have received in the US, Europe, and Asia, are those from *Macworld, MacHome, MacNN,* and *MacAddict.* In France, *UniversMacWorld* recently awarded NetBarrier their 2000 trophy for the best Internet program.

Again, quoting Laurent Marteau, CEO of Intego: "All Macs connected to the Internet are susceptible to security problems without exception. Some Internet users falsely believe that using a modem or ISDN dial-up connection does not expose them to hackers. Hackers can get in through flaws in the OS. For example, a flaw discovered in port 49152 of Mac OS 9 allows hackers to send data that instantly freezes up a Mac, a problem that NetBarrier solves easily."

New NetBarrier Features include:

- Quick access to many settings via a new Control Strip module
- New Aqua interface
- Spam filtering
- Filtered spam is deleted directly on POP3 servers
- Filtering of message subject, author, and sender
- Filtering of URLs
- Updates to the program's Firewall settings
- Definition of port intervals
- Predefined rule sets
- Ability to monitor data traffic by protocol or application
- Blocks cookies and counts the number of cookies received
- Allows the user to erase cookies received by Internet Explorer, Netscape Communicator, and iCab
- Blocks banner ads
- Allows the user to filter information sent when connected to a Web site
- Choose to not send your type of computer and browser
- Choose to not identify the last Web page visited
- Support for the new version of NetUpdate
- Information on Macintosh network configuration

System requirements are a MacOS compatible computer with a Power PC processor, OpenTransport, Mac OS 8.1 or higher, and 32-MB RAM. It is also compatible with Mac OS 9.1. A Mac OS X version will be available Q1 2001. Also available in French and Japanese versions.

NetBarrier is available immediately. It can be purchased from www.intego.com, from retailers including buy.com, CompUSA, MacZone,

Outpost.com, Computertown, Club Mac, MacWarehouse, MacMall, ComputerWare, Computer Store Northwest, J&R, Microcenter, CDW, Developer Depot, and from 200 Apple Specialists (see list on the Intego Web site) and online at htm://www.intego.com.

Intego, the i-security software company, publishes security software for the Macintosh, and its products are currently sold in 65 countries. With three essential products, Intego focuses on all aspects of the computer security market, that is, antivirus protection, intrusion prevention and content control.

In less than two years, NetBarrier has become the world leader in personal firewalls for the Macintosh. VirusBarrier, Intego's acclaimed antivirus solution, has been a resounding success since its launch in July 2000. And ContentBarrier, Intego's new parental control program, introduced to reinforce its product line, became available in January 2001.

Intego was founded in May 1999 by a collection of highly motivated engineers and high-profile marketing, finance and sales managers to leverage their extensive knowledge of network security and the Mac environment to corporate, individual and educational users worldwide. Intego grew 500% in the year 2000, and 2001 will help maintain this exceptional growth through the release of other new and innovative computer security products. The privately held company has its headquarters in Miami, Florida and in Paris, France.

Company name: Network ICE
Address: 2121 S. El Camino Real, Suite 1100; San Mateo, California 94403
Phone number: (650) 532-4100
E-mail address: info@networkice.com
URL: www.networkice.com
Category: Personal Firewall
Product name: BlackICE Defender
Product description: An easily installed personal firewall combined with a hacker detection system. Everyone on the Internet is at risk of attack by hackers. "Always-on" DSL or cable modem, and dial-up Internet connections provide hackers with the ability to violate the security of your computer.

BlackICE Defender is an industrial-strength anti-hacker system that automatically blocks unauthorized intrusions into your computer. It scans your DSL, cable modem, or dial-up Internet connection looking for hacker activity. When it detects an attempted intrusion, it automatically blocks traffic from that source, keeping intruders from accessing your computer. BlackICE Defender works silently in the background, keeping hackers at bay so you can safely stay connected to the Internet.

BlackICE Defender installs automatically and is up and running in a matter of seconds. It has a simple easy-to-use interface, provides audible or visual alerts, and a display that identifies who's trying to break into your computer.

BlackICE technology has been recognized with over 12 industry awards for superior technology and usability by leading publications such as *Business Week, PC World, Network World, PC Computing, PC Magazine, Info World,* and *Internet Week*.

Company name: Open Door Networks, Inc.
Address: 110 S. Laurel Street; Ashland, OR 97520
Phone number: (541) 488-4127
E-mail address: sales@opendoor.com/doorstop/
URL: http://www.opendoor.com/doorstop/
Category: Personal Firewall
Product name: DoorStop Server Edition
Product description: A software-based "firewall" product for Macintosh servers. Unlike conventional firewalls, which are usually expensive dedicated hardware devices, DoorStop is software that you install directly on the servers you wish to protect. DoorStop is significantly easier to set up and use than a hardware firewall and provides the same capabilities at lower cost. With DoorStop, you can specify precisely which machines should have access to which services, and you can keep track of both allowed and denied access attempts to those services. DoorStop works well with a wide range of Macintosh-based Internet servers, including AppleShare IP, WebSTAR, and Open Door's ShareWay IP product line. This product or service will protect a PC on the Internet by acting as a machine-specific firewall to deny TCP access attempts as desired. Also logs access attempts.

Company name: Open Door Networks, Inc.
Address: 110 S. Laurel Street; Ashland, OR 97520
Phone number: (541) 488-4127
E-mail address: sales@opendoor.com
URL: http://www.opendoor.com/whosthere/
Category: Personal Firewall
Product name: Who's There? Firewall Advisor
Product description: Who's There? Firewall Advisor helps users analyze and react to access attempts detected by their firewall. Who's There? is essential for understanding the ever-increasing access attempts from the Net. It provides advice and helps users take action to combat access attempts. It works with Open Door's DoorStop and Symantec's Norton Personal Firewall for Macintosh. This product or service will protect a PC on the Internet by allowing users to understand and react to access attempts detected by their machine-specific firewall.

Company name: Presinet Sytems
Address: 645 Fort Street, Suite L109; Victoria, BC V8W 1G2
Phone number: (250) 405-5380
E-mail address: Solutions@PresiNET.com
URL: http://www.PresiNET.com
Category: Personal Firewall
Product name: Deadbolt Managed Internet Firewall and Virtual Private Networking Services
Product description: PresiNET provides a range of managed Internet Firewall security services, Network Activity Reporting, and Virtual Private Networking services for small to enterprise-sized organizations for their computer networks of 1 to 250 units. As part of the service, PresiNET provides its robust firewall server, firewall management and reporting services, event and activity monitoring services, expert consulting, and support wherever your business is located.

Company name: SOLSOFT
Address: 130 rue Victor Hugo; 92300 Levallois Perret, France
Phone number: 00 33 1 47 15 55 00
E-mail address: info@solsoft.com
URL: www.solsoft.com/np-lite/
Category: Personal Firewall
Product name: Solsoft NP™-Lite 4.1
Product description: Solsoft NP-Lite 4.1 is a free version of Solsoft NP™ specially created for Linux users. Combining a powerful visual interface and compiler engine, Solsoft NP-Lite automatically translates visual representations of a security policy into consistent, error-free IP Filters. Solsoft NP-Lite configures up to three interfaces on Linux IP Firewall 2.0.x, Linux IP Chains 2.2.x and Linux NetFilter version 1.2. Solsoft NP-Lite 4.1 is a free security solution and can be downloaded from Solsoft's Web site (www.solsoft.com/np-lite/).

Solsoft NP-Lite is the ideal solution for any user or small companies directly connected to the internet (ADSL, Cable, high-speed connection) that want to protect themselves without wasting time.

Company name: SonicWALL, Inc.
Address: 1160 Bordeaux Drive; Sunnyvale, CA 94089
Phone number: (408) 745-9600
E-mail address: info@sonicwall.com
URL: www.sonicwall.com

Category: Personal Firewall
Product name: SonicWALL SOHO2 Internet Security Appliance
Product description: Integrated Internet Security. The SonicWALL SOHO2 Internet Security Appliance is a high-performance, integrated security platform. It includes a stateful packet inspection firewall, IP address management, and support for an expanding array of SonicWALL security services, including VPN (virtual private networking), network anti-virus, and content filtering. The SonicWALL SOHO2 is an ideal solution for broadband connected small offices to provide Internet security for all the computers on a LAN. By offloading security from each PC on the LAN to a high-performance appliance, security is dramatically enhanced.

A1.5 Physical Security

Company name: Codex Data Systems, Inc.
Address: 143 Main Street; Nanuet, New York 10954
Phone number: (845) 627-0011
E-mail address: sales@codexdatasystems.com
URL: www.codexdatasystems.com
Category: Physical Security
Product name: PC PhoneHome
Product description: Tracks and locates a stolen computer throughout the world.

Company name: Digital Asset Protection
Address: 617 Myrtle Street; Arroyo Grande, CA 93420
Phone number: (877) 752-7364
E-mail address: Info@DAProtect.com
URL: www.DAProtect.com
Category: Physical Security
Product name: Lock & Go™
Product description: Lock & Go offers premier mechanical protection for notebook computers. Nearly 700 pounds of resistance offers a level of asset protection unmatched by traditional cables. For quick and effective notebook protection the Lock & Go simply snaps into place, no awkward cabling is required. Upon your return, one twist of the key allows you to access your computer.

Company name: Digital Asset Protection
Address: 617 Myrtle Street; Arroyo Grande, CA 93420
Phone number: (877) 752-7364
E-mail address: Info@DAProtect.com
URL: www.DAProtect.com
Category: Physical Security
Product name: DAP Watchman™
Product description: The DAP Watchman is a standalone electronic alarm that may be used to protect a single piece of computer hardware or other electronic equipment. Ideally suited for the SOHO, or isolated equipment distributed throughout a large facility. If the sensor is removed, or the wire severed, an 85-dB tone notifies personnel in the vicinity of an attempted theft.

Company name: Digital Asset Protection
Address: 617 Myrtle Street; Arroyo Grande, CA 93420
Phone number: (877) 752-7364
E-mail address: Info@DAProtect.com
URL: www.DAProtect.com
Product name: DAP Marshall™
Category: Physical Security
Product description: Ideally suited for environments that contain notebooks that are frequently taken on the road, the DAP Marshall is a standalone electronic alarm system for computer hardware that combines state-of-the-art asset protection with hassle-free mobility. The DAP Marshall's infrared remote access allows the end-user to engage the system from a distance of up to 20 feet and protects your computer hardware without compromising the mobility of portable equipment.

Company name: Digital Asset Protection
Address: 617 Myrtle Street; Arroyo Grande, CA 93420
Phone number: (877) 752-7364
E-mail address: Info@DAProtect.com
URL: www.DAProtect.com
Category: Physical Security
Product name: DAP Sentry™
Product description: Ideally suited for environments with distributed computer hardware, the DAP Sentry is a standalone electronic alarm system that allows for complicated configurations with minimal impact. Touch pad or optional remote infrared access allows authorized users to quickly and effectively engage the system.

Company name: Digital Asset Protection
Address: 617 Myrtle Street; Arroyo Grande, CA 93420
Phone number: (877) 752-7364
E-mail address: Info@DAProtect.com
URL: www.DAProtect.com
Category: Physical Security
Product name: DAP Guardian™
Product description: The DAP Guardian is a standalone electronic alarm system for computer hardware that pinpoints the exact location of a security breach. In the event of an attempted theft of your high-tech equipment, the information provided by the alarm panel allows your personnel to execute an effective stealth response.

Company name: Digital Asset Protection
Address: 617 Myrtle Street; Arroyo Grande, CA 93420
Phone number: (877) 752-7364
E-mail address: Info@DAProtect.com
URL: www.DAProtect.com
Category: Physical Security
Product name: DAP Monitor™
Product description: The DAP Monitor is an integrated system ideally suited for unsupervised environments where round-the-clock protection of computer hardware is critical. The DAP Monitor provides an interface with a central alarm system point panel. The DAP Monitor uses a zone within a normally open or normally closed alarm loop circuit to protect computer equipment and allows organizations to take advantage of their existing access control infrastructure.

Company name: Fastening Solutions, Inc.
Address: 15230 Burbank Boulevard, Suite 106; Van Nuys, CA 91411
Phone number: (818) 994-3698; (800) 232-7836
Category: Physical Security
Product name: LockGuard
Product description: Provides fastening protection in combination with a key and lock security system. Can be used with PCs, and peripherals.

Company name: Kensington Technology Group ACCO Brands
Address: 2855 Campus Drive; San Mateo, CA 94403
Phone number: (650) 572-2700
Category: Physical Security
Product name: Notebook MicroSaver Security Cable

Product description: A lock and cable device that can be attached to the security slot of a desktop sytem or notebook.

Company name: PC Guardian
Address: 1133 E. Francisco Boulevard; San Rafael, CA 94901-5427
Phone number: (415) 459-0190; (800) 288-8126
E-mail address: pcg@pcguardian.com
URL: www.pcguardian.com
Category: Physical Protection
Product name: Perma Dome Cable Anchor
Product description: Security cable anchor.

Company name: PC Guardian
Address: 1133 E. Francisco Boulevard; San Rafael, CA 94901-5427
Phone number: (415) 459-0190; (800) 288-8126
E-mail address: pcg@pcguardian.com
URL: www.pcguardian.com
Category: Physical Protection
Product name: Partition Furniture Cable Anchor
Product description: Security cable anchor that can be inserted into cublic walls.

Company name: Philadelphia Security Products, Inc.
Address: 405-R Baily Road; Yeadon, PA 19050
Phone number: (800) 456-1789
E-mail address: info@flexguard.com
URL: www.flexguard.com
Category: Physical Security
Product name: FLEXGUARD security system
Product description: Anti-theft security hardware for laptop computers, desktop computers, and other electronic equipment.

Company name: Se-Kure Controls, Inc.
Address: 3714 Runge Street; Franklin Park, IL 60131-1112
Phone number: (847) 288-1111; (800) 322-2435
E-mail address: secure@se-kure.com
URL: www.se-kure.com
Category: Physical Security
Product name: Laptop Holder #PTR-200
Product description: Provides protection for the glass screen with a metal enclosure.

A1.6 User Authentication

Company name: American Biometric Company
Address: DFW Engineering & Development Ltd.; 3429 Hawthorne Road; Ottawa, Ontario, K1G 4G2 Canada
Phone number: (613) 736-5100; (888) 246-6687
Category: User Authentication
Product name: BioMouse Fingerprint Scanner
Product description: Plug and play peripheral that uses a desktop fingerprint scanner to replace password protection.

Company name: Ankari
Address: 3429 Hawthorne Road; Ottawa, Ontario K1G 4G2 Canada
Phone number: (613) 736-5100, or 1-(888) 246-6687
E-mail address: info@ankari.com
URL: www.ankari.com
Category: User Authentication
Product name: BioMouse
Product description: Combined fingerprint scanner and smart card reader. The BioMouse Plus integrated fingerprint scanner and smart card reader lets you store credentials on a secure portable token whose use depends on a method of positive identification that cannot be lost, stolen, shared or forgotten—your fingerprint. When applied to Internet security, a user can store a Verisign digital certificate on a smart card and use a fingerprint instead of a password to enter secure Web sites.

Company name: Ankari
Address: 3429 Hawthorne Road; Ottawa, Ontario K1G 4G2 Canada
Phone number: (613) 736-5100, or 1-(888) 246-6687
E-mail address: info@ankari.com
URL: www.ankari.com
Category: User Authentication
Product name: Trinity
Product description: Trinity is a software authentication infrastructure that enables secure and convenient verification of user identities to protect access to a wide range of platforms and applications. Trinity allows a user to consolidate all their Web-based passwords into a single digital identity and protect that identity through the use of a biometric or smart card.

Company name: Litronic Inc.
Address: 17861 Cartwright Road; Irvine, CA 92614

Phone number: (949) 851-1085
E-mail: info@litronic.com
URL: www.litronic.com
Category: User Authentication
Product name: NetSign
Product description: Stores identity on a Smart Card which is compatible with Newscape2 and Microsoft@suites. This allows the user to conduct secure transactions over the Internet.

NetSign secures the Internet for communications by adding smart card functionality to Microsoft and Netscape email/browser packages. A user's digital identity is stored on the smart card to increase security. Mission-critical security functions such as private key storage and digital signature are performed on the smart card for significantly greater security that is completely portable for use with a desktop or laptop at the office, from home, or while traveling.

NetSign includes SecureDial , SecureStart@, and CardStart features that enhance network and desktop security and control desktop applications.

NetSign CardStart Features:

- Automatic registration of new certificates
- Windows log-off capabilities when the smart card is removed from the reader
- Automated launching of applications upon insertion of the smart card into the reader

NetSign SecureDial Features:

- Secure remote network access using the RAS, RADIUS, TACACS or PPTP protocols to enable smart card secured dial-up sessions and ISP access
- Storage of account information on the smart card to protect dial-up passwords

NetSign SecureStart Features:

- Log-on protection for Windows 95/98 and Windows NT PCs requiring the insertion of the user's smart card and PIN for PC access (Windows 2000 support provided through native Windows 2000 Logon)
- Locking capabilities for Windows PC NT stations upon the removal of the user's smart card
- System lock override with the use of an administrator card

Browser and E-mail Security Features:

- Authenticated Web page access with SSL
- Digitally signed and encrypted e-mail using S/MIME (VeriSignTM Digital ID included)
- Form and object signing using Microsoft Internet Explorer 4.0 or higher, Outlook 98/2000 or Outlook Express 4 or higher, or Netscape Communicator 4.05 or higher

- Support for custom smart-card enabled Java applets

Company name: Litronic Inc
Address: 17861 Cartwright Road; Irvine, CA 92614
Phone number: (949) 851-1085
E-mail: info@litronic.com
URL: www.litronic.com
Category: User Authentication
Product name: Profile Manager
Product description: Allows the user to create and maintain smart cards and to expert PKCS#12 files using a variety of Certificate Authorities.

Profile Manager provides organizations with a flexible solution by offering token interoperability. Because Profile Manager can initialize and maintain both smart cards and the exporting of PKCS#12 files, organizations can implement an adaptable PKI scheme that supports a multilevel security approach. Profile Manager is integrated with a variety of Certificate Authorities (CAs) offering trusted certificate issuance and integrated directory service. The CAs currently supported are Microsoft@ Certificate Management Sytstem, and CyberTrust@. In addition, Profile Manager supports international standards such as SSL, S/MIME, PKCS#11, and PC/SC while enabling the generation of X509v3 certificates, RSA keypairs, and other custom data objects.

Efficiency and security are critical to the success of a large-scale PKI deployment. Profile Manager enables organizations to quickly generate security tokens for any user in the system. To increase efficiency and to decrease the risk of third party interception, token generation is removed from the user's desktop and performed by the security administrator for fail-safe installation of the certificate on the token. Security administrators can control security by generating and backing-up keys and certificates in a restricted environment.

Profile Manager conveniently integrates with your existing employee or customer database so that the security administrator does not have to re-key user data for token personalization. User information can be imported from several sources including existing ASCII files, directories, and various databases. For large-scale deployments, Profile Manager integrates with DatacardTM printers to provide bulk smart card initialization and custom printing.

The ability to recover user information, including keys and certificates, is necessary to replace lost or damaged tokens. Profile Manager provides optional secure database integration for the recovery of token information. User data and profile information is encrypted with the security administrator's Triple DES key/PIN-protected smart card and stored in the database.

The security administrator can access this information from the database to issue a user a duplicate smart card when a card is lost or damaged.

The routine maintenance of a PKI can be burdensome for security administrators without the proper tools for the management of security tokens. Profile Manager can be used to modify user privileges or alter user data by adding, deleting or modifying items on an existing user token. If necessary, a user's keys and certificates can be revoked using Profile Manager. Data on a card or other token can be changed and updated after that token has been issued using Profile Manager. Changing user data after token issuance also creates a new backup entry in the database.

Profile Manager Supports:

- Hardware key generation
- Integration with leading X.509v3 Certificate Authorities.
- Security policy profiling
- Integration with various databases and directories
- Bulk token issuance .Key recovery
- Certificate revocation

Profile Manager Includes: Profile Manager Software. Two NetSignia™ Smart Card Reader/Writers, Argus 2000 PC Card Reader/Writer, Chrysalis Luna 2 PCMCIA Token, thirteen smart cards.

Company name: Mytec Technologies, Inc.
Address: 1220 Sheppard Avenue E., Suite 200; Toronto, M2K 2S5 Canada
Phone number: (416) 467-6000
E-mail address: sales@mytec.com
URL: www.mytec.com
Category: User Authentication
Product name: Mytec® Gateway
Product description: Compares the user's fingerprints with those contained in an encrypted template.

Company name: Recognition Systems, Inc.
Address: 1520 Dell Avenue; Campbell, CA 95008
Phone number: (408) 364-6960
E-mail address: Sales@regosys.com
URL: www.handreader.com
Category: User Authentication
Product name: Id3D-R Handkey
Product description: A biometric access control system that responds to and recognizes people.

Company name: Secure Computing Corporation
Address: One Almaden Boulevard, Suite 400; San Jose, CA 95113
Phone number: 1-(800) 379-4944
URL: www.securecomputing.com
Category: User Authentication
Product name: SafeWord 5.1
Product description: Allows authentication methods to be mixed and matched as needed.

Company name: SHYM Technology Inc.
Address: 75 Second Ave.; Needham, MA 02494
Phone number: (781) 455-1100
E-mail address: info@shym.com
URL: www.shym.com
Category: User Authentication
Product name: snAPPSecure™
Product description: Allows the user to securely move offline processes onto the Web. The snAPPsecure targets organizations moving offline processes to the Web to achieve increased efficiencies. Most of these organizations do not have the vast resources required to implement a custom-built infrastructure for strong authentication and eSignatures. Initial target market segments include healthcare, manufacturing, financial services, pharmaceuticals, and government. Every organization is working rapidly and furiously to determine which core processes should be e-enabled. However, without the necessary security precautions, mission-critical Web, e-mail, and enterprise applications, such as SAP and PeopleSoft, are at serious risk. The latest version of Microsoft's server operating system, Windows 2000, has been developed with built-in security capabilities including a standards-based public key infrastructure (PKI) to deliver a complete Internet-enabled business operating system. SHYM's snAPPsecure utilizes no-cost certificates from Microsoft's Windows 2000 as a low-cost and easy to deploy solution for small and medium enterprises to secure critical applications.

SHYM's snAPPsecure is a turnkey application security solution powered by the Microsoft Windows 2000-based public key infrastructure (PKI) that dramatically accelerates the deployment of application security using digital certificates to protect today's e-business initiatives. The snAPPsecure allows organizations to look beyond individual security point solutions to a complete product solution that is centrally managed, covering all organizational domains. Also, snAPPsecure lets organizations easily leverage the integrated PKI of Windows 2000 with their choice of Web, e-mail and client/server applications without the time-consuming and costly custom integration traditionally needed for a complex and powerful PKI security. Further, snAPPsecure combines PKEnable', SHYM's flagship product, the Windows 2000 Certificate Server and professional services to enable organizations to rapidly secure critical e-business applications in just a few days, as opposed to the months of integration needed with today's digital certificate toolkits.

SHYM's application library includes support for popular Web, e-mail, and enterprise applications, providing snap-in application security, eliminating the pain of integrating and maintaining custom development. However, snAPPsecure does not require a homogeneous Windows 2000-based network. It provides clean integration with existing Windows NT, Novell, and UNIX environments.

Today, enterprises engaging in business over public networks are doing it at a great risk. The idea of conducting high-value transactions, such as contract negotiations and the exchange of product ideas with today's security technology gives most organizations reason for concern. The PKI is poised to meet these security needs with its combination of strong authentication, message integrity, and eSignature capabilities, but PKI is still too difficult to integrate, manage and deploy. Recent PKI projects that were expected to be in full-scale deployment are still mired in the pilot stages, while other projects have been completely cancelled. Those very few who have started to roll out a PKI now realize that just issuing certificates is not enough, and that there must be a way to validate that credentials are trusted to perform certain transactions. SHYM's snAPPsecure is the solution to this problem because it makes PKI less expensive, faster to deploy, and easier to manage.

SHYM's snAPPsecure enables organizations to leverage the underlying digital certificate capabilities of their Windows 2000 operating system, thereby leveraging digital certificates for greater efficiency and competitive advantage. snAPPsecure enables e-processes that result in greater efficiencies and competitive advantage. SHYM's snAPPsecure also removes application security integration barriers, making the product far easier to install and manage. With Microsoft's integrated PKI software, customers can deploy PKI-based security services quickly, easily and, most importantly, cost effectively. SHYM's solution lets organizations reap the promise of streamlined business processes, without breaking the bank or missing the market window. SHYM's solutions have the added advantage of being both snap-in simple, and customized to fit each organization's needs. A snAPPsecure pilot implementation can usually be installed in one day as opposed to weeks or months.

SHYM's snAPPsecure allows companies to build strong strategic online relationships with suppliers, distributors, customers, and other entities. They can share important business information knowing that interactions are private, that the identity of each party is authenticated, and that any agreements cannot be forged or repudiated. These assurances allow companies to replicate the best practices of the brick and mortar marketplace in the e-business realm.

Company name: Silanis Technology Inc.
Address: 398 Isabey, 2nd Floor; Saint Lauren, Quebec H4T 1V3
Phone number: 888-SILANIS (745-2647)
E-mail address: info@silanis.com
URL: www.silanis.com
Category: User Authentication
Product name: ApproveIt
Product description: Silanis ApproveIt is an award-winning, electronic signature software that enables organizations to securely capture multiple, legally binding signatures in electronic documents and Web forms without additional hardware, software or programming. Supported software includes Microsoft Word, Excel, Outlook, Adobe Acrobat, JetForm FormFlow, PureEdge and X.509 v3 digital certificates.

Company name: Secure Computing Corporation
Address: One Almaden Boulevard, Suite 400; San Jose, CA 95113
Phone number: 1-(800) 379-4944
URL: www.securecomputing.com
Category: User Authentication
Product name: SmartFiler
Product description: Allows control of Web access throughout the entire organization.

A1.7 Virus Protection

Company name: Computer Associates International, Inc.
Address: 1 Computer Associates Plaza; Islandia, NY 1788-7000
Phone number: (516) 342-5224; (800) 225-5224
E-mail address: info@ca.com
URL: www.ca.com
Category: Virus Protection
Product name: eTrust AntiVirus

Product description: Provides antivirus protection. Has built-in identifiers of new virus.

Company name: F-Secure, Inc.
Address: 675 N. First Street, 5th Fl.; San Jose, CA 95112
Phone number: (408) 938-6700; (888) 432-8233
E-mail address: info@f-secure.com
URL: www.F-Secure.com
Category: Virus Protection
Product name: F-Secure Anti-Virus
Product description: Provides protection against virus and other attacking codes for both mobile and site-based workers.

Company name: InDefense
Address: 303 Potrero Street, #42–204; Santa Cruz, CA 95060
Phone number: (831) 471-1413; (877) 472-3372
E-mail address: info@indefense.com
URL: www.indefense.com
Category: Virus Protection
Product name: Achilles' Shield
Product description: Provides a patented protection from virus. It detects worm, viral, and Trojans.

Company name: Intego, Inc.
Address: 6301 Collins Avenue, Suite #1806; Miami, Florida 33141
Phone number: (305) 868 7920
Contact name: Olivier Depoorter
E-mail address: odepoorter@intego.com
URL: www.intego.com
Category: Virus Protection
Product name: VirusBarrier
Product description: Provides anti-virus protection for the Mac.
VirusBarrier features are as follows:

- Simple, fast and nonintrusive
- Scans compressed files and checks all types of archives recognized by Stuffit Expander (Zip, CompactPro, DiskDoubler, tar Bzip, arc, etc.)
- Turbo Mode makes scanning from 4 to 40 times faster
- Contextual Menu module for quick scanning
- Self-protection ensures that VirusBarrier doesn't get infected
- Scans RAM after detection of system viruses
- Faster manual scans
- Compatible with Mac OS 9.1

The upgrade from VirusBarrier version 1.x is free for registered users. Available from the Intego Web site, www .intego.com. System requirements are a Mac OS compatible computer with a Power PC processor, OpenTransport, Mac OS 8.1 or higher, and 32-MB RAM. It is also compatible with Mac OS 9.1 A Mac OS X version will be available Q1 2001. Also available in French and Japanese versions.

VirusBarrier is available immediately from retailers including buy.com, CompUSA, MacZone, Outpost.com, Computertown, Club Mac, MacWarehouse, MacMall, ComputerWare, Computer Store Northwest, J&R, Microcenter, CDW, Developer Depot, and from 200 Apple Specialists (see list on the Intego Web site), and online at httQ://www.intego.com.

In less than two years, NetBarrier has become the world leader in personal firewalls for the Macintosh. VirusBarrier, Intego's acclaimed antivirus solution, has been a resounding success since its launch in July 2000. And ContentBarrier, Intego's new parental control program, was available to reinforce its product line in January 2001.

Intego was founded in May 1999 by a collection of highly motivated engineers and high-profile marketing, finance and sales managers to leverage their extensive knowledge of network security and the Mac environment to corporate, individual and educational users worldwide. Intego grew 500% in the year 2000, and 2001 will help maintain this exceptional growth through the release of other new and innovative computer security products. The privately held company has its headquarters in both Miami, Florida and Paris, France.

Company name: McAfee
Address: 3965 Freedom Circle; Santa Clara, CA 95054
Phone number: 1-(888) VIRUS-NO
URL: www.mcafeeb2b.com
Category: Virus Protection
Product name: VirusScan TC
Product description: As the Internet becomes the hub of an increasing number of business transactions, and users—especially mobile users—depend on network availability to perform mission-critical functions, bandwidth becomes an essential resource for IT to manage. And in a circular scenario, this trend leads to a lack of available bandwidth. VirusScan TC (Thin Client) not only requires less bandwidth to deploy and manage than any other antivirus solution on the market today, but it intelligently uses the little bandwidth it does require. Working in concert with McAfee's ePolicy Orchestrator, which sets the standard for enterprise anti-virus management, VirusScan TC allows you to centrally update, configure, manage, and gather information about your entire network, while minimizing the bandwidth impact to your network.

Because ePolicy Orchestrator uses standard protocols to communicate between the desktop and the server (secured HTTP), managing remote sites across the Internet is a breeze. Got an office in Australia, but no VPN connectivity between here and there? Using ePolicy Orchestrator and VirusScan TC you're still secure. Remote users who dial in for e-mail and became frustrated with their anti-virus protection because it took a long time to download updates will forget they ever had a problem once VirusScan TC is installed. Not only is the download speed of VirusScan TC's incremental update technology quicker, but you will have the peace of mind that secured agent-server communication gives you.

Company name: Midwest Systems, Inc.
Address: 1303 Corporate Center Drive; Eagan, MN 55121
Phone number: (651) 406-4100; (888) 800-8339
E-mail address: moreinfo@midwest-sys.com
URL: www.midwest-sys.com
Category: Virus Protection
Product name: Midwest Systems
Product description: A services company that specializes in storage, network, and messaging solutions that are secure.

Company name: SaferSite
Address: 2130 Walnut Bottom Road; Carlisle, PA 17013
Phone number: (717) 243-6588
E-mail address: brose@safersite.com
URL: www.safersite.com
Category: Virus Protection
Product name: PestPatrol
Product description: PestPatrol detects and can delete any malicious non-virus software found on PCs. Everyone knows what a virus scanner is and what it does. What people don't realize is that there is a wide variety of malicious software that can be more harmful than viruses, and they are not being detected by your antivirus software.

"Pests" represent a whole new category of things, which threaten the stability and integrity of your computer or network. You may not have been aware that these threats exist. Wouldn't you be surprised to find files containing information about hacking your PBX, password cracking, mail bombing, or a variety of hacker tools on your network or even on your own computer?

Where Do These Pests Come From? In some instances, these pests can be planted on your machine by "hackers." Such things as Trojans, worms, or hostile applets are among the most common items that arrive from the "outside." Other items can be brought into your network, knowingly or unknowingly, by your own employees. In any event, as a Webmaster or system administrator, you should be aware that they exist . . . and that they can be a source of disruption.

Some pests can cause a great deal of damage, and some can live on your machine without you even knowing about them. There are thousands of pests and new ones are found each day and added to SaferSite's PestPatrol database. You should be as rigorous about scanning for pests as you are about scanning for viruses.

There are dozens of categories of pests. Some include: worms, Trojans, spyware, hacker toolkits and password crackers. With such a large variety of pests out there, doesn't it make sense to protect your network from these types of things? PestPatrol only needs a few minutes to identify unwanted pests on your entire network. PestPatrol can also be updated in seconds to detect new pests as soon as they are discovered.

Company name: Trend Micro, Inc.
Address: 10101 N. De Anza Boulevard, 2nd Fl.; Cupertino, CA 95014
Phone number: (408) 257-1500; (800) 228-5651
E-mail address: sales@trendmicro.com
URL: www.antivirus.com
Category: Virus Protection
Product name: InterScan Virus Wall
Product description: A three-in-one product that scans SMTP mail, HTTP, and FTP traffic. All this is done in real time.

Company name: Trend Micro, Inc.
Address: 10101 N. De Anza Boulevard, 2nd Fl.; Cupertino, CA 95014
Phone number: (408) 257-1500; (800) 228-5651
E-mail address: sales@trendmicro.com
URL: www.antivirus.com
Category: Virus Protection
Product name: ScanMail for OpenMail
Product description: A virus protection system for Hewlett-Packard's e-mail.

APPENDIX 2

TCP/IP Reference

Do you remember the talking animated Santa Claus you received from a "friend" of yours via e-mail during the holidays? Yes, it took over an hour to download and rewarded you with a chuckling fat man. At the same time, you might not have received those e-mails you got from your loved ones. All of this, in both its splendor and annoyance, is possible because computers can "talk" to each other via the Internet and, more specifically, via a protocol called TCP/IP.

In Chapter 1 we talked about the glue that holds the Internet together. This glue is the TCP/IP protocol. In order to understand how to set up a home network you will need to understand a bit about TCP/IP. So let's start off with an analogy. There is a street, in your neighborhood, a nice street that does not have junked cars all over the place. A clean street—OK, you get the idea—a street. On this street are two houses, one house will be the sender house and the other house is the received house. Okay, we want to send a piece of mail from one house to the other. Now we are talking about postal mail, or snail mail. In reality the postal person (or mail dude or dudette) will pick up the mail, take it to the post office and then return it back to the same street. We will suspend reality for a moment and believe that the postal person will pick up the mail and deliver it directly to the destination house. So what components are required for this postal mail to be picked up and then delivered?

- A postal person
- A source house (with a source address)
- A destination house (and it has a target address)
- A letter or a package
- On the letter or package is some type of addressing information
- A street (with a list of addresses)—(and a street name)

Here is the process: You are at 123 Bubba Street. You want to send a message to 124 Bubba Street. You create a message and place it into an envelope, address the envelope and send it to 124 Bubba Street. Okay, as shown here in Figure A2.1, not bad, this will work.

Now, let's see how the computer does it by checking Figure A2.2. The source computer, Computer 123, sends a packet of data on a network. This network is called Network A. The data packet travels over the network looking for Computer 124. Once found it delivers the packet to the computer.

The Transmission Control Protocol/Internet Protocol (TCP/IP) address works much like the postal mail analogy. Every computer has a source address and if you want to send data to another computer you need to know its "target" address.

The TCP/IP provides connectivity between equipment from many vendors over a variety of networking technologies. The Transmission Control Protocol (TCP) is intended for use as a highly reliable host-to-host protocol between hosts in packet-switched computer communication networks.

The Internet Protocol (IP) is specifically limited in scope to provide the functions necessary to deliver an envelope of data from one computer system

FIGURE A2.1

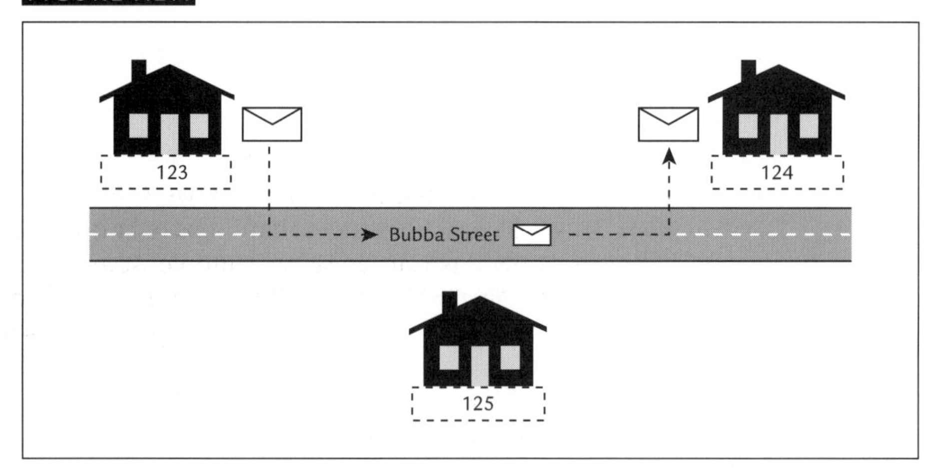

FIGURE A2.2

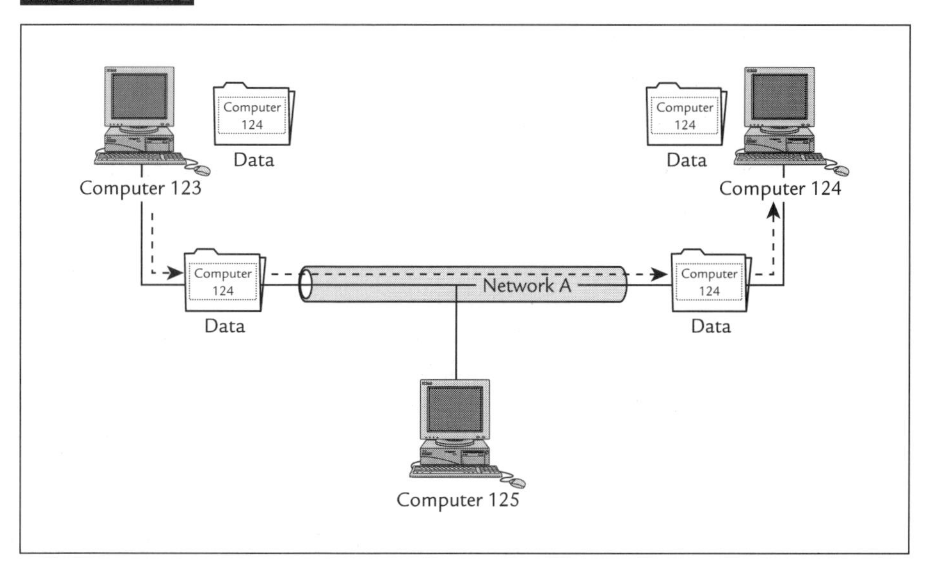

to another. Actually we are not limited to PCs, as this can be any network-connected device, for example, a computer, a printer, a cell phone (see WAP in the glossary). Each computer or device on a network will have some type of address that denotes where it is on the network. Every device will have one of these addresses, assigned via a permanent mechanism or a temporary addressing scheme. You will notice that we are referencing a network; IP and TCP are used on the Internet but also can be used on any network. Many networks use TCP/IP as their primary protocol.

When data is sent via a network (e-mail note or a Web page), the data (or message) is carved into little chunks called packets. The packets contain the information required to determine who sent the message as well as the recipient of the message.

An Ethernet LAN typically uses some type of cable or special grades of twisted pair wires. Basically, the computer is connected to the cable via a card (or NIC—Network Interface Card) and that card puts the data onto the cable. In our examples for your home network we will be discussing the Ethernet LAN. This is a complex system that keeps data from running into each other and is known as Carrier Sense Multiple Access with Collision Detection (CSMA/CD). Every NIC card will have some type of address, and this address is known as a MAC address. This is typically a 48-bit address that is unique for every card. All Ethernet data is crafted into packets, and each packet has the information needed to find its target computer and knows where it came from. Table A2.1 is an example of an Ethernet Packet.

TABLE A2.1

6 Bytes	6 Bytes	2 Bytes	46–1500 Bytes	4 Bytes
Target Address	Source Address	Protocol Type	Data	CRC

As you can see there is a "target address" and a "source address." Each byte shown is an 8-bit byte—so we end up with 48 bits for each address. See the IEEE 802.3 for a description of the address assignments (http://www.ieee.org/). The protocol type tells the computer that is receiving the data what the packet is, for example: 0800 = IP4 or Internet packet, 0806 = ARP packet (ARP used by TCP to determine what other computers are on the network). The 1500 bytes of data are where TCP/IP lives. The CRC is a checksum to make sure the packet did not get corrupted in transmission.

We have just described the first layer in the TCP/IP model. This is similar to the OSI (Open Systems Interconnection) model. The OSI is a standard reference mode for how network data is transmitted between any two points in a computer network. The TCP/IP supports the Defense Advanced Research Projects Agency (DARPA) model of internetworking and its network-defined layers: Network Interface, Internet, Hosts-to-Host, and Process/Application. This model was developed in the early 1970s, and preceded the Open Systems Interconnection Reference Model (OSI). Much like the DARPA model, the OSI was designed to connect dissimilar computer network systems. The OSI reference model defines seven layers of functions that take place at each end of a network communication. As shown in Table A2.2, OSI divides the communication into seven layers.

TABLE A2.2

OSI	
Application	**Application layer:** This is the layer at which programs are identified, user authentication, and privacy are implemented.
Presentation	**Presentation layer:** This is a layer, usually part of an operating system, that converts incoming and outgoing data from one presentation format to another.

(continued)

Session	**Session layer**: This layer sets up, coordinates, and ends conversations, exchanges, and dialogs between the applications at each end of the dialog.
Transport	**Transport layer:** This layer manages the end-to-end control and error-checking.
Network	**Network layer:** This layer handles the routing of the data. The network layer does routing and forwarding.
Data Link	**Data link layer:** This layer provides error con trol and synchronization for the physical level.
Physical	**Physical layer:** This layer transmits the bit stream through thet network at the electrical and mechanical level. Cables, Cards, . . .

The TCP/IP also has a protocol model; shown here in Table A2.3, this is a much simpler model.

There is no direct correlation between the TCP protocol model and the OSI model. But they are roughly equivalent in the services that are provided. Table A2.4 shows a comparison between the models.

TABLE A2.3

Process Layer	**Process Layer:** This is the layer where each process is defined and communicates. FTP, Telent, . . .
Host-to-Host Layer	**Host to Host:** This is where TCP lives. This is the mechanism that actually ports the data to the correct application. TCP ports are defined here.
Internet Layer	**Internet Layer:** IP address is used to direct the packet to the correct destination. Routing protocols live here along with ARP and ICMP.
Network Interface Layer	**Network Interfact Layer:** This is the physical connection to the network .Ethernet, token ring, etc. The packets are placed onto the network at this point. Also the CRC is done here.

TABLE A2.4

Protocol Implementation

DARPA Layer				OSI
Process/ Application	FTP SMTP TELNET RFC: 959,821,854		TFTP NFS SNMP RFC: 783,1094	Application
				Presentation
				Session
Transport	Transmission Control Protocol (TCP) RFC793		User Datagram Protocol (UDP) RFC 768	Transport
Internet	(ARP) Address Resolution RFC826,903	**(IP) Internet Protocol RFC791**	Internet Control Message Protocol RFC792	Network
Network Interface	Network Interface Cards: Ethernet, Token Ring RFC894 RFC 1042			Data Link
	Transmission Media: Twisted Pair, Coax, Fiber, Wireless, etc.			Physical

The first layer of the DARPA model is the Network Interface Layer, and it links the local host to the local network hardware. This loosely maps to the Physical and Data Link layers of the OSI reference model. The Network Interface Layer makes the physical connection to the network cable whether it is Ethernet or Token Ring. In each case a frame is generated with data from the upper layers. The Internet Layer transfers the packets from one host to another host. Each packet will contain address information relating to the source and destination of the packet. The third level of the Internet software is called the Transport Layer. It is responsible for providing communication between applications residing on different hosts. This can also be called the host-to-host layer. Depending on the application, the Transport Layer will provide a reliable service (TCP) or an unreliable service (UDP). In a reliable service the receiving station acknowledges the receipt of a datagram. The top layer of the DARPA model is the Application Layer. This is where actual applications such as TFTP and Telnet reside.

Thus we have seen the Ethernet Packet and where it lives in the TCP/IP model. Next, let's look at the IP packet. The IP packet is how the TCP packet finds to which computer it is destined. The Internet Protocol is defined in RFC 791 (http://info.internet.isi.edu:80/in-notes/rfc/files/rfc791.txt). The IP provides the most basic level of service in the Internet, and is the basis upon which the other protocols stand. The IP provides the protocol above it with a basic service model. Also, the IP is really similar to the Postal Service. Using its address scheme, a packet is routed from a source to a destination much like a letter having a street address. Overall, IP does not promise the best service, hence it is known as a "Best Effort Service." If you send a postal message from your house, you rely on "best effort" that the message will arrive at its destination. Without special handling you will not know if the letter (a.k.a message) has been delivered to its destination. The IP routing is outside the scope of this document; see the following URL for a basic overview: http://www.sangoma.com/fguide.htm.

The Ethernet packet carrying TCP/IP is shown in Table A2.5. Notice that IP precedes TCP.

TABLE A2.5

6 Bytes	6 Bytes	2 Bytes	46–1500 Bytes			4 Bytes
Target Address	Source Address	Protocol Type	IP	TCP	Data	CRC

Table A2.6 shows how it looks in each section.

TABLE A2.6

6 Bytes	6 Bytes	2 Bytes	46–1500 Bytes			4 Bytes
Target Address	Source Address	Protocol Type	IP	TCP	Data	CRC

4 Bits	4 Bits	3 Bits	5 Bits	2 Bytes	2 Bytes	2 Bytes	1 Byte	1 Byte	2 Bytes	4 Bytes	4 Bytes
IP Version	IP Version	Precedence	Type of Service	Total IP Length	ID#	Fragment	TTL	Protocol	Check Sum	Source IP Address	Target Address

This is how an address is accomplished on the Internet. As we mentioned before, all network-connected devices will have an address. Keep in mind that every NIC card has a 48-bit address, but this is how the packet finds its way to a specific NIC card. Addressing between applications happens using the IP address. Figure A2.3 provides an example.

In this figure the laptop computer is sending an IP packet to the Server. The source address is 192.9.200.21 and the target address is 192.9.200.23. Using this nomenclature the server now knows how to respond back to the laptop computer, assuming the application needs to do that. This address scheme is how computers talk to each other on the Internet or any IP network. Thus back with our postal analogy: the IP address is much like the address on the letter, or the address on your house. Hence, the letter (packet) is dropped into the postal box and it is sent via a network of postal employees, with one finally dropping the letter at your house or mailbox.

Part of the IP architecture is the address methodology. From the 32 bits of which it is comprised there are approximately 4 billion possible addresses. The addresses are categorized into five different classes of addresses: A,B,C,D, and E. The IP addresses are broken down into octets and each octet represents a part of the address. Example: "192.168.0.1." This address, as with all IP addresses, contains four octets. Each portion of the address is separated with a Dot (.). This is known as Dotted-Decimal IP addressing. The address range for any octet is 0–255. Also each address, via octet, can be displayed in binary:

Binary—			**Dotted-Decimal**	**IP Address**
11000000	10101000	00000000	00000001	192.168.0.1

Each octet is 8 bits with a maximum decimal value of 255.

FIGURE A2.3

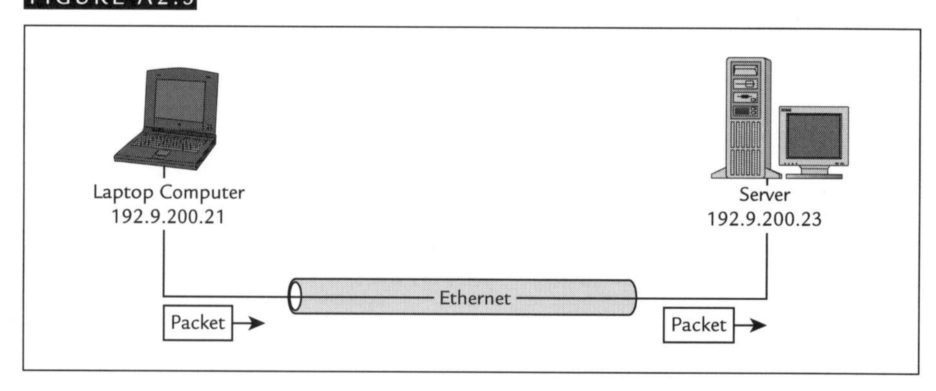

An important part of TCP/IP is subnetting. However, this is too important to be covered in the limited space in this book. Now you are really confused. A subnet is a network that is created by using, or borrowing, bits from the host portion of an IP address. This is needed to split out the address from the various classes. Why is this so important? Subnetting can be utilized to get full use of an assigned address from an ISP. (We will discuss address assignments later.) One of the best books on this subject is: *EXAM CRAM—TCP/IP Hudson, Certification Insider*. (This is a good book, even if you are not trying to pass the TCP/IP exam for MCSE.)

A2.1 IP Address Classes

Class A addresses are used with large networks with many hosts. The leading bit in the address is 0 (Bit 0 = 0). Mathematically, 128 networks are available, but the architecture reserves address 0 and 127. Bits 8–31 will make 16 million (16,777,214) addresses available to assign as hosts:

0		31
0	Network ID 1–7	Host ID 8–31

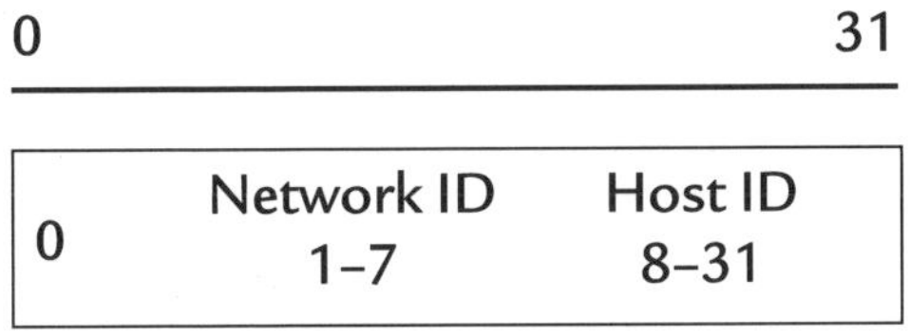

Class A Address

Class A:
Networks: 126
Hosts: 16 Million
Leading Bit = 0
Address 0 and 127 as reserved.
Octet range: 1–126.x.y.z
Host component of address: x.y.z
Default subnet Mask: 255.0.0.0

Class B addresses are used with medium-sized networks with many hosts. The leading bit in the address is 1 (Bits 0,1 = 10). Mathematically, 16,384 networks are available from bits 2–15. Bits 16–31 will make 65,000 (65,534) address available to assign as hosts:

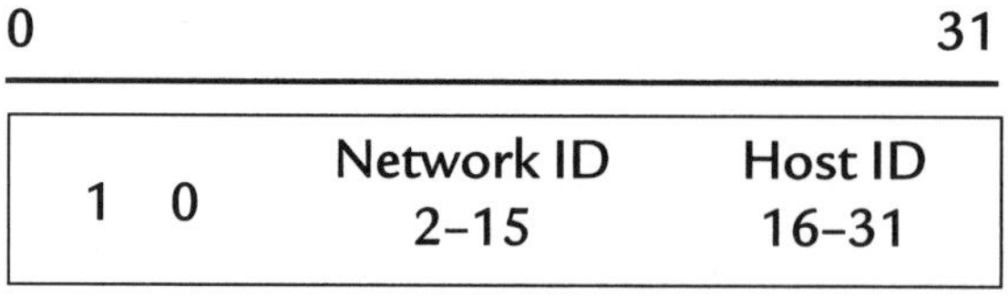

0		31
1 0	Network ID 2–15	Host ID 16–31

Class B Address

Class B:
Networks: 16,384
Hosts: 65,000
Leading Bits= 10
Octet range: 128-191.x.y.z
Host component of address: y.z
Default subnet Mask: 255.255.0.0

Class C addresses are used with small networks with few hosts. The leading bit in the address is 1 (Bits 0,1,2 = 110). Mathematically, 2 million (2,097,152) networks are available from bits 3–24. Bits 25–31 will make 254 addresses available to assign as hosts:

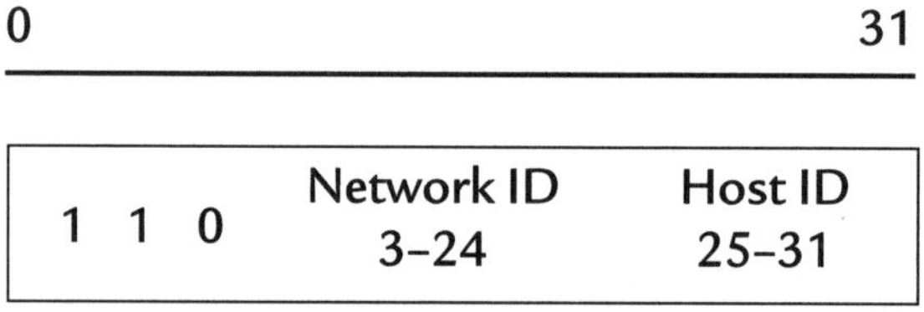

0		31
1 1 0	Network ID 3–24	Host ID 25–31

Class C Address

Class C:
Networks: 2,097,152
Hosts: 254
Leading Bits= 110
Octet range: 192–223.x.y.z
IIost component of address: .z
Default subnet Mask: 255.255.255.0

Classes D and E are not used for addressing. Class D, leading bits 1110, is used for multicasting, and Class E, leading bits 1111, is reserved.

Example and uses of the addressing classes follow.

Class A: By definition a class address of 9.2.3.4 is on a different network than an address of 11.2.3.4. The reason is by definition of the class. If computer A is on 9.2.3.4 and computer B is on 9.3.4.5, then they are considered to be on the same network. If that is the case, then they can communicate without the need of a gateway (router).

Class B: By definition a class address of 130.2.3.4 is on a different network than an address of 131.2.3.4. Again if computer A is on 130.2.3.4 and computer B is on 130.2.4.5, then they are considered to be on the same network. But 130.2.3.4 is on a different network from 130.3.4.5. See the difference? Look at the host component of the address to understand the address of an IP address in Table A2.7.

Class C: By definition a class address of 193.2.3.4 is on a different network than an address of 194.2.3.4. Again, if computer A is on 193.2.3.4 and computer B is on 193.2.3.5, then they are considered to be on the same network. But 193.2.3.4 is on a different network than 193.2.4.5. See the difference? Look at the host component of the address to understand the address of an IP address in Table A2.7.

Address Components, based on the format w.x.y.z with each letter representing an octet, are shown in Table A2.7.

TABLE A2.7

Address Class	IP Address Range	Network Component	Host Component	Example
Class A	0–126	w	.x.y.z	**9.2.3.4**
Class B	128–191	w.x	.y.z	**131.2.3.4**
Class C	192.223	w.x.y	.z	**193.2.3.4**

So far in our review of TCP/IP we have discussed Ethernet and IP. Our new stop down the network trail is Transmission Control Protocol (TCP). This is a connection-oriented, end-to-end reliable protocol designed to work within a hierarchy of protocols, which support networked applications. The TCP provides for reliable communication between pairs of processes (applications) in host computers attached to separate but interconnected computer networks. The TCP is designed for error-free bulk data movement and provides error detection, and recovery. This can make up for IP's best effort delivery service. Also, TCP will set up a connection between two hosts before the actual data transmission begins, break the data into chunks, add some sequencing information, and then place these chunks into IP packets. The IP will actually route the data through the Internet to its destination:

6 Bytes	6 Bytes	2 Bytes	46–1500 Bytes			4 Bytes
Target Address	Source Address	Protocol Type	IP	TCP	Data	CRC

The TCP rides in the Ethernet packet after the IP packet. The TCP packet contains information about the application. Although IP routes packets through the Internet using the destination address, more information is needed to identify which application on the destination host should receive the data once it arrives. This is accomplished via ports. Both sending and receiving applications are assigned port numbers to send and receive data.

Coupled with the source and destination IP address, the source and destination port number, a small integer number, identifies which application is associated with any given data transfer. As mentioned before, the IP address is like the addressing scheme of the Postal Service. Once the Postal Service delivers the letter to your house, further addressing on the letter determines who actually gets the letter. This is where TCP helps out:

2 Bytes	2 Bytes	4 Bytes	4 Bytes	4 Bits	4 Bits	1 Bytes	2 Bytes	2 Bytes	2 Bytes
TCP Source Port	TCP Target Port	Seq Number	ACK Seq Number	TCP Header Length	Res	Flags	Win Size	Check Sum	Urgent Data Size

The TCP port addresses, Source and Target, provide a mechanism to direct data to a specific application. Once the IP packet arrives at the host then the port determines which application receives the data. With 2 bytes of data you can have up to 65,000 different addresses. These address are defined by RFC 1700 http://info.internet.isi.edu:80/in-notes/rfc/files/rfc1700.txt. In this RFC the ports are categorized. The TCP/IP port numbers below 1024 are special in that normal users are not allowed to run servers on them. These ports are called "well-known ports." There are a number of commonly used well-known ports; these include the SMTP mail service (25), the network news (NNTP, port 119), Telnet (23) and the FTP service (21). The normal port number for Web access and server is port 80.

The sequence number and ACK sequence number are used as part of the TCP handshake process. The header length is used to tell the target computer the size of the current TCP header in 32 bit words. The session flags are used to control the various data elements sent to the target computer, for example: Urgent points, Valid Ack, Push Request, and Sync sequent number. The Window size is the number of bytes that the sending computer will accept from the target computer without requirement or acknowledgment. The CheckSum is an error check for the TCP header fields. The Urgent data size can be used if the target computer is congested and it will clear the buffer space as needed to receive and process the data.

So far, so good. Now how can I access a Web site? Let's say you want to go to a site. You will need an address. Let's use 207.69.200.100. Easy to use and remember, but what about remembering numbers for 20 or 30 sites. A process known as DNS solves this problem. Today, we access Web sites via domain names. Domain names are a method of looking up addresses without having to remember some long number. Remembering a 32-bit number (that really maps to a 48-bit number) can be difficult. Thankfully, the Domain Name System was created.

The following extract describes how domains work (from Request for Comments: 1591): http://info.internet.isi.edu:80/in-notes/rfc/files/rfc1591.txt.

A2.2 Domains

Getting where you want to go can often be one of the more difficult aspects of using networks. The variety of ways that places are named will probably leave a blank stare on your face at first. Don't fret, there is a method to this apparent madness.

If someone were to ask for a home address, they would probably expect a street, apartment, city, state, and zip code. That's all the information the post office needs to deliver mail in a reasonably speedy fashion. Likewise, computer addresses have a structure to them. The general form is:

A person's e-mail address on a computer: user@somewhere.domain
A computer's name: somewhere.domain

The user portion is usually the person's account name on the system, but not necessarily so; somewhere.domain tells you the name of a system or location, and the kind of organization. The trailing domain is often one of the following:

com Usually a company or other commercial institution or organization, like Convex Computers (convex.com).
edu An educational institution, for example, New York University, named nyu.edu.
gov A government site; for example, NASA is nasa.gov.
mil A military site, like the Air Force (af.mil).

net Gateways and other administrative hosts for a network (it does not mean all of the hosts in a network). One such gateway is near.net.

org This is a domain reserved for private organizations, who don't comfortably fit in the other classes of domains. One example is the Electronic Frontier Foundation (EFF) [see Section 8.3.3 (EFF publication), p. 66, named eff.org].

Each country also has its own top-level domain. For example, the US domain includes each of the fifty states. Other countries represented with domains include:

Au Australia

Ca Canada

Fr France

UK The United Kingdom. These also have subdomains of things like ac.uk for academic sites and co.uk for commercial ones.

The proper terminology for a site's domain name (somewhere.domain in the preceding) is its Fully Qualified Domain Name (FQDN). It is usually selected to give a clear indication of the site's organization or sponsoring agent. For example, the Massachusetts Institute of Technology's FQDN is mit.edu; Similarly, Apple Computer's domain name is apple.com. While such obvious names are usually the norm, there are the occasional exceptions that are ambiguous enough to mislead such as vt.edu, which on first impulse one might surmise is an educational institution of some sort in Vermont; not so. It is actually the domain name for Virginia Tech. In most cases it is relatively easy to glean the meaning of a domain name; such confusion is far from the norm.

The DNS is a distributed database of name-to-IP address mappings. Give the DNS the name of a computer and it returns the address, for example: www.lotus.com is 198.114.68.10. To look up a name the computer sends a request to a remote domain server. This server will answer the query and return an actual 32-bit IP address. This address is then used by the application to access the resource and return the data.

A2.3 ARP and Routing

The acronym ARP stands for address resolution protocol. This is the mechanism that IP uses to get the Ethernet address for a packet. The ARP resolves IP addresses to hardware addresses, also known as MAC address. Each network adapter has a unique hardware address, which it uses for identification on the network. When there is a need to locate a computer/peripheral on the TCP/IP network, ARP first checks its local cache to see if it contains the hardware address for the computer/peripheral to which it is trying to connect. If the address is not in the ARP cache, ARP broadcasts a message to the known IP address for its hardware address. The computer it is trying to locate will receive the broadcast and send a reply with its IP and hardware addresses. Once the hardware address has been attained, ARP stores the resolved IP and hardware addresses in cache, then proceeds with communication. But this is only part of the story. The IP really only communicates on its own network. Remember we talk about the various classes of networks, A, B, and C. Let's look at some examples for a Class C Network:

Computer	Address
Computer A	192.9.200.2
Computer B	192.9.200.3
Computer C	192.9.201.5

Computer A and Computer B are in the same IP network. Computer C is on a different IP network. In our example as shown in Figure A2.4, all computers are connected to the same physical network. So from an IP perspective, Computer A and Computer B can communicate, but Computer C can not communicate with Computer A or Computer B. Why? The answer

FIGURE A2.4

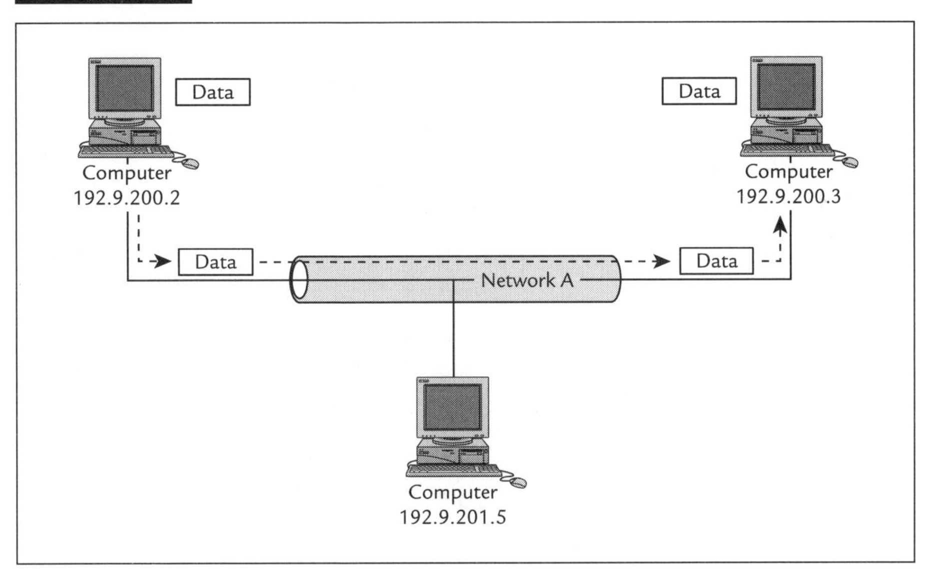

is Routing. Routing in IP is based entirely upon the network number of the destination address. Each computer has a table of IP network numbers. If these IP numbers show that the destination computer is in the same network, then the computers can establish a point-to-point communication. If the computers are not in the same network then a "gateway" will be needed. A gateway is an IP communication facilitator.

In Figure A2.5 we have two IP networks 192.9.200.x and 192.9.201.x. How can Computer A (192.9.200.2) establish a connection with Computer D (192.9.201.5)?

FIGURE A2.5

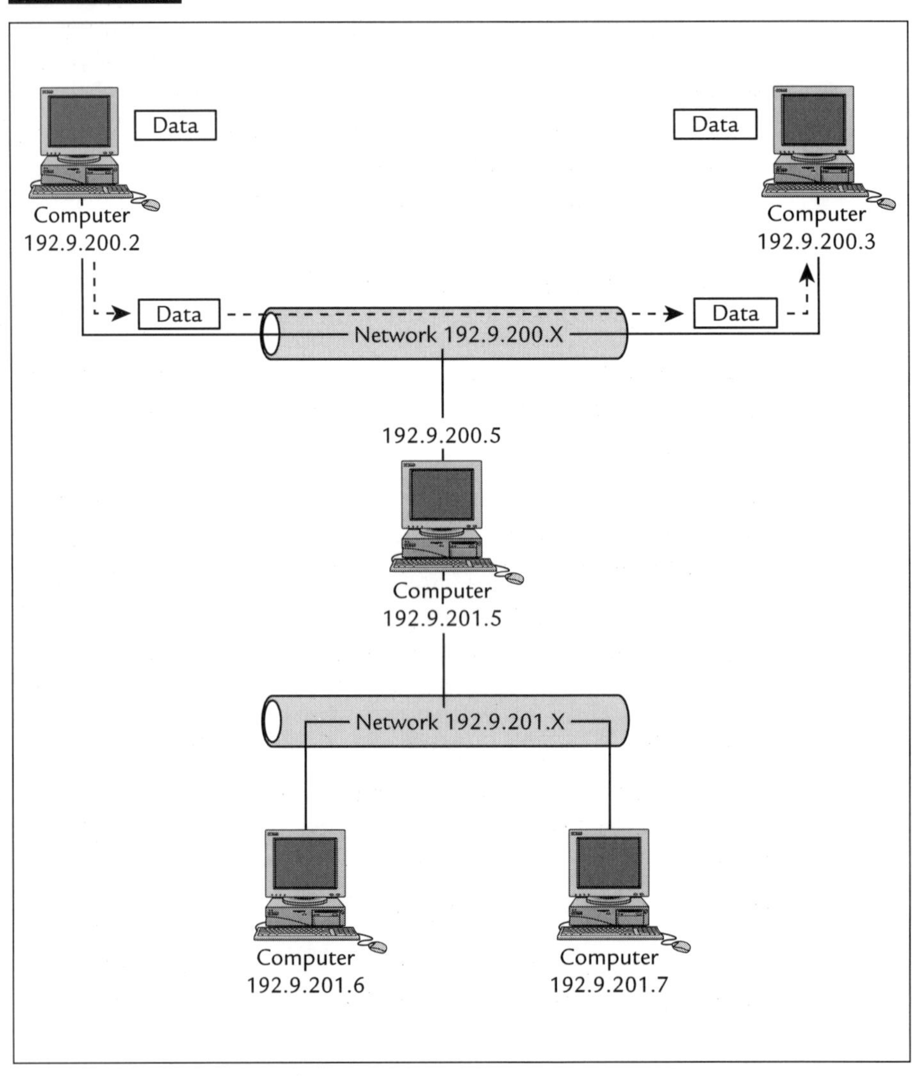

Let's follow the steps:

- When a computer wants to send a packet of data, it first checks to see if the destination address is on the system's own local network.
- If yes, then the data is sent point-to-point.
- In our example the computers are not in the same IP network so the data will be sent to a gateway that is on the source network.

In our example the gateway (also known as the default gateway) is at IP address 192.9.200.5. Thus as the target computer is not on the local network, then all "unknown" traffic will be sent to the gateway. All traffic for 192.9.201.x will be sent to 192.9.200.5, and that computer will then route the data (traffic) to 192.9.201.x network. This concept is very important, because if you are going to set up your own private network, then you will be using these simple routing concepts.

Now at this point you may be thinking that this routing stuff is easy and it is easy as long as you have a small network. There are books, courses, and companies that are dedicated to routing implementation, software, and hardware. The IP routing can get very complicated very quickly. Remember, this book is trying to give you the concepts to set up and protect your home network. If you need to set up a business, then you need a different book or a consulting service.

A2.4 Ports

At this point we need to return to our postal analogy. Remember that when you want to send a message from one house to another you will use an addressing scheme in which you have a source address and a target address. In the IP world this is managed by the IP address. In our example you sent that message to your friend at the end of the block, but in our analogy the address was not complete. You put the house address on the message, but you did not put to "whom" the message was going. The "who" part of the message is very similar to a concept known as ports. The port in TCP/IP (actually just the TCP part) tells the computer what application needs this data (or message).

TABLE A2.8

Protocol Implementation

<table>
<tr><th colspan="5">DARPA Layer</th><th colspan="2">OSI</th></tr>
<tr><td rowspan="3">Process/
Application</td><td colspan="2" rowspan="3">FTP
SMTP
TELNET
RFC: 959,821,854</td><td colspan="2" rowspan="3">TFTP
NFS
SNMP
RFC: 783,1094</td><td>Application</td><td rowspan="3"></td></tr>
<tr><td>Presentation</td></tr>
<tr><td>Session</td></tr>
<tr><td>Transport</td><td colspan="2">Transmission
Control
Protocol (TCP)
RFC793</td><td colspan="2">User Datagram
Protocol (UDP)
RFC 768</td><td>Transport</td><td>Who
(App)</td></tr>
<tr><td>Internet</td><td>(ARP) Address
Resolution
RFC826,903</td><td colspan="2">(IP) Internet
Protocol
RFC791</td><td>Internet Control
Message Protocol
RFC792</td><td>Network</td><td>Street
Address
(IP Addr.)</td></tr>
<tr><td rowspan="2">Network
Interface</td><td colspan="4">Network Interface Cards:
Ethernet, Token Ring
RFC894 RFC 1042</td><td>Data Link</td><td>Street Name
(NIC Card)</td></tr>
<tr><td colspan="4">Transmission Media:
Twisted Pair, Coax, Fiber, Wireless, etc.</td><td>Physical</td><td>The Street
(Cable)</td></tr>
</table>

In our analogy we can compare each feature to the OSI reference mode (see Table A2.8).

1. At the physical layer, which is the cables, wires, and so forth, the street is how the message gets from house to house.
2. At the data link layer would be the same as the street name. Example: the MAC address lives here.
3. The street address of the house would be the same as the IP address at the Network layer.

4. The transport layer would have the persons name on the letter (or the message). At the TCP layer the port would point to the application receiving the message.

TCP port numbers are divided into three basic ranges: the Well-Known Ports, the Registered Ports, and the Dynamic Private Ports. The Well-Known Ports are those from 0 through 1023. The Registered Ports are those from 1024 through 49151. The Dynamic Private Ports are those from 49152 through 65535

The Well-Known Ports are controlled and assigned by the IANA and on most systems can only be used by pre-defined system processes or by programs executed by privileged users. The Registered Ports are not controlled by the Internet Assigned Numbers Authority (IANA) and on most systems can be used by any program or processes.

Here is an example of the Well-Known Ports:

- Ftp-data 20/tcp File Transfer [Default Data]
- Ftp 21/tcp File Transfer [Control]
- Telnet 23/tcp Telnet
- Smtp 25/tcp Simple Mail Transfer
- Http 80/tcp World Wide Web HTTP
- www-http 80/tcp World Wide Web HTTP
- Pop3 110/tcp Post Office Protocol—Version 3
- nntp 119/tcp Network News Transfer Protocol
- imap2 143/tcp Interactive Mail Access Protocol v2
- Https 443/tcp https

Thus why all this fuss about ports? Hacking into computers can include port scanning or surfing. The essence of port surfing is to pick out a target computer and explore it to see which ports are open and what a hacker can do with them. If you understand ports, then you can understand what hackers can do to you and/or your systems.

Scanning, a method for discovering exploitable communication channels, has been around for ages. Over time, a number of techniques have been developed for surveying the protocols and ports to which a target machine is listening. They all offer different benefits and problems. The TCP port scanning is used to find any TCP ports that are "listening." If the port is listening, then the scan will succeed, otherwise the port isn't reachable. Later, you will learn how to block ports from the bad dudes.

A2.5 DHCP

Dynamic host configuration protocol (DHCP) is a network protocol that enables a DHCP server to automatically assign an IP address to an individual computer. This process is controlled by a server but initiated by a client computer. The DHCP server assigns a number dynamically from a predefined range of numbers. In DHCP terms this is called a "scope." If the DHCP is configured properly then the IP address and DNS address can be assigned at the same time.

The following is the transaction that a server and client will implement:

1. The client is started.
2. The client computer sends a broadcast request out on the network looking for a DHCP server to answer its request.
3. A DHCP Server returns a DHCP OFFER packet.
4. The DHCP client sends a DHCP REQUEST packet back to the server.
5. The client then sends out a DHCP ACK packet.
6. The DHCP server then assigns an IP number according to the scope range defined in its DHCP configuration.
7. As part of the process the DHCP server may also send the DNS information.

Let's look at the configuration for a DHCP client on Windows 98 using Figure A2.6. First, open the control panel in Windows 98 and select Networks.

Once in the Network configuration select the Configuration Tab. Select TCP/IP. If you do not see TCP/IP listed then you will need to add it to the list. A big assumption is that you have a network card (NIC) in your system at this time.

As shown in Figure A2.7, select the TCP/IP binding and then select the Properties button.

The next screen (Figure A2.8) shows the TCP/IP Properties dialog box. Select IP Addresses, then select "Obtain IP Address automatically." Press OK and reboot your system.

When your system re-starts then you should have an address that was assigned to you. But what if you wanted to check out the IP address that was assigned to you. Again, if you are using Windows 98, here are the steps:

At the Start button select Run—and type "WinIpcfg" (Figure A2.9).

FIGURE A2.6

The WinIPcfg utility allows a user to view the current IP address and other useful information about your network configuration. The user can reset one or more IP addresses. The **Release** or **Renew** buttons can release or renew the assigned P address. The user can also release or renew all IP addresses by simply clicking **Release All** or **Renew All**.

Once you press OK, on the run dialog box you will see the dialog box shown in Figure A2.10.

FIGURE A2.7

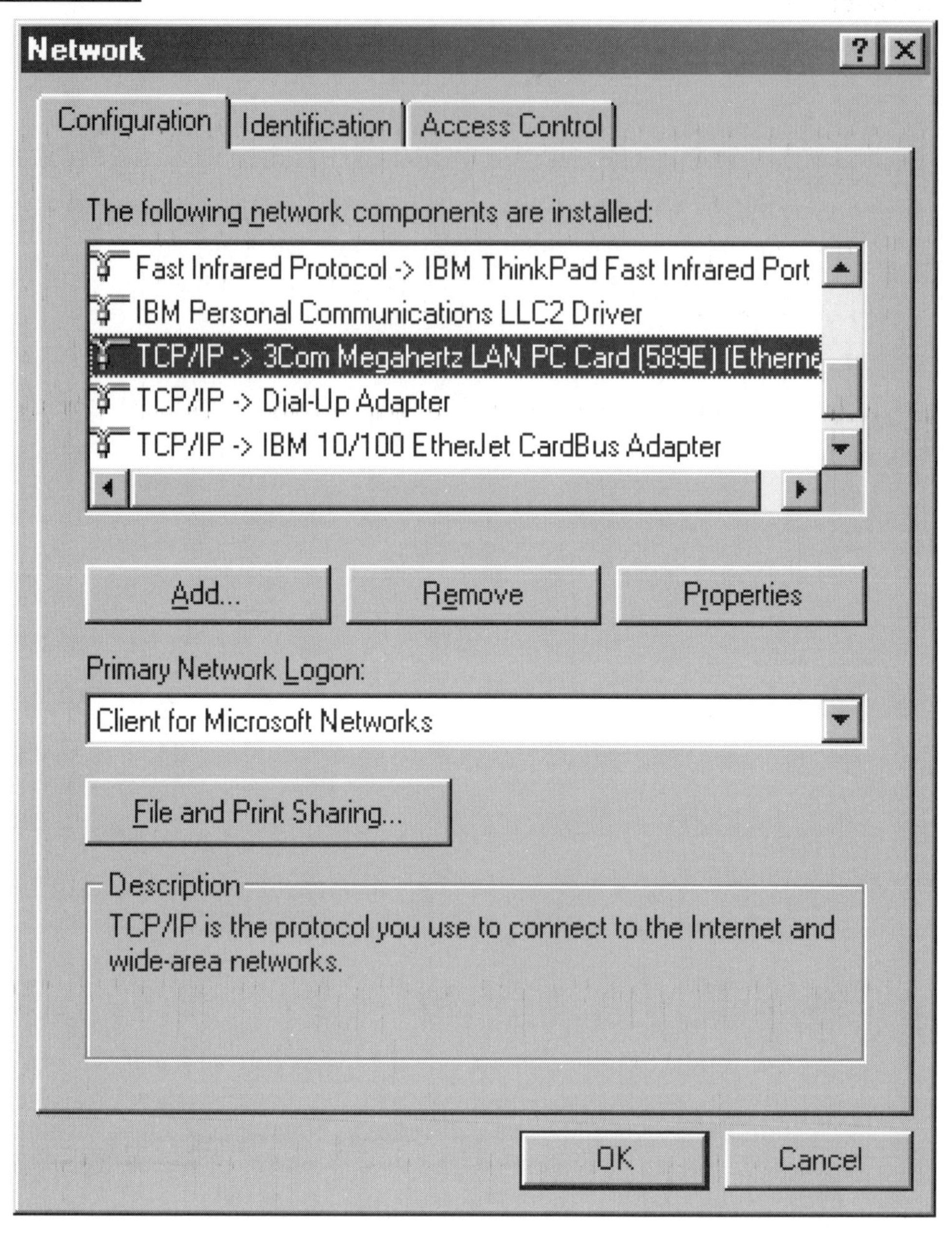
Network
Configuration
Identification
Access Control
The following network components are installed:
Fast Infrared Protocol -> IBM ThinkPad Fast Infrared Port
IBM Personal Communications LLC2 Driver
TCP/IP -> 3Com Megahertz LAN PC Card (589E) (Etherne
TCP/IP -> Dial-Up Adapter
TCP/IP -> IBM 10/100 EtherJet CardBus Adapter
Add...
Remove
Properties
Primary Network Logon:
Client for Microsoft Networks
File and Print Sharing...
Description
TCP/IP is the protocol you use to connect to the Internet and wide-area networks.
OK
Cancel

FIGURE A2.8

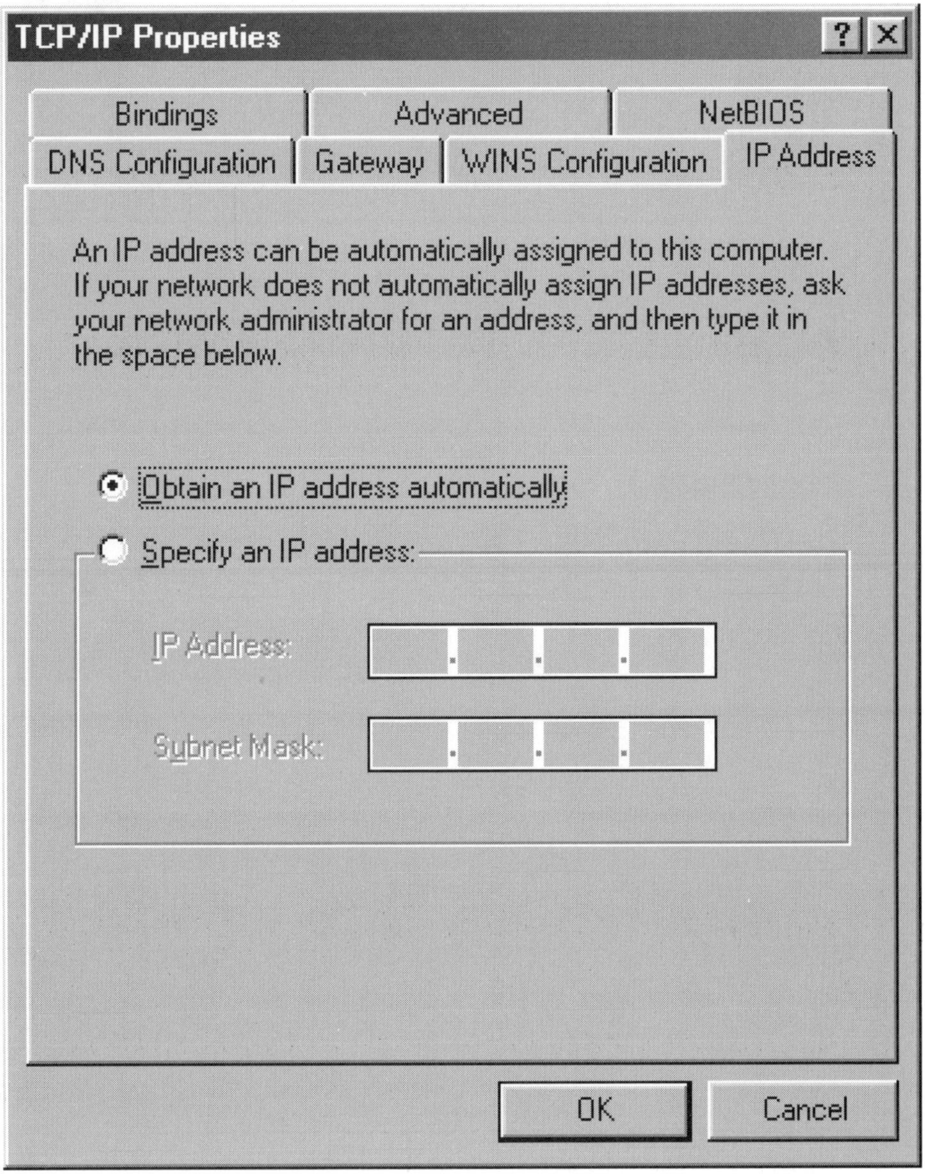

TCP/IP Properties

Bindings | Advanced | NetBIOS

DNS Configuration | Gateway | WINS Configuration | IP Address

An IP address can be automatically assigned to this computer. If your network does not automatically assign IP addresses, ask your network administrator for an address, and then type it in the space below.

Obtain an IP address automatically

Specify an IP address:

IP Address:

Subnet Mask:

OK

Cancel

FIGURE A2.9

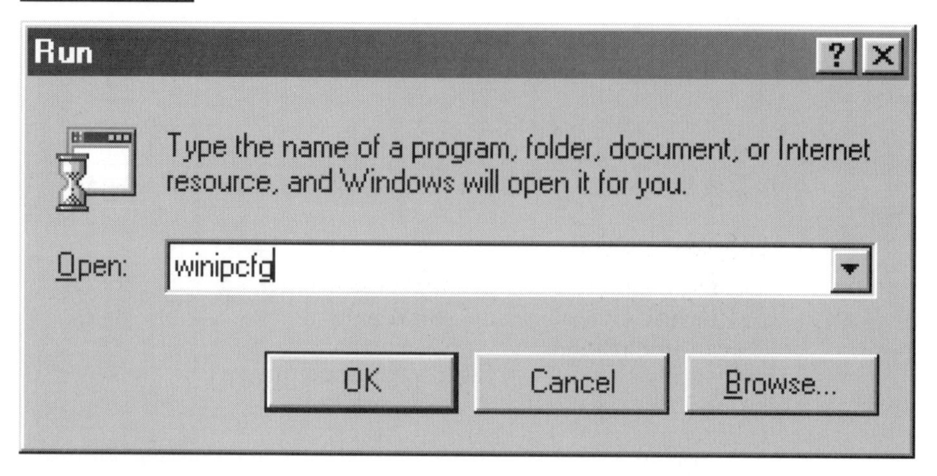

FIGURE A2.10

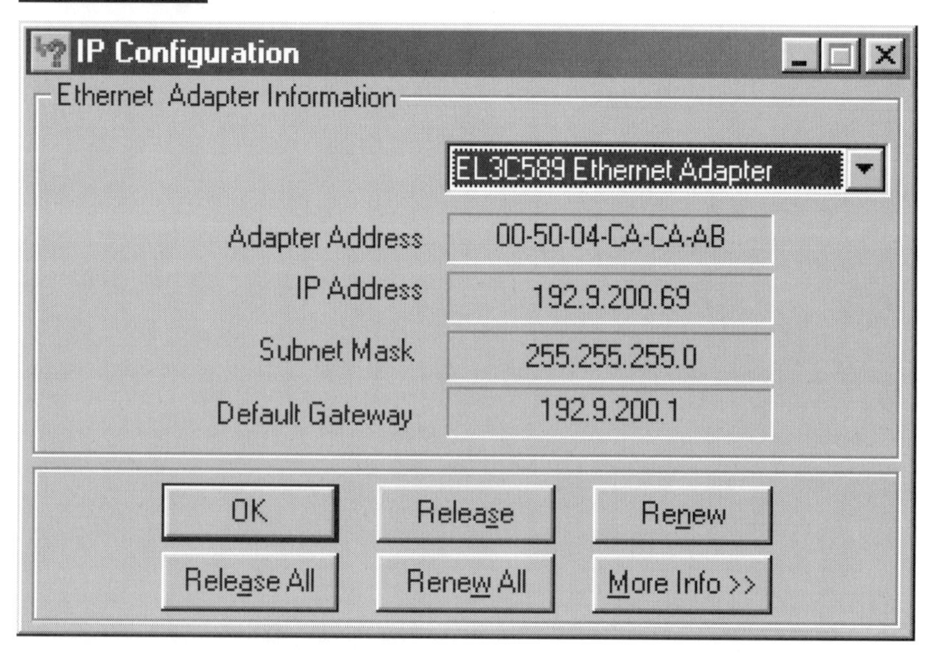

Select your network card in the drop down list as show in the preceding. This will display the following:

- Adapter Address—This address is the address of the card, in this case the MAC address.
- IP Address—The IP address is one of the addresses in the "scope" of available addresses.

- Subnet Mask—This is the make used for subnetting (not covered in this book).
- Default Gateway—The gateway address to other networks.

Press "More Info>>." As shown in Figure A2.11, this will display more detailed information about the address that was assigned and any DNS names and address that have been assigned to your computer.

FIGURE A2.11

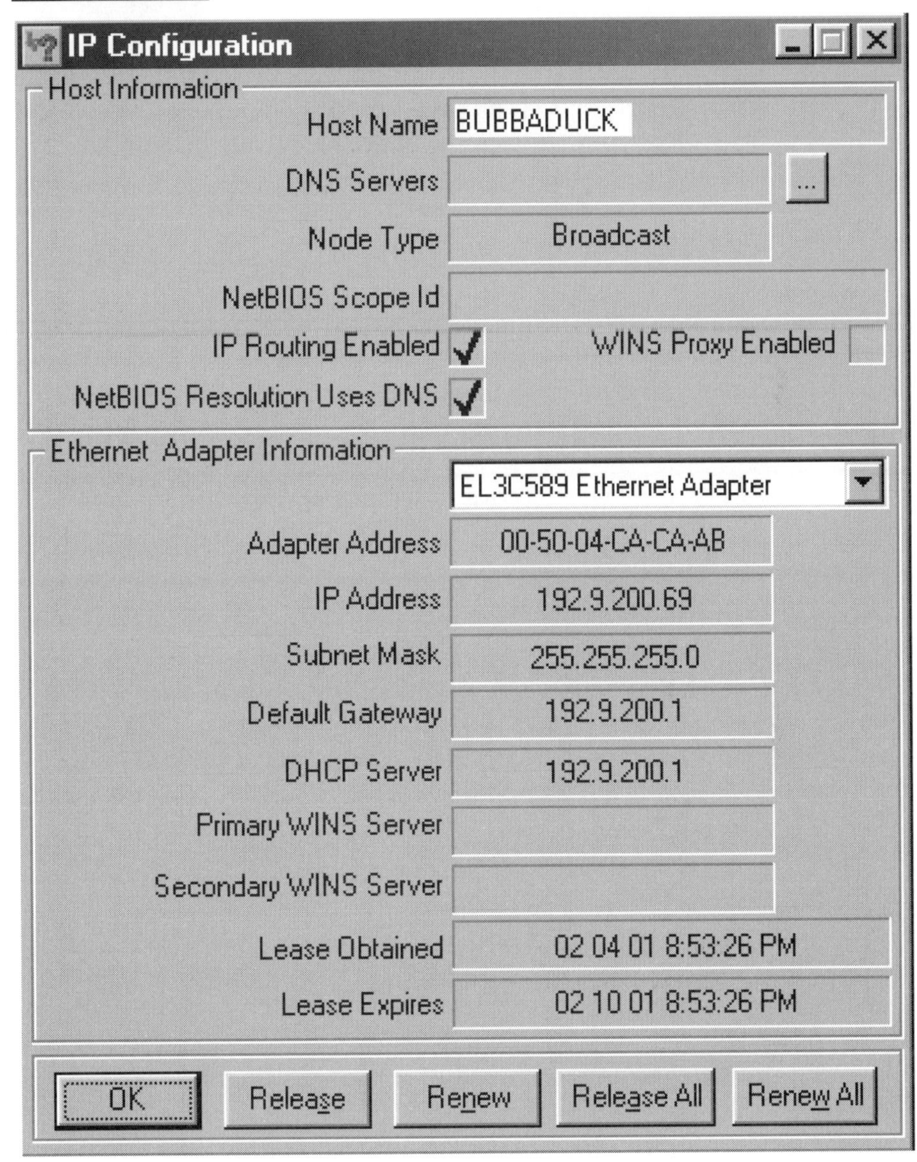

Okay, so why all this talk about IP addresses? As we already mentioned, every computer on the Internet has an IP address. Of the 32 bits of an IP address there are just a limited number of addresses (the potential is 4 billion, but true registered addresses are much fewer than that). If you want more information about the registration process then check out http://www.arin.net/regserv.html. At this point we are running out of what is known as IP4 addresses. How can we deal with this issue? One answer is known as Ipv6. This is a new IP addressing scheme that will have 128 addressable bits, and as we say in Texas, that is a truckload of addresses. But for now IPV6 is not as widespread as IPV4. One method is to use a system known as 10- net;[1] RFC 1918 discusses the 10-net address allocation. The Internet Assigned Numbers Authority (IANA) has reserved the following three blocks of the IP address space for private Internets:

10.0.0.0—10.255.255.255
172.16.0.0—172.31.255.255
192.168.0.0—192.168.255.255

These addresses are not registered and cannot be allocated to anyone on the Internet. But we can use these address for our internal networks. So how do we communicate with addresses that cannot be registered? The answer is Network address translation (NAT). Network address translation is the technique that was discussed in Chapter 4. So hold onto your hat, horse, or cat and we will take you back into Chapter 4 (for the answer).

1. http://info.internet.isi.edu/in-notes/rfc/files/rfc1918.txt

GLOSSARY

ActiveX. ActiveX controls are software modules based on Microsoft's component object model (COM) architecture. They add functionality to software applications by incorporating modules with the basic software package.

Application. Part of the OSI reference model (see OSI-open systems interconnection). The application layer is also known as layer 7, the highest layer in the OSI model.

Arpanet. The network that became the basis for today's Internet. Funded by the US military, the Arpanet was composed of a number of individual computers connected by leased lines and that used a packet-switching scheme.

Attack. An attempt to subvert or bypass a system's security.

Authentication. Verification of a claimed identity.

Back Orifice. This is a program that can let unwanted people **access and control your computer** by way of its Internet link. It runs on Windows 95/98 systems. Once installed, Back orifice (BO) runs invisibly. It has to be **run** to be installed, but it is seldom recognizable to the victim. It can be packaged with legitimate software, attached to any program or file, or run all by itself. It installs itself quietly, usually erasing the original, and opens an "orifice" into your system. It is configurable in a variety of ways. Back orifice allows a very high degree of access and control by the remote operator, who uses a simple pushbutton client program to access the "server" on your machine. Once "in" your system, he can perform practically any of your computer's functions, most of them without any outward indication to the user at the console. The hacker can see passwords, run a DOS session, use your computer as a relay point for communications (so as to make himself untraceable), read your mail, track your keystrokes . . . , and lots more. Back orifice has been in use since August, 1998.

Biometric. Biometric is a unique, measurable characteristic or trait of a human being used for automatically recognizing or verifying identity.

Bubba. A dude who does not know much about computers and drives a truck.

Bubbette. A dudette who does not know much about computers and drives a truck.

Certificate Authority (CA). A CA is an authority that issues and manages security credentials for a PKI.

The CA Private Root Key. A cryptographic key known only to the CA. It is used to certify the user or server certificate requests.

Cat. A small furry animal.

A Cable Modem. A device that enables you to hook your PC to the Internet via a cable connection from your TV cable provider.

CERT. The CERT Coordination Center is an organization that grew from the computer emergency response team formed by the Defense Advanced Research Projects Agency (DARPA) in November 1988 in response to the problems generated during the Internet worm incident. http://www.cert.org/

Certificate. digital identifier linking an entity and a trusted third party in order to confirm the entity's identification. Typically stored in a browser or a smart card.

Certificate Owner. A person or system is bound to the certificate. The owner is the person who has access to view and manipulate the certificate.

Certificate Policy. A set of rules that indicates the applicability of a certificate to a particular environment or application with common security requirements.

Certification Authority (CA). A trusted entity issuing certificates to end-users or systems.

Certification Practice Statement (CPS). This is a statement of the practices which a certification authority (CA) employs in issuing certificates.

Cipher. Alternative term for an encryption algorithm.

Ciphertext. Text (or data) that has previously been encrypted.

CRL. The certificate revocation list. A database of certificates no longer valid within a given PKI infrastructure.

Cryptography. This is a discipline that embodies principles, means, and methods for the transformation of data in order to hide its information content, prevent its undetected modification, and prevent its unauthorized use.

CSMA/CD. Carrier sense multiple access/collision detect or CSMA/CD is the protocol for carrier transmission access in Ethernet networks.

DAP. Directory access protocol.

DARPA. Defense Advanced Research Projects Agency (DARPA), is a research branch of the US Department of Defense (DOD), was one of the founder's projects that led ultimately to the development of the Internet.

Data Link. Part of the OSI reference model, this layer provides error control and synchronization for the physical level.

DDOS. This is a distributed denial of service attack. This DOS attack exploits several machines to make the attack.

Denial-of-Service Attacks (DOS Attack). This is any act intended to cause a service to become unavailable or unusable. In an Internet environment, a service might be an application such as a web or mail server, or a network service.

DES. Data encryption standard is a method of data encryption using a private (secret) key. The DES uses a 56-bit key to each 64-bit block of data.

Digital Certificate. A digital certificate is an electronic mechanism that binds a set of credentials to a particular person or system. A CA will issue the certificates.

Digital Signature. This is data appended to, or a cryptographic transformation of a data unit that allows a recipient of the data unit to prove the source and integrity of the data unit and protect against forgery.

DMZ. The demilitarized zone is a network inserted as a "buffer zone" between a company's private, or trusted network and the outside, untrusted, network.

DNS. A DNS system is a method by which Internet domain names are converted into IP addresses.

Dog. Another small furry animal. Or a computer that will not work properly or consistently.

DSL. Digital subscriber line.

Decryption. The process of transforming ciphertext back into plaintext.

Encryption. A process of disguising information so that it cannot be read or interpreted by an unauthorized person.

Ethel. Based on our extensive research (about 5 minutes), this person may have loved William Shakespeare at some point in time.

Ethernet. A network that is specified in a standard IEEE 802.3. Xerox, DEC, and Intel originally developed Ethernet.

Ethical Hackers. These are legal hackers and this means they will hack into your system only after obtaining legal and company permission. These hacking companies are paid to perform this operation and will provide a report on their findings after hacking into your systems.

Firewall. This is hardware and/or software that will protect the trusted resources of a private network user from attacks by untrusted networks.

Footprinting. Also known as profiling, this is the process of obtaining data about a particular individual or company. This information can be obtained from various resources, including public resources.

FTP. File transfer protocol uses TCP/IP ports 21 and 22.

Hacker. A bad person who wants to get into your computer systems without authority.

HTTP. Hypertext transfer protocol is the protocol used via the www. See http://www.w3.org/Protocols/ for more information.

HTTP 1.0. http://www.w3.org/Protocols/rfc1945/rfc1945

HTTP 1.1. ftp://ftp.isi.edu/in-notes/rfc2616.txt

HTTPS. (Secure hypertext transfer protocol) is a protocol developed by Netscape that will encrypt the data at the "network" layer. See SSL for more info.

IEFT. Internet Engineering Task Force http://www.ietf.org

IMAP. (Internet message access protocol) is a standard for accessing electronic mail from a server. Typically used on port 143 or IMAP for SSL is on 993.

IP. Internet Protocol is a method by which data is sent from one computer to another on any network (public or private).

IPSec. Internet protocol security is a standard (in development) for security at the network layer of network communication. This protocol can be used with **VPN**. Virtual private network.

ISDN. Integrated services digital network.

ISO. International Organization of Standards http://www.iso.ch/

ISP. Internet service provider is a company that provides individuals and/or companies access to the Internet and other related services.

Key. A series of numbers used by an encryption algorithm to transform plaintext data into encrypted data.

Key Generation. The process for creating keys in a browser. See <keygen>tag at http://users.knoware.n1/users/schluter/doc/tags/TAG/_KEY-GEN.html

Key Management. Systemic processes associated with the secure generation, transport, storage, and destruction of encryption keys.

Key Recovery. This is a PKI key management process associated with the retrieval of a key lost by the keyholder.

Key Serial Number. This is a 128-bit number associated with a certificate.

KEYRING FILE. This is a file that can house the certificate.

L2F. Layer two forwarding protocol used in VPNs.

L2TP. Layer two tunneling protocol used in VPNs.

LDAP. This is the Internet standard for simple directories for use in messaging and similar applications.

LDIF. LDAP data interchange format is a file format used to import or export data from a lightweight directory access protocol directory. These files are ASCII text files. In many cases the files can be exported from one source and imported into another type of software, for example, export data from the LDAP directory and then import it into a private data source to register users.

Local Registration Authority (LRA). Evaluate and approve or reject certificate applications on behalf of a CA.

Macro. A macro is a series of instructions designed to simplify repetitive tasks within a program such as Microsoft Excel or Word. Macros execute when a user opens a file that has been associated with a program. Example, Bubba.doc is associated with Microsoft world.

Macro Virus. A macro virus is an evil (or it may not be evil but it is malicious) macro. These macro viruses are written with an embedded macro programming language and they attach to a document file.

Mapped Drives. Network drives assigned local drive letters and locally accessible. For example, the directory path \\MAINNT\Jsmith\ might be mapped as drive E: on a computer.

Marcel Marceau. French MIME who, as far as we know, has nothing to do with e-mail or encryption.

MD2—Message Digest. An algorithm that takes as input a message of arbitrary length and produces as output a 128-bit "fingerprint" or "message digest" of the input. http://info.internet.isi.edu:80/in-notes/rfc/files/rfc1319.txt

MD5—Message Digest. An algorithm that takes as input a message of arbitrary length and produces as output a 128-bit "fingerprint" or "message digest" of the input. http://info.internet.isi.edu:80/in-notes/rfc/files/rfc1321.txt

MIME. Multipurpose Internet mail extensions is a method to exchange different kinds of data files on a network: video, audio, images, and others. MIME will be transported via the SMTP protocol.

Modem. A modem is a device that modulates an outgoing digital signal from a computer into analog signals for a twisted pair telephone line and demodulates the incoming analog signal and converts it to a digital signal for the digital device.

NIC. Network interface card.

NNTP. Network news transfer protocol is a protocol used by computers for managing the notes posted on UseNet newsgroups.

Nonrepudiation. Cryptographic assurance that a message sender cannot later deny sending a message, or that the recipient cannot deny receipt.

Nontrusted Network. This is a network that is defined by a company as not being trusted. In many cases this would include the Internet.

Open Systems Interconnection. OSI open systems interconnection, also known as the OSI reference model. This describes a standard for how messages should be transmitted between any two points in a network. The reference model defines seven layers that take place at each end of a communication.

Password Attacks. A password attack is an attempt to obtain a user's password. Hackers can use cracking programs, password dictionaries, and password sniffers in password attacks.

PCI. Peripheral component interconnect is an interconnection system between a microprocessor and its attached devices in which expansion slots are spaced closely together for high-speed operation.

PGP. See www.pgp.com for information and product descriptions.

Physical. The first layer of the OSI reference model. This layer connects the bit stream through the network at the electrical and mechanical levels.

Physical Access. This can define access to a particular computer or site. Physical access should be controlled in a security environment.

PIN. Personal identification number.

Ping. This is a program that lets you verify that a particular IP address exists and can accept requests. Ping is typically used as a diagnostic.

Ping of Death. A technique that hackers use to overwhelm a computer with ping requests.

PKCS. Public-key cryptography system is a set standard protocol developed by RSA for secure information exchange. http://www.rsasecurity.com/

PKI. Public key infrastructure.

PKIX. A set of standards for PKI from the IETF. See http://www.ietf.org

POP. Point-of-presence is a location where a network can be accessed.

Pop3. Post office protocol 3 is a standard protocol for receiving e-mail. POP3 typically uses TCP/IP port 110.

Port. In our definition it is a mechanism for TCP to communicate with an application.

POT. This is an illegal substance. As far as we know there is no relationship to POTS.

POTS. "Plain old telephone service."

PPP. Point-to-point protocol is a protocol for communication between two computers.

PPTP. Point-to-point tunneling protocol is a protocol that allows corporations to extend their own corporate network through encrypted "tunnels" over a non-trusted network (a good example would be via the Internet).

Presentation. Another layer of the OSI reference model. This layer can be part of an operating system that converts incoming and outgoing data from one presentation format to another.

Private Key. A cryptographic key known only to the user, implemented in public key cryptography in decrypting or signing information.

Protocol. The special set of rules for communications that computers use when sending signals between and among other computers.

PSTN. Public switched telephone network.

Public Key. A cryptographic key implemented in public key cryptography to encrypt data to the key's owner, or to verify the key owner's signature. The public key can be published, for example in LDAP, without revealing the owner's corresponding private key.

Public Key Infrastructure (PKI). See PKI, PKIX, and PKCS.

Public/Private Key Pair. A form of asymmetric encryption where all parties possess a pair of keys, one private and one public, for use in encryption and/or digital signing of data.

RC2. A block cipher encryption method. Data is encrypted in blocks instead of by character (stream cipher/RC4). Block ciphers are slower than stream ciphers as data is encrypted only when a block is full. http://info.internet.isi.edu:80/in-notes/rfc/files/rfc2268.txt

RC4. A stream cipher encryption method. Each plaintext symbol/character is dynamically translated to ciphertext.

Registration Authority. As part of PKI, this is the mechanism or person involved in verifying and enrolling users.

RFC. Request for comments is an Internet document or standard that is the result of committee drafting and subsequent review by interested parties; see http://www.ietf.org

RSA. This is the encryption algorithm invented by Rivest, Shamir, and Adleman (RSA) in 1976.

S/MIME. Secure multipurpose mail extensions, a standard for secure e-mail.

Script Kiddies. These are entry-level hackers, newbies and cyberpunks. They have little skill, use other hackers' programs, and cause malicious damage such as the defacing of Web sites.

Service Provider. See ISP.

Session. Another layer of the OSI reference model; this layer sets up, coordinates, and terminates conversations, exchanges, and dialogs between the applications at each end.

Service Provider. See ISP.

Sex. If you don't know what this is then you need a lot of help.

Shared Drive. A disk drive made available to other computers on a local network. Most shared drives use the universal naming convention to differentiate themselves from other drives.

SLA. Service level agreement.

Smart Card. A small plastic card with a microprocessor that can store information (e.g., X.509v3 certificate).

SMTP. Simple mail transfer protocol is a TCP protocol that is used for sending and receiving e-mail, normally over TCP port 25.

Snail mail. Postal mail that is delivered by a person.

Sniffer. A software program that monitors network packets. Hackers use sniffers to capture IP data transmitted via a network.

SSL. Secure sockets layer was created by Netscape for managing the security of message transmissions in a network.

Stupid User. This is a computer user who is really stupid.

TCP. Transmission control protocol.

TCP/IP. Transmission control protocol and Internet protocol.

Transport. This OSI layer ensures complete data transfer and manages the end-to-end control and error checking.

Trinoo. A tool used by hackers as a DDOS.

Tripwires. A mechanism or tool that detects hack attacks and alerts someone (like an administrator) to the attack.

Trojan. A program (a.k.a. Trojan horse) in which malicious or harmful code is placed inside an apparently harmless program or utility. This Trojan is constructed in such a way that it can get control of various parts of the PC (or any computer) OS and inflict damage. We don't know if any links between a Trojan horse and the ©1999 Carter-Wallace Trojan® Brand Condoms. So don't get the two confused, one is a computer virus and the other can keep you from getting or giving a virus.

Trusted Network. This is a network that has been defined by a company as trusted.

UDP. User datagram protocol.

URL. Uniform resource locators (http://info.internet.isi.edu:80/in-notes/rfc/files/rfc1738.txt).

USB. Universal serial bus.

VBS. Visual basic script. Visual basic script is a programming language that can invoke a system function. Some of these functions can include starting, using, and shutting down other applications without the user's knowledge.

Vinton Cerf. The father of the Internet.

Virus. A virus is a piece of programming code that causes some unexpected and usually undesirable event on a computer.

Virus Hoaxes. Hoaxes are not viruses, but usually deliberate e-mail messages that warn people about a virus or other malicious software program. Some hoaxes cause as much trouble as viruses by causing massive amounts of unnecessary e-mail. Look out for these types of messages:

- Fake comments from government sources.
- Warnings about alleged new viruses.

VPN. Virtual private network.

WAP. Wireless access protocol.

Worms. Viruses that attack several computers.

www. World Wide Web.

X.500. A directory standard; see http://www.itu.int/

X.509. A certificate standard; see http://www.itu.int/ and http://www.ietf.org

Index